Social Media Marketing Mastery

3 in 1

Proven Strategies to Stay Ahead of Your Competition, Leverage the New Viral Trends, and Build a Massive Brand Using Facebook, Instagram, YouTube, Twitter

Table of Contents

Book #1

Social Media Marketing 2020

Cutting-Edge Strategies to Grow Your Personal Brand, Reach Millions of Customers, and Become an Expert Influencer with Facebook, Twitter, YouTube, and Instagram

Introduction

If you are reading this, chances are, you are not a stranger to the Internet. You are already aware that with the right resources, the rest of the world is only one finger tap away from you. So, it makes a lot of sense financially and logically to bring your business online so that you can reach a broader audience without necessarily leaving the comfort of your office space. However, just because you are taking this grand step to get your business online does not guarantee success overnight—or any time soon, for that matter.

As with all things in life, there are rules and processes to follow to get to that destination and depending on the novelty of your niche, you may have to create your own path sometimes. There are a lot of articles, books, and resources on different topics—all of which are geared towards helping you and your brand thrive online—from marketing the traditional way to utilizing the various digital marketing tools embedded deep in the virtual sphere. The problem with these materials is that they all profess to possess this one trick that you can apply and transform your online business operations overnight.

The problem with those kinds of promises is that you do not have the complete picture. Every trick is focused on one aspect and that aspect is stuck in a specific timeframe. So, as the digital marketing world evolves, these tricks quickly become obsolete so trying to apply them in the world today would leave you with very disappointing results. I know because I have been there. When I started my first online business, it was in an industry that was just "awakening" and I was among the first influencers in that era. The rules back then were very simple. Get the product, take some great pictures, put it online, and then market it. To make things even more impressive, I signed up three major socially recognized celebrities to represent my brand.

Business was great. In the first three months, I was already making six figures in sales. Life was beautiful. When I made my first million, I couldn't believe it—especially since my initial investment was under $1,000. A few months after making my first million, sales tanked. I could barely make five figures in sales and even then, I would have had to pour in a lot of money in adverts to make that much. I thought the problem was the industry I was in so I sold the company and packed things up. I set up a new base in a different niche which was just awakening at the time. I applied the same techniques that worked for me the first time and to my amazement, the results were abysmal. People were interested in the products I was selling but I just wasn't making sales.

I combed through several articles and books telling me how I can get the sales figures I wanted. When that wasn't working, I trained my focus on increasing my followership on all platforms. I did increase my followers but that did not directly translate to sales for me either. I was frustrated and began to feel like a one-hit wonder. I made the decision to convert my frustrations into productive efforts in growing my brand. I went back to the drawing board and started from the basics. It has been four years now since the day I made the choice to be more deliberate in my marketing efforts online. I have three businesses actively doing very well in their respective industries. My journey to this point has been characterized by a lot of ups and downs. I have suffered great losses that could have been avoided if I had the right kind of information. And I have made some major strides just because of simple but effective choices. I decided to compress my experiences over the years and put it here on paper for you. And that is what this book is about.

The social media marketing sphere is constantly evolving but if you get the basics right, you and your business can stay on top of those changes and continue doing well no matter what level you are in right now. Whether you are starting from ground zero or looking to take things to the next level, the content of this book is meant to help you make the right marketing choices that would bring about tremendous growth for you. The truth is that there are so many opportunities to grow and expand your business or brand and with this book, you can plot your way to the top. But before we climb to the top, we need to start at the bottom. So, turn over to the next chapter to begin your journey.

PART ONE

THE ROLE OF MARKETING IN BUSINESS TODAY

Chapter One

Marketing 101 for Brands and Businesses

"Even when you are marketing to your entire audience or customer base, you are still simply speaking to a single human at any given time."

Ann Handley

One of the first things you will learn as you get into business is that there is still so much for you to learn. This is especially true for those who are running their businesses solo. You have to learn to multitask and function in different capacities. One minute, you are a business developer, the next minute, you are building your website. Today, you are comfortably wearing the CEO badge and the next day, you could find yourself down in the trenches playing a more hands-on role with your customers. The more passionate you are about your business, the more flexible you will have to be. To make the most of this book, you have to wear the marketer's hat. If that is something you have never done before, don't fret. This chapter will get you up to speed in a bit.

Growing a Business from Ground Zero

Every business has to start from somewhere. A lot of aspiring entrepreneurs make the mistake of thinking that the very first thing needed to start a business is financial capital. They get carried away with the glamorous side of business with the location, the finished product, and the monies needed to get that started. I was in this category until I learned different. My heroes back in the day were the greats of our time: Bill Gates, Oprah Winfrey, Warren Buffett, and even J. K. Rowling were my icons. They have an impressive resume boasting of assets, earnings, and investments that run into billions. But they all have one thing in common: they started from zero. If you are currently starting out with nothing, you are in great company. If you have already made some strides in business or in the development of your brand, that's okay too. We are just going to go over the essentials and ensure that you have covered the basis.

1. Define Your Business

This is the very first thing you need to do to put your business on the map. Because, even if you have the capital you need to start right now, without a clear definition, you would find your brand drifting on the ocean of the opinions of other people. Every step that you need to implement in the process of growing your business is heavily reliant on the clarity of purpose that powers your business. It is like building a house. The first thing you do is hire an architect to clearly interpret the dreams you have for your home. Without this, your building contractor is going to keep putting up walls where there should be windows and toilets where there should be rooms. Now, building a business is slightly different from building a home in the sense that the parameters of your business is constantly expanding. In some situations, you may need to adjust your vision to match the growth. However, the foundation must be right. Be clear on who owns what percentage, what you are hoping to achieve, and the problem you are trying to solve.

2. Rate Your Passion for What You Do

Forget the glamor of running a business for a minute. Take your eyes off the perks of being your own boss and let go of the fulfillment that comes from satisfying a customer thoroughly. There is a dark side to this "journey" that many people do not talk about. This is the side that robs you of your sleep or wakes you up in a jolt if you manage to sleep. It is the side that will bring you to your knees in tears and have you questioning your existence. I know of business owners who have been driven to a mental low that was so bad that they contemplated giving everything up. On this side, your money or support group may not be effective in pulling you back into the light. The only thing that gets you going is your passion. Without passion, your business might be dead on arrival. Even if everything works out on the bright side for you, passion is that ingredient that would see you going the extra mile to ensure that your customer is satisfied. If you feel that you have lost the spark for what you do, now is a good time as any to reignite it. You might want to start by going on a relaxation retreat to help you reconnect with your purpose. Having a gratitude journal also helps. For me, going all the way back to the beginning works like magic. I read the notes I put down, reflect on the progress I have made, and find the feelings I lost along the way.

3. Reacquaint Yourself with Your Market

You know what you want to sell, and you know why you want to sell it. The next step is to know who you want to sell it to. People don't buy things simply because they are programmed that way. There are a lot of factors that lead people to the choices that they make. People buy sweaters and clothing made from thick fabrics when it is winter. This is because they want to keep themselves protected from the cold. If you live in a region that alternates the four seasons and run a fashion business, it would be wise to model your products and marketing campaigns after these changes. However, when you go online in the hopes of taking your products to more people, working with the same assumption about the four seasons might not be effective. There are regions that have two seasons: hot and wet or hot and hotter. Selling sweaters to people here would tell the customer that you don't really know them. Their reluctance to buy your product has more to do with their need for it than your product itself. Know your target market as much as you can. The more detailed you are in defining your market, the more effective you will become in making sales. Your marketing strategies will be more effective if you understand your customer base.

4. Set Goals

I am going to go out on a limb that you understand the game of soccer (football to the rest of the world). The game is set to last for 90 minutes. In that time frame, each team tries to put the ball at the back of the net belonging to the opposing teams. This is the objective of the game (coincidentally, we scream goal every time this is done). Now imagine if these 22 players just ran all over the pitch without this objective in mind. The game would be pointless and devoid of the passion that we have come to associate with the game. This is the same thing that happens when you get into business without setting clear goals. It becomes a pointless endeavor and any one you sign up to work with you would have a problem helping get your business off the ground because there is no sense of direction. So, it's unclear if you are going up, sideways, or even down.

5. Execute Those Plans

An idea will always remain an idea if no step is taken to implement it. Just because you have figured out the what, the why, and the who does not mean business has started. I know some people who procrastinate their launch date because of fear. Some people say they are trying to ensure that the product is perfect. They want the right font for the logo, the perfect camera for the images, or something that would add that extra pizzazz to their product. Any businessman or woman who has made their mark in their field would tell you that if you started after that thing you were waiting for, you started too late. Stop holding yourself back and start today. It is scary. But postponing the launch is not going to make it any less scary. The only thing you would succeed in doing is stopping your growth to the next level. Start now.

Basic Marketing Concepts You Should Know

Modern marketing cannot be discussed without referencing Phillip Kotler. And the marketing guru is quoted as defining marketing as "the science and art of exploring, creating, and delivering value to satisfy the needs of a target market at a profit." Whether you are running a brick and mortar business or making your mark in the digital space, marketing management is an essential skill to have if you want to meet your business goals. Don't worry, I am not about to rain down a bunch of marketing lingo in this segment.

What I want to do is bring up the very foundational knowledge that could make a difference in how you create your marketing campaigns, how you choose the kind of products to sell, and how you communicate your brand/product essence to your customer base. We all want that viral campaign that sets our sales on fire and while there are videos that go viral without any conscious effort, having a basic knowledge of how things work would go a long way in ensuring that you are consistently able to replicate success. This is an essential quality for business growth. So, grab a pen. Let us explore some of those fundamental concepts.

For starters, a marketing concept looks at how you market your products to your customers. This is informed by the kind of product you have, your sales and business goals, as well as the location of your business. Some of these concepts could mean long term stability in the industry you find yourself in. Some of them might mean success in the short-term which would translate to dormancy as there will be no recurrent sales. Go over them briefly and let this define your direction.

Product Marketing vs Production Marketing

There is always going to be the debate of quality versus quantity. Do you want to sell your product as that unique item specially designed for the customer at a higher price? Or would you rather hit a larger audience at a lower price? If that question was confusing, let me make it simpler. Would you rather sell one product at $70 to one customer or would you rather sell a $7 product to ten people? One requires an attention to detail so as to ensure quality while the other one means having the means to mass produce the same product quickly.

On social media, this would tell you where to concentrate your marketing effort. If you are going for quality, an effective marketing campaign would mean being very particular with your target market because you are not looking for the crowd...just that one paying customer at a time. If you prefer quantity, you want to reach a wider audience as more people would mean more sales. For people whose businesses are strictly online and find themselves in unconventional roles as influencers, there might be some problems getting definition.

But don't get confused by the details. Structurally, it is still the same. For instance, you could sell online classes for followers who are looking to get to where you are. Product marketing would look at customizable classes where you give one-on-one tutorials and you are more hands on with your students, whereas production marketing would see you putting up several classes with the same prices across the board for clients to just click, pay, and start attending the classes with little to no additional input from you. This is something you should be clear about in your early start-up stage.

If your business or brand went ahead to become established without attaining clarity on this, you are in good place to revisit this.

Marketing vs Advertising

Contrary to popular opinion, marketing is not the same thing as advertising. Advertising is directed towards creating awareness about your product while marketing is about getting your product to the right market. Your market research will dictate the direction of the advert, which in turn boosts sales. Understand these basic terms and how they apply to your business. Putting up a YouTube ad does not mean you are marketing your product. That is an advert. A proper marketing strategy will have you questioning the decision to put your adverts on YouTube in the first place because you have to be sure that your market is really out there on that platform.

The inability to differentiate between marketing and advertising is the reason some brands get a lot of engagement but are struggling with converting those engagements to sales. And as you know by now, sales are critical to the success of a brand or business.

Elevator Pitch

Every entrepreneur has come across the phrase "elevator pitch" at some point on their journey. However, many of us (yours truly included) have taken this to mean the pitch that we make to potential investors. During my early years, I was given a talk by one of my mentors and that talk stayed with me the rest of my life. See, the elevator pitch is basically a summarized version of your business description. However, summarized does not necessarily mean leaving out the good parts. On the contrary, it should be like those tasty appetizers they serve at high-profile events. They give you a taste of what is to come without really satisfying your hunger, thus making you salivate over the main course in anticipation. When you meet a potential investor, your elevator pitch should get their attention and keep them excited about your business prospects so much so that they are willing to invest in you.

The talk my mentor gave me was to try and see my customers as investors and that every purchase they make is an investment that, if managed right, could lead to more business. With this in mind, I learned to create an elevator pitch for my customers too. This is an essential part of marketing. Your ability to summarize your business to potential customers will play a prominent role in the success of your marketing strategy. On platforms like Facebook, Twitter, or Instagram, there are sections labeled as "bios." This is an elevator pitch version of an "about us" page. Nail it and you can change how your market finds or accesses your brand.

Think of what your product or brand says every time you encounter a potential customer. If you find yourself trying to explain things every time, you are not doing it right. If you nail the elevator pitch, by the time people get to you about enquiries, they should be eager to buy in. Of course, there are a lot of other factors that will tip your customers to the buying point and that is what the rest of the book is about. As I mentioned earlier, we are just covering the basics here.

Customer Building Practices for Your Business

Years ago, a very close associate of mine asked me if I wanted more customers or more sales. I looked over at her questioningly. "Duh, I want more sales." And then she said, "But wouldn't more customers mean more sales?" At this point, I wasn't so sure of my answer anymore, so I gave a weak "Yes?" in response. She smiled and then she asked me if I would rather have customers who kept buying more products or more buyers who kept increasing. Here, I paused for a while before I chose the latter.

Seeing my confusion, she decided to put me out of my misery by making her point. She told me that the key to building a sustainable business is ensuring that my current customers are satisfied. Based on her logic, if my current customers are satisfied with my products and services, they would keep coming back for more. And more than that, they would keep advertising my products and services to the people in their circle. If I maintain the same attitude that I have for my current customers when dealing with the new clients that come through them, that brand loyalty that they have would spread like an infection. And that's just how my client base and sales will keep increasing. This, according to my mentor, is the key to building a business that lasts.

Anything outside this will bring you customers in the short term but without having a solid customer retention plan, you will lose all of them in the long term. The moral lesson in all of this is that no matter how fantastic your social media marketing plan is, no matter the quality of people you hire to execute your marketing strategy, without a solid customer service, it will be almost impossible to retain customers. You may be of the opinion that the quality of your product speaks for itself and because your product or service is awesome, people should be happy to buy. But the truth is, people are willing to pay more for the way you make them feel when they come to buy your product than for the actual product itself. Your product answers their need; your advert gets their attention. Your marketing gets your product to them, but it is your customer service that will keep them coming.

This is the reason why you would leave the grubby store flashing a sales sign and walk into a high-end store instead. Because there you would find an assistant attending to you the second you walk through the doors. You will be ushered into a special room where you will be offered drinks of your choice and snacks to nibble on while you make a decision on what you want to purchase. You can get that same product somewhere else but because the customer service in this store makes you feel superior, warm, and welcome, you prefer to pay that little extra amount of money for that product or service. This is the key to building a business that lasts.

On a final note for this segment, I thought it would be nice to include here that another crucial factor for building your customer base is trying as much as possible to retain the human element. The world is automated now. Everything is done at the click of a button, but that can seem a little cold for humans who crave interaction and connection with one another. The automated system may work for certain products. So, in this stage while you are still formulating your marketing strategy, determine if you absolutely fall in that category. If not, you should start planning on keeping certain aspects of your marketing strategy as humane as possible. Social media has a way of making us feel as though we are interacting with emotionless entities who only care about making sales. Now that you are still in the foundational process of your marketing strategy, you should strive to include things that are interactive and engaging that would simulate human connectivity.

Simple things like the following can make a difference in how people interact with your brand:

1. Have a very short response time to customer enquiries
2. Celebrate your customers in thoughtful ways
3. Use relatable content for your advert and marketing campaigns

Old Marketing Strategies that are Still Effective

There is a popular poem I learned as a kid:

"Make new friends, don't leave the old. One is Silver and the other Gold."

Times have changed. The players have changed. Even the structure has changed. But the game is still very much the same. For starters, the objective of making your product accessible to your client is something that businesses from the 16th century can say they relate with 100%. Now, the way we go about achieving this objective is a little different. The differences in the way things are done does not in any way render the old practices completely useless. In the next few minutes, we are going to look at some of those practices that are very old, but very relevant in the kind of results they deliver even in this present age.

Signage

Picture posters on buildings in the middle of nowhere are a thing of the past but cute images on taxis are giving life to this old marketing hack. Taxis are one of the most sought-after things in major cities. With signage, your customers are getting more of you and your brand.

One-on-One marketing

There are so many digital marketing tools that have sought to take the place of one-on-one marketing, but to date one-on-one marketing remains one of the most effective methods of converting interest into sales right after cold calling. Business owners these days tend to look at one-on-one marketing as outdated and unsexy. As effective as digital marketing is you cannot replicate the effect that comes from interacting with your clients face-to-face. And, in my opinion, I believe that it has something to do with that connection that we crave as humans.

Direct Marketing

Email marketing targets anyone who has ever signed up on your platform. This gives you a wider reach of audience, and to an extent a foot in the door of people who might be interested in the products or services that you offer (at least that's how I see it). Direct marketing, on the other hand, is a personalized form of email marketing; if done right, you might be taking your product directly to your target market, and the results usually translate to an increase in sales. The personalized touch has a way of reaching your customer better than an email newsletter, which seems to be addressing everyone without really talking to anyone.

Summary

There is a need to understand the basic concept of business and marketing. This will help you retrace your steps if you have already established your business and give you a solid foundation if you are yet to start.

Task

If you haven't opened a book or an article on the fundamental knowledge of the business process this season or in the last one year, dust off your old books and notes and then get yourself reacquainted.

Chapter Two

Social Media Marketing

"The first rule of social media is that everything changes all the time. What won't change is the community's desire to network."

Kami Huyse

If you operate a business in today's world, it is very unlikely that you have not come across the term "social media marketing." In fact, I would go as far as saying that there is a very high possibility that you are already involved in social media marketing on some level. This chapter is understanding the basic concepts of social media marketing, and its application. As we grow deeper and deeper into the knowledge of the subject, we will get to the point where we understand each of the platforms individually as well as practical knowledge on how to harness the advantages that they provide in our favor. But for starters, let us break this down for those of us who are new to the concept and refresh our minds for those of us who know what it already is.

Growing Your Business Online

One common mistake a lot of us make is the assumption that growing your business online means the same thing as growing an online business. They sound the same, but the inference is different. The first part of that sentence implies that you already have a brick-and-mortar business and the online platform is a way to expand your outreach and provide access to clients who may not be able to reach your business otherwise. The second part is basically saying that your business is based online. There is nothing wrong in belonging to either of these categories. However, it is important that you clearly distinguish which one you belong to because it is an important factor in determining the best social media marketing solutions for you.

For this segment, we are going to look at solutions that can be beneficial to both business models. Another area of focus will be on solutions that don't require tons of money and even if you happen to have the cash for it, it would serve to amplify the results that you get from applying these suggestions.

1. Choose a platform that is mobile-friendly

According to statistics, more than 50% of the people who are using the Internet today are accessing it from a mobile device. By choosing a platform that is easy to use on a phone or tablet, you immediately bring your brand to the doorstep of at least half of your customer base. That number is higher if your target market is in the younger age demography. Even if you are going to stick to using a website alone, there are still a lot of features you can integrate into your site design to make it mobile-friendly like:

- Ensuring that the images you put up on the site are optimized for mobile view
- Installing larger buttons to make them easy to click on with the thumb
- Using a menu that can be easily managed on a small screen

2. Creating high-quality content to drive your brand

When it comes to online experience, the visuals you incorporate into your site content becomes everything for your clients and potential clients. For brick-and-mortar businesses, clients can be a little more forgiving, as you have plenty of chances to make things right with them from the moment they walk through your doors right up to the point where they make a purchase. Online, you barely have 30 seconds. With the wrong visual content, your potential clients may not even take the time to browse through your store much less make a purchase. Ensure that the content you put up is an instant hint visually. Here are a few tips to get you started:

- Avoid lengthy posts (unless that is what your brand is about)
- Choose images that are of high quality and your readers can relate with
- The design layout should be top-notch but also provide a functional experience

3. Take your business operation process online

There are a lot of applications and software products/tools that are designed to enable the seamless running of your business. If you are going to make your transition to the digital sphere, it makes sense that you would operate some key aspects of your business online. For those of us who belong to the school of thought who believe that bookkeeping should always involve an actual book (and stacks of them as your business grows older), that's cute. But there are so many tools and programs that are very functional and address your concerns about losing data.

These programs come fully integrated with business solutions that will make the cost and process of running your business easier, faster, more effective—and the best part is that despite the sophistication of the services provided, it is so easy to operate that even a novice with basic training can navigate around it. As for data loss, there are ways to prevent this from happening and in the unlikely event that it does happen, there are excellent data recovery options. That said, here are a few programs to get you started on your brand/business transition to online platforms.

- Wrike: This is a project management software that can help you automate business workflow.
- HubSpot: Bring all your marketing efforts to one place and track its growth with this advanced software system.
- Zenefits: This HR software comes with some very impressive HR solutions to help you manage your workforce, whether you are small scale or large scale.

There are so many business solutions out there. If you are a small business owner, look for business tools that are focused on running day-to-day operations at your scale. Also, if you are just starting out, pay attention to the running costs of some of these software. You want something that gives you excellent service without necessarily breaking the bank. Start out with a basic package to help you determine if they (the software) are going to be the right choice for you.

In this chapter, I am pretty sure that you have observed the fact that I did not mention anything related to social media—which is what you signed up for when you bought this book. Well, your patience and diligence are about to be rewarded because going forward, our focus is going to be on social media. And to kickstart that, we are going to look at what being a business owner in this present age would mean for you.

Digital Marketing for the 21st Century Business Owner

Despite the horror stories you may have heard, this is an excellent time to be a business owner. This is not necessarily a pros and cons list because I feel that the successes and failures that we attain along the way are dependent on the choices that we make along the way. While there are standard practices that can influence the outcomes and results that you get, at the end of the day, it all boils down to those nail-biting decisions you make behind closed doors. Business today is not based on a recipe handed down by the greats that is guaranteed to get you the same results every time. Oh no sir. It is a lot more complicated than that ma'am.

Today, you would take the formulas that the business giants and pros have graciously given to us and then you would make some tweaks and adjustments to this formula in order to arrive at what you can now say is your own brand of success. For the business owner in this day and age, you can take your business to explosive heights in a matter of hours (thanks to the power of viral content) whereas businesses from the previous era had to work hard at creating a name for themselves. And that process could take years. That is not to say that today's business owners do not have to work hard. I am just saying that with the right tools, your business growth can be automated and at the click of a button, things can happen.

The downside to this evolution is that business can crumble just as quickly overnight. And again, you have the viral content that I talked about earlier to thank for that. In today's world, the advent of social media has blurred the lines when it comes to how you do business. You can sell a product that you don't have (Drop Shipping) and you can make a tidy income from products that you didn't sell (affiliate marketing). You can source for a product in China, negotiate with a client just down the block, have your product or service delivered to your client in the Middle East, and make a sale of over $1,000—all before you are done with your first cup of coffee in the morning.

Today's business owner has a wealth of opportunities accessible to them at their fingertips but most importantly, the major capital that determines how far you go is not the amount of startup capital you can raise. It is not even determined by your current physical location...no matter how exotic it is. Your biggest asset right now is knowledge, and I am not referring to the knowledge you gained yesterday. When you have a smartphone, one of the key things that ensures it stays relevant is not by buying a new phone each time an upgrade is released. It is the software updates. For your business to stay relevant, you need to stay updated on the latest events. In marketing, the general lingo is "keeping your fingers on the pulse of what is trendy." This is not different for digital marketing. For starters, you can adapt some of these habits to keep you updated on what is going on in your business niche:

- Keep up with the news: Start off by updating your newsfeed and then take things up a notch by subscribing to journals, magazines, and blogs that are focused on industries that are a perfect match or related to what you do.
- Keep an eye on your competition: Your competition, as well as bigger brands in your niche, can give you clues on where your next wave of customers might be coming from or going to.
- Use SEO and Tags: Google Alert tells you what people are looking for and with an excellent understanding of this, you should be able to determine how you can fill a need by looking at what people search for.

Is Social Media Right for You?

At some point on this journey, you are going to ask yourself this question and while there are right or wrong answers for this, there is a fact you need to consider. The truth is that, whether you choose to be on social media or not, social media is influencing your business. As long as the people who patronize your products and services are online, your business will find its way there. People will write reviews of their experiences with you. This can prove to be a good thing or a bad thing and the outcome may affect you negatively if you are not online to respond to the questions that may arise from the reviews. Some people will even list you as a provider in your niche. This is good but if you are not online, you miss out on an opportunity to connect with a new market.

If not for any reason, get online to take control of your brand's narrative. Information these days travels at the speed of "now." Being offline would only make it easier to target and hurt your brand. Apart from controlling customer perception of your brand, here are a few more reasons to get on a social media platform today:

1. It helps you connect with your customers and vice versa

According to a report by Smartinsights, 63% of your customers expect you to offer customer services via your social media channel and even more startling is the fact that 90% of those social media users have used social media as a communication channel for brands that they either patronize or plan to. On the flip side, it also gives you an opportunity to interact directly with your customers and get into their heads to find out how you can be better for them.

2. It helps you increase sales

It does not matter what product or service you provide, if you get it on social media, you can sell it. With your social media accounts, you can widen the process through which an interested contact can become your most loyal client. The number of people who use social media is expected to keep growing as time goes by. Keeping your accounts active means you can access this market. With the right tools, you can always find leads and drive sales for your business.

3. It helps keep your business or brand on the mind of your customers

You know that saying, "out of sight is out of mind"? Well, many businesses suffer from this syndrome. Traditional marketing can only keep you relevant for so long and even then, it takes a very hefty budget to retain that kind of relevance. For a significantly lesser amount, your services and the products can remain in the minds of people. Whenever they have a need that you can service, your presence on social media can ensure that in the very least, you are one of the first people they think of.

The Goals of Social Media Marketing

We have looked at how social media affects you in this age. We have even gone ahead to help you answer the question of having your business on a social media platform. In the last segment, we explored some of the benefits of being on social media. Whether you are hoping to generate $1 billion in sales or have a massive following, your marketing strategy must include SMART goals. These goals will help you accurately measure the level of success or failure that you make on this journey. In the next chapter, we will go into extensive details of what these SMART goals should be but for now, let us examine the main goals of social media marketing.

1. Creating awareness about your brand

Don't assume that people already know what you are about. People will always formulate their own opinions about you based on their experiences, perception, and deductions. Your social media marketing strategy should be targeted at addressing all three areas as you create awareness and promote your relevance to the right audience.

2. Generate sales and pursue leads

If your strategy is not generating leads and sales, you may not be doing it right. Social media marketing is a softer version of the cold calling technique often used by traditional marketers because it allows you to engage your customer, understand their preferences, and gauge their responses before making your pitch. This has proven to be very effective in sales conversion.

3. Build a community

A satisfied customer can become your most ardent marketer. I learned this firsthand. When I started my health-based ecommerce business, I was finding it difficult to find the right influencer for my brand (we will talk about influencer marketing later). I had this customer who reached out to me for my product. I addressed her questions and moved on to sales. She was skeptical but eventually made a purchase. A week later, I reached out to her to find out her experience. She had several complaints. I took notes of her complaints, made a few modifications, and sent her a free sample when it was ready. She was ecstatic and shared it with her followers (turns out she runs a blog with a massive following). Soon, I was flooded with comments, suggestions—and, of course, demand for my product. I was able to create a small army of influencers through that singular act. That should be your social media marketing goal.

4. Research and development

You can also infer some lessons from the experience I just shared for this purpose. Apart from making sales, one of your goals in business should be to improve your services and be better, generally speaking. Using customer feedback and complaints, you can make modifications to your product and bring your customers to a place where they feel like they are more than just consumers. They become key contributors to shaping the future. This way, you are able to truly provide solutions that are meeting the needs of your customers in the best way possible. I have always been told that the key to building sustainable businesses is growth. And growth should not just be in your client base or sales volume. It should be in the evolution of the solutions that you provide.

5. Improve public relations

In 2019, a feud between beauty vloggers on YouTube led to a series of allegations that saw one party losing over a million subscribers in less than 48 hours. In the months following that, there was a sharp decline of interest. The moral lesson? People are watching. The way you handle your brand or business online can lead to more opportunities or more shut doors. Crises are bound to happen. Your goal should be to have an effective strategy in place to help you manage the situation better.

Summary

- Today's business technology sets you up for phenomenal growth in a shorter time frame. But a few wrong moves can pull your business to the ground just as fast.
- There is a difference between having an online presence for your business and running your business online.
- Social media impacts your business whether you are online or not.

Task

Engage someone in your circle who you think might be in the demography of your client. Ask them questions about the products that you plan to sell and get their input. Take note of the responses you get and go back to the drawing board. Are you on the right track? Are there modifications that you need to make?

Chapter Three

Creating a Social Media Marketing Strategy

"Strategy is about setting yourself apart from the competition.
It is not a matter of being better at what you do.
It is a matter of being different at what you do."

Michael Porter

And now, we are getting into the main aspects of this book. Before now, we have been cruising on the parameters trying to set a tone and get our bearings. I'd like to think that we have done that. I also hope that you have been carrying out your tasks so far. Remember, this is not a race to finishing the book. It is about internalizing the contents of the book.

Evaluate Your Current Marketing Plan

Before you set out to create new goals and plans for your business, it is necessary to go back to the plans you had before you came across this book. If you are working from a clean slate (as in, you are just starting up completely), then go ahead and read through to the next segment. You don't need to take action now but in the future you will, as you'll have to evaluate your performance based on the strategies you implemented in the first place. If this is not your first rodeo ride, whip out your pen and notes. It is time to see how far you have come.

Objectives: Your objectives are the compass that leads you to your goals. What are those things you laid out as your objectives? How far have they taken you? Would you say that your current objectives are SMART-oriented? Do your best to answer these questions as honestly as possible. Try not to water down failures or overplay your successes and vice versa. You need to be very objective in evaluating your objectives (pun intended).

KPIs: Your key performance indicators are those things that you can use to accurately determine how much growth or sales you have had. For example, your objective may have been to increase sales by 50% by the end of the month. A good KPI would be the amount of deliveries that were fulfilled at the end of that time frame. A poor KPI would be the number of followers you got. KPIs give you a metric to help you measure your success. As we have all come to learn, success means different things to different people. In your case, it may be a higher following. For others it might mean an increased number of clicks and so on.

Create SMART Goals

Now that you have successfully worked out where you are coming from, it is time to work towards where you are going to. Now, there is a possibility that you already have a vision, or at least an idea, of what you want your marketing strategy to look like. Ensure that they are written down so that you can measure them against these SMART goals that I am about to share with you. The purpose of this, as I hinted earlier, is to help you ensure that you are able to better evaluate the successes or failures you will record when you get to the end of the time frame. Before we go further here, I want to offer a few words of advice: ***never be afraid of failure***. Yes, it stings, but it also provides valuable lessons for success. That said, let us continue.

S – Specific

Try as much as possible to be clear on what you achieve. Vague goals will only bring about vague results. Being specific will help you focus your efforts on the problem areas that need to be resolved.

Example of a vague goal: I want a new look for my brand.

Example of a specific goal: I want a new brand logo and website redesign.

M – Measurable

The goals that you set should be something that you can measure. This almost wants to tie in with being specific except that this time, you are attaching figures to it. By attaching measurable elements to your goals, you are better able to track your progress.

Example of a bland goal: I want to increase followership.

Example of a measured goal: I want 100 new followers.

A – Attainable

In some places, this would read as achievable. Personally, I put it in my notes as actionable. The concept is the same. You want to set a goal that you can act on immediately. Now, here is something of note. Just because your goals need to be attainable shouldn't mean that your dreams should become smaller. Keep your dreams big. It is the steps that you take to achieving those dreams that need to be small.

Example of an unrealistic goal: Get half of my clients to use my website as their homepage.

Example of an attainable goal: Create relevant content on social media pages consistently.

R – Relevant

Now this is where you keep the dreams and aspirations that you have for your business in focus. The goals that you set now should be relevant to the dreams that you have for your business. The relevancy of your goals depends on the vison that you have for your business.

For example, your want to be a recognized thought leader in your niche.

Example of a relevant goal: Creating content centered on hot topics in your niche.

T – Time Oriented

Time is a crucial factor in measurement. It gives you a starting point and ending point. This in turn helps you in assessing your plans to reach your goals. These milestones keep you accountable.

Example of a goal without schedule: Get 100 new followers on Instagram.

Example of a time-oriented goal: Get 100 new followers at the end of the week.

If you are going to apply everything you have learned in this segment, going forward, your goals should look something like this:

At the end of _____ (insert time frame), I should be able to grow my _____(insert relevant objective) by _____(insert the right measurable value). I will achieve this by_____ (insert specific action to carry out).

It takes some practice to get used to writing out your goals this way, but eventually, you will get the hang of things.

Choosing the Right Platform for Your Brand

There are so many social media platforms to utilize for your marketing strategy and while they all serve the same purpose of getting your product and service to the doorstep of your client, not all of them would be able to do that effectively for you. This is because each platform appeals to a particular group of people and the appeal could be based on gender (Pinterest is a female-dominated platform), age (Facebook has the highest growing number of people above 40) or profession (LinkedIn is mostly utilized by professionals).

There are three main things to consider when choosing the right social media network for your business or brand and by now, I would think that you have sorted them out. If not, here is a chance for you to do so.

Consideration 1: The identity of your customer

I kind of eased into that in the introduction of this segment but let us get into it anyway. You need to know who your customers are. Ask yourself questions like:

1. Is my client male or female?
2. What age bracket do they fall under?
3. Are my clients income earners? If so, how much do they earn?
4. Are they educated? If yes, to what level?
5. What are their interests?

The answers that you get will help you profile your clients and predict or determine where they are most likely going to socialize online.

Consideration 2: Your goal for your customers

Now that you know who your customers are, what are you hoping to achieve with them? Do you want to sell your products to them? Do you want them to subscribe to your service? Or do you just want them to come and interact with each other on the platform that you have created for them? The answers can point you in the best direction to go. Instagram, for instance, is great for getting your customers to your store to buy.

Another thing you can do is decide on what platform can best serve the goals you have for your customers (that is if you have more than one goal). For example, Instagram can show off your products. Twitter can be used to address and resolve customer complaints while LinkedIn can be used to showcase your company culture.

Consideration 3: Go into the social media sphere and seek your audience

Statistics come in very handy here. Look at the numbers pulled from each social media platform. Look at the kind of people who use which platform and also what they are mostly interacting with there. Compare what you see with the list of answers to the questions you asked yourself previously, and determine what becomes the right fit for you.

If you are still unsure, in the next five chapters, we will be looking at some of the most utilized platforms for both businesses and individuals and break them down for you. Right now, let us look at the force behind your new movement: your team.

Building the Team Behind the Dream

If you are just starting out and are limited when it comes to resources, it is okay to start out alone. But you have to understand that implementing a social media marketing strategy is more than tweeting or using fancy lingo like growth hacks or algorithms. The core of effective social media strategy is having a workflow and thought process that is centered on the goals that you have established.

That said, from the onset, you need to determine the level of commitment needed to get you to your goals. Figure how much you are willing to allocate to social media marketing and the time frame for that budget. Then, finally, look at the resources that will be needed to pull off your strategy. Do you need design at the forefront? Or will a writer play a prominent role? Remember, this is about knowing where you will need to concentrate your effort the most to get maximum result.

Even if you have the budget to accommodate all of this, these are things you still need to look into before you hire.

Summary

- Start your strategy by getting an understanding of where you are coming from.
- Articulate your goals in such a way that they are Smart, Measurable, Attainable, Relevant, and Time-oriented.
- Know where your market is before choosing a platform and get a team that understands the goals you have set explicitly.

Task

What skills are you bringing to the table if you are handling your social media management yourself? What skills are you lacking the most when looking at what it would take to implement your strategy? Answer these questions and proffer solutions.

PART TWO

GROWING YOUR BRAND AND INCREASING CUSTOMER REACH

Chapter Four

Instagram

"Instagram is a personal subscription.
It's like your own personal magazine.
It's like doing a photoshoot for no money, which is cool."
Goapele

Before we delve into Instagram properly and all of its incredible marketing features, let us take a quick trip down memory lane and marvel at the numbers that these guys do. In 2010, when the app was first launched on the iOS platform, it garnered a usership base of two million and within a year, over a million people were already using Instagram. As of May 2019, Instagram has more than one billion users with an estimated half of that number using the story feature. What does any of this mean for businesses and brands on Instagram? For starters, it opens you up to a demography of under 35 urban dwellers, which constitutes about 135 million of the one billion users. On the flip side, Instagram is censored in a few countries and unless that is where you or the bulk of your clients are located, this shouldn't bother you so much.

We all know Instagram for its amazing picture editing and sharing tools, but it has evolved from this basic feature since it was first launched in 2010. As of now, it has become a very powerful business platform. And just in case you were thinking that Instagram is best utilized by individual brands and businesses, it would shock you (I know I was) to know that Instagram is such a disruptive ecommerce force that businesses are integrating it into their ecommerce platforms. As long as your business can find visual expression, Instagram can be the right place for you.

The Basic Element of Instagram Marketing

One of my favorite things about Instagram is its simplicity. On the surface, it looks like something that the kids can just roll with (and in reality, the kids are rolling with this) but in reality, Instagram has so many incredible features that would appeal to brands and businesses regardless of their size. Despite the simplicity of the app, people are still unable to key into the rewards that come with it and that is because your marketing strategy has not been optimized to use the full features of Instagram.

By now, you know how setting up an Instagram page for business works. You have nailed the bio for your brand and compiled your specialized hashtags and you even know how to organize your posts for a synchronized aesthetic appeal. Good for you! But that is just a part of the equation. There are other elements to consider that could determine the overall performance of your marketing strategy. Thankfully, these are quite easy to navigate once you get the hang of it. To get you started on the second part of the equation that we talked about earlier, you need to have a clear understanding of what Instagram algorithm means and how to work this into your marketing plan.

When I was doing the research for this particular topic, I came across lengthy definitions and heavily worded descriptions that had an instant snooze-inducing effect on me. I decided to spare you the long yawns and keep it simple.

Instagram algorithm helps to ensure that a user is only shown images that are relevant to them (in theory). There are factors that would determine the performance of your post in this Instagram algorithm deal and I have them listed out below.

1. The interests of your ideal client on IG

When a user goes to their Instagram feed, what they see there is not a chronological listing of contents that were posted up by the people that they follow. Back in the early Instagram years, the key to driving customer engagement with your post was figuring out the active time of your ideal IG demography and putting up your post during those times. Well, those days are gone. However, it still doesn't mean that your cause is lost. To hack this, pay attention to your posts. You have to ensure that the following elements are in place:

- Your niche is very, very specific.
- Create content that is relevant and relatable to your audience.
- Be vocal about your brand and the services that you offer.
- Put up high-quality images on your page. There are so many tools to help with that.
- Have a human element. Great pictures are awesome, but it is the captions that drive conversations.
- Be perfectly imperfect. Errors and flaws humanize us. When you look too perfect, you risk looking too artificial, which people don't like.

2. The time line for your posts

The Instagram algorithm gives priority to posts that are put up recently. So, while your older posts may show up occasionally on the feed of your target audience, Instagram is committed to preventing that from happening. The only way to bypass this is to put up posts regularly. That is not to say that you should bombard your page with hourly posts. The best thing to do is schedule your posts to come up at a particular time even though you are not online. Space them out in such a way that your page is active, but your audience is not overwhelmed by the content you put up. There are apps that can help you manage your post schedule effectively. Now these apps are not going to put up images on your page directly, but they help you plan ahead and notify you when you are due to post. I am sharing a few of my favorites with you:

UNUM: Along with helping you manage your post schedule, this app is great for improving the aesthetics of your Instagram page. From my personal experience, however, this is more suited for a brand that is heavily invested in Instagram. It has great editing tools, saves your captions for posting, and my personal favorite—it can temporarily delete images on your feed to give you an idea of what your feed would look like without them. While it can be adapted to suit all kinds of businesses, I feel it works best for pages targeted at the female demography.

PREVIEW: Is your Instagram page for a personal brand? Then this app is just perfect for you. As the name implies, one of the features is that you can get a preview of what your page is going to look like before you upload the image you have in mind. I like to think of it as having a bird's-eye view of your feed. My personal favorite is that you can curate your feed to get it to that place where you want it to be without having to delete anything. Just swap until you get what you want. And the best part, you can get your post up just in time for your midday crowd!

HOOTSUITE: This platform is not unique to Instagram alone. It is a social media management platform that helps you sync your account across the board (Facebook, Twitter, Instagram, and so on). However, its primary purpose is to make content scheduling very easy and this comes in very handy on those days when you don't have the time to be active online. You simply create the content you want to put up there and schedule it for a specific time. And when that time comes, you can handle other projects while Hootsuite ensures that your posts are put up on time.

Essentially, if you want to remain relevant on Instagram "city," you have to ensure that you are putting up your posts consistently. However, it is important that you try not to flood the time line of your followers with content. This kind of habit can get you red flagged by followers.

3. Engage your followers and people who try to connect with your brand

It is not enough to just put up content on your page and hope that you will connect with people. To improve the performance of your content/post on Instagram, you have to take things a step further by connecting with the people who reach out to your brand. One of the easiest ways to do that is by responding to comments on your page. If your page typically generates a lot of comments on each post, it may seem like a lot of work to individually respond to all the comments are coming on the post. What I used to do, basically, is respond to the first three to five comments. And then any other comment that comes in, I would either like the comment if it is favorable for my brand or respond to it directly if it is an inquiry.

What this does is that it feeds the Instagram algorithm with information telling them that people are connecting to this content and the more you do that, the higher your chances of your content popping up on people's feeds. If my manual response process is a lot of work and responding to comments becomes a little bit tedious, there are applications that have been developed for this very purpose. A lot of these applications that offer this kind of service are paid platforms, but if you don't have the resources to do so, you can simply go to the settings on your Instagram page and turn on the notifications. This way, any time a comment pops up, you are notified, and you have the option of responding to that comment.

Another thing you can do to increase your engagement on Instagram is to use the "tap and hold" tag. Now, this is not a tag or feature on Instagram, however, Instagram brands are really into it at the moment because of how it affects or impacts your algorithm. When you put up a story on your Instagram story, you encourage your viewer to tap and hold so that they can view the content to the end. You can use stickers or GIFs to make this happen. There are so many cute options right now. This presents a win-win situation because your followers are able to view the contents that you have put up to the end without missing out on all the juicy details and behind-the-scenes; this engagement feeds the Instagram algorithm with a notification that Instagram users are interacting with your content.

How to Become an Instagram Influencer

As you probably know already, Instagram is a powerful marketing platform that is currently worth almost two billion dollars, if not more, and people are constantly trying to get their own share of this cake. One way to do that is to become an influencer on the platform. Instagram influencers are basically people who have built and created a large following on Instagram. More than that, these people are very much engaged with their followers to the point that they can influence their decision in terms of the kind of products to buy or service to patronize. The rise of influencer marketing came as an answer to the need for brands to connect with an audience that require their products or services. This method of marketing is very effective because bronze or businesses are able to connect with their customers in such a way that feels more genuine than traditional marketing. A proof of influencer marketing is Kylie Jenner's tweet of 2018 that ended up costing Snapchat over one billion dollars. She is currently one of the highest paid influencers on Instagram with about $1 million per product-related post.

If you were feeling sleepy while you read this book, I'm pretty sure that Kylie's influencer earnings woke you right up. You may not have the general or Kardashian name to back you up, but there are things that you can apply to help you climb up that ladder quickly. And I'm going to break all of that down into seven steps; this is not something that's going to happen overnight. Also, you are going to need to put in some work, but if you apply each of these seven things consistently, within a short time you will become an influencer in your own right.

1. Choose a specific niche

You can't be everything to everybody. So, pick an area of interest or expertise and stick to it. What this does for you is that you become a voice of authority in that particular niche. When you decide on that niche, offer information and tips that provide solutions to the problems often encountered by people in that group. This will establish you as a voice of authority. Right now, your focus shouldn't be about the number of followers you have. It should be about ensuring that the people who come to your page are basically looking for the kind of information you offer. To achieve this you need to try and be as specific as possible from the description in your bio, to the hashtags that you use, and even to the contents that you put up—everything should connect people to this niche.

2. Create high-quality engaging content

Think of Instagram as a crowded marketplace and your attempts to build an influencer brand as setting up a stand. You would see the millions of people moving around you but most likely not noticing you. However, using some attention-grabbing antics, you are able to get their attention. To keep their attention, you need to let them know what you are about. This would sieve those who genuinely want to know what you are talking about from those who are simply just looking. At that point, you have their attention and whatever it is you sell to them, most likely they will buy it, but we will get to that later on. Right now, the plan is simple. Grab the attention of the crowd you want on your platform and quickly let them know what you are about.

3. Maintain a cohesive aesthetic

Your page is like a store except that the only perception that customers can get off your page is what they see. Of course, the stuff that you write can also be engaging, but from the very first moment they get on your page, it is what they see that reels them in and keeps them there. When your content is jumbled and in disarray, it can be visually off-putting and can drive your customers away without you saying a single word. Pick a theme to create a general ambiance for your page and stick to it. You could decide to go minimalistic and keep things black and white or you can choose the eclectic route and bring a lot of color to your page. Some people prefer to use monochromatic colors. That way, they can keep things colored yet minimalistic. Choose colors that will help you create the ambiance you want on your page.

4. Be consistent with your post schedule

No matter your goals in business and whatever the platform you are using, the key to success is consistency 90% of the time, and you have to bring the same energy here. When it comes to building your brand as an Instagram influencer, choose the specific times you want to put up your content (which should typically align with the time that your users are most active on Instagram) and ensure that those posts go out on schedule. More importantly, ensure that you can maintain the same level in the quality of the content that you put up. A compromise in the quality of the content that you put up is easily noticeable and may not speak well for your brand.

5. Engage with your followers

Thankfully, there are so many tools and features on Instagram that helps you stay connected with your followers. To be an influencer means that you have a certain level of influence over your followers. And for you to create that platform where you can influence your followers, you have to be able to engage with them first. Start this by connecting with them at the level that they understand by putting out relatable posts. Secondly, show that you are more than just the posts you put up by commenting on the pages of other people or even your followers. Respond to comments on your posts, reply to DMs, and use the features that Instagram has to generate feedback. One of those features that I happen to love is the Instagram polls. Put up engaging stories on your Insta story and generally encourage your audience to reach out to you. As we mentioned earlier, all of this is great for your Instagram algorithm

6. Network with other influencers in the same niche

You know that saying, "we rise by lifting each other up"? Well, that is very effective in this case. There are other influencers (or aspiring influencers) who may either be in the same boat as you or have gained more experience in the field. Reach out to them and see if you can collaborate with them in creating content that would appeal to both your audiences. Collaborating with other influences can boost your profile as a brand influencer. With the right kind of boost, you can improve the visibility of your brand. This in turn opens the doors to brands that would want to work with you.

7. Send out your portfolio to brands that you want to work with

When you feel that you have found your footing as well as a voice in your community, you can take the bold step of reaching out to specific brands that are in your niche (that is, if they haven't reached out to you already). A lot of influencers cringe when it comes to this point because they worry about the number of followers that they have. While numbers are good and improve your chances of securing good deals with good brands, these brands are more interested in your engagement with your community. It is possible for someone to have a following of over 100,000 and still not be able to generate 100 comments or likes on the post that they put out there. You, on the other hand, may have a following of 10,000 people but every time you put up a post, you draw out likes from at least 20% of the people following you and out of that 20%, you are still able to get 10% of the people to comment. That is an influencer with an impressive record, and this is the kind of person a brand would like to work with. So, if you feel that you are here, you can simply reach out to the brand that you want to work with.

Effective Instagram Advertising Practices

Whether you are a brand or a business, one way to generate engagement with your content on Instagram is to advertise. Advertising on Instagram is more than just putting out content and paying for it. There are simple, albeit not too known, techniques that can be applied to amplify your marketing efforts. The objective is to reach a wider audience and gain more traction from it so that every penny you pay comes back to you a hundred-fold. To get started on Instagram ads, you need to complete the following checklist:

1. Create a page on Facebook to help you manage your Instagram ad
2. Convert your account on Instagram into a business page
3. Link your Facebook page to your Instagram
4. Decide on what your budget should be
5. Do a little research on who your target market is going to be
6. Create the ad material that you feel best represents your brand

Now that we have gotten that out of the way, there are some concepts that you need to familiarize yourself with to help you make the most of your advert experience on Instagram. We are going to start off with the different types of adverts that you have on Instagram.

1. Story ads

These are the ads that you put up in your Insta story. Since your Insta story has a shelf life of about 24 hours, these kinds of ads are great for short-term marketing objectives like flash sales. You can also use it to alert your viewers about a new post that you have put up on your website platform.

2. Picture ads

This is a type of Instagram ad that utilizes high-quality images that have been formatted specifically for the Instagram platform. If your page already has excellent visual content, the picture ad is a perfect way to ensure that they reach more people in a shorter time frame.

3. Video ads

Video ads give you the option of telling a very compelling story about your brand in the most creative way possible. Of course, there is a limited time for the video if you want to keep it on the most visible platforms, but with IGTV, you can extend that time for even longer. Video ads give you the opportunity to include a lot of interesting details in your adverts.

4. Carousel ads

Rather than compressing everything you want to say about your brand into a single video or image, the carousel ad gives you the option of separating the images or videos (or both) that you want to use. However, it is important that you keep it in the same theme so that your viewers can understand the message you are trying to get across better.

5. Collection ads

If you are a product-based company and you want to create an ad that will compel your viewers to buy, the collection ad is an excellent way to go about it. This is because it includes the option to make a purchase directly from the ad. It brings all the elements of direct marketing, image, and video ads together on one platform.

6. Explore ads

Every Instagram user goes to the explore page to search for content outside their usual go-to platforms. With the explore ad, you can reach this unique demographic of people who want to try something new. It is not a very common practice for advertisers, but if you put in the basic elements of a successful Instagram marketing campaign, you could get massive results from it.

Now that you know the different types of adverts on Instagram and can determine what kind of advert would work best for you, let us look at some of the basic principles that you need to employ in your Instagram advertising. This will ensure that your minimum effort can you bring maximum results for your business online. I am going to assume that you are not entirely a novice to this process. So this is something you have probably done before and the only reason you are here is because you were not able to get the results that you were hoping to get and since that is the case, I am not going to focus on guiding you on how to create Instagram ads. I am going to guide you on how you can get the most out of your Instagram ads.

1. Before you do anything, look at your previous posts

The way people interact with your page basically informs you of the kind of content that people in your niche connect with the most. This should, in turn, form the foundation for your ad. Look for pictures that have the highest number of interactions and make it your goal to replicate that same image in your advert. The factors you could look out for when determining interaction is the number of likes, saves, shares, comments, and so on. Your search should not be limited to your Instagram profile. Check on your other social media platforms, like your website, to see the post that had the highest number of views and clicks as well.

2. Be strategic in the creation of the content for the ad

Now that you know the kind of posts that generated the highest number of engagement on your platform, it wouldn't do to just use that image or video as the ad for your brand. For starters, the image may not completely represent what your brand stands for. So, you need to ensure that the content that you create for it is a very apt representation of your brand. It should be immediately captivating while at the same time establishing you as an authority in your field. And most importantly, it should make your viewer want to know more about you or your brand. If the content you choose is effective, viewers should be able to connect with your ad and at the end of it be compelled to make a decision concerning your product or service.

3. Be focused on your niche

When setting up your advert for Instagram, it can be tempting to try and reach everybody at once. A lot of people make the mistake of assuming that the wider your demography is, the more people you will reach and the more people you reach the more chances you have of getting your product or service patronized. But here's the thing—widening your target demography without being specific when activating your Instagram ads is like taking a basket to fetch water from the ocean. There is a very strong possibility that you end up with nothing. Rather than focus on fetching the water, it is better to focus on the fish (pardon my use of fish as an analogy here). Your adverts will perform better if you are specific about the kind of people you want to present your product or service to.

On a final note, one thing you need to consider here is your goal for marketing. If you are hoping to make sales through the Instagram platform, then yes, be as specific as possible with your demography. Make sure that you focus on the kind of people who are most likely going to buy your product. This is why the researches, your foundational fact-finding mission, and the information I have shared earlier is very valuable. Now, outside of that, if your goal is to create awareness about your brand, then it makes sense to try and reach a wider group of people.

With this goal in mind, you can afford to be as generic as possible with your ad. And even then, I will say there are certain areas that you need to be specific about. For instance, if you are a real estate person, you should know that not every 18- to 20-year-old can afford to buy a house on their own, as they do not have the purchasing power to that capacity even though they are strong buyers in certain industries, like fashion. That sort of product is better suited for an older market. So even if you are creating awareness about your product or service, you will get better results if you go to the people who are most likely going to do something with the information you have given them.

How to Write Captions that Increase Followership and Create Engagement

Instagram is an image-based platform but you get exceptional results with your caption game. When I first started doing ads on Instagram, I remember thinking to myself that I am going to create these fantastic images and put them out there. These images were so engaging and from an artistic perspective, beautiful. I had the graphics team do their thing on them and the final result was this exotic creation. For lack of words, it was very beautiful. However, when I put them out there with a little caption, the results I got were crickets. I imagine Instagram as a noisy marketplace and the ads that we put up are like those traditional marketers trying to get attention. The ad I created generated a lot of likes but outside that, it was just silence. It wasn't because people didn't like the image I had put up. It was just that the concept was so abstract that they couldn't relate it to my brand or what my product offering was about. And on top of that, there was just nothing telling them where to go or what to do with this beautiful thing I had given them.

A lot of people hesitate when it comes to writing captions, mostly because they feel that it is something that professionals should do. I can categorically tell you that I was neither a professional writer nor copywriter to write my own Instagram captions. However, it was a process for me. I didn't get it right overnight. First of all, I had to understand what my audience wanted and then also understand the right kinds of words and phrases to use that would compel them to connect, or at least take an action, about my product. It was a learning process for me, and I am going to share some of my experiences on that journey.

1. Keep it short and to the point

Instagram allows you to use all 2,000+ characters to create a caption for your post. However, you do not need to exhaust these characters in your text in order to get your message across. The attention span of the average social media user is less than ten seconds. If you cannot capture your audience within that time frame, you'll probably lose them. We will go into more of that later, but for now, let us just focus on the brevity of your post. Digital readers have this method of reading called skimming which essentially means that they are scanning the content of your post for the major points. When these kinds of readers see that the post that you put up is lengthy, most likely than not, they will be discouraged to continue reading your post. They will focus on the image and unless the image has an engaging concept that will pull them into your platform, you will lose your potential market. So, keep it short but interesting.

2. Get visual with your texts

We are all adults, however, in every one of us is that little kid who enjoys reading comics and books that don't have too many words in them. Interspersing the contents of your caption with interesting emojis create an overall visual appeal that just makes your caption that much more interesting. Emojis have a way of visually connecting the viewer or reader to your post and presenting you and your brand as more human. Having a bunch of words written out (even if they are written articulately) can make you seem too plastic. Even if your brand is a corporate one, there are ways to go about this. However, regardless of your industry or social media brand voice, ensure that you do not use too many emojis. Because too much emojis can make your readers or viewers feel that you are not a serious person or at least, unserious about what you do.

3. Create a captivating line

When I talk about creating a captivating line, I am not talking about creating the caption that would singularly transform your business. Because, quite frankly, it is unrealistic to expect that. There are different types of businesses and each of them have their own social media strategies that are effective for them. And it is from the strategies that we then go on to determine the appropriate caption for posts. While there are basic elements that need to be included in every caption you use for your Instagram post, the right caption for your brand is something you are going to have to discover all on your own. You can kick off the process by ensuring that the first line of your captions are absolutely engaging because Instagram only shows the first line of your post. The rest of the content is hidden behind the ellipsis and Instagram users will have to click on that sign to see the rest of caption. We expect the people will automatically click on that ellipsis, however, it is the write-up in the visible part that will compel them to either click or move on.

4. Drive engagement with a call to action

An old mentor in business used to tell me that people don't really know what they want until you show it to them. And I believe that when it comes to marketing, especially on Instagram, this type of thinking also plays out. People see your content but they are not always sure what to do, or even if they find the content engaging they might not interact with that post the way you want them to. This is where a call to action, or CTA, comes into play. It is basically telling the customer what you want them to do at the height of post engagement. This, in turn, helps you meet your marketing goals. For instance, if the objective is to direct traffic to your website, a call to action such as "click on the link" will ensure that this happens. If you want people to engage more with your post, something as simple as "comment below" could ensure your comment section is lit and that, on its own, can become a major attraction to your posts.

5. Check your spelling and grammar

This goes without saying. A post that is riddled with errors and grammatical blunders is a turn-off and is as good as hiring a very terrible actor to do an advertorial pitch for you. Not only does it fail at effectively communicating the message you want to pass across to your audience, it also gives a very poor representation of your brand. I think the biggest issue of all is the fact that grammatical blunders in your post can call your own integrity into question. That is how much of a big deal it is. So, ensure that when you are putting up your posts on Instagram, keep it simple. Avoid using words and phrases out of context and most importantly, try to avoid using words and phrases that might be offensive.

I know that we have covered a lot of ground on the subject of Instagram, and while you are still processing all of this information, let me give you a quick recap. This way, you get everything in a condensed version and know where best to apply efforts if you feel that you want to go over it again.

1. Instagram is the best platform for brands looking for visual expression.
2. To maximize Instagram for growth, you need to pay attention to the Instagram algorithm which capitalizes on factors such as the interest of users, the consistency of your posts, as well as your ability to engage people on your platform.
3. Becoming an Instagram influencer is about becoming a voice of authority in a specific niche. Pick an industry where you are either an expert in or have a very strong passion for. Identify your role in it and then be consistent as a voice in that niche.
4. To effectively advertise on the Instagram platform and get the results that you want, you need to be strategic about the content of your post.
5. A great Instagram caption is precise, engaging, has a call to action, and is free of grammatical errors.

Task

With everything that you have learned so far, do you think that your brand is compatible with the offerings that Instagram has? If yes, why? If no, what are the things you think you can do with Instagram that might bring some beneficial results to you? Also, if you are thinking of going with Instagram as the ideal social media platform for your brand or business, what do you hope to achieve in the areas of...

- Brand awareness
- Frequency of reach
- Conversion

Use the answers that you get to define your marketing goals for Instagram.

Chapter Five

Facebook

"Facebook was not originally created to be a company. It was built to accomplish a social mission—to make the world more open and connected."

Mark Zuckerberg

More than <u>one billion</u> people use Facebook daily. This figure has gone on to establish Facebook as the go-to platform for social media marketing strategies that are seeking to reach a wider audience. With the tools and features available on the platform, you can open up your business to a broader niche without necessarily sacrificing a lot of money in the process. The platform is updated consistently and so the rules of engagement change from time to time. In this chapter, we are going to look at some of the fundamentals, especially in the areas of advertising rules on Facebook. Beyond that, we are going to look at how you can drive engagement on the Facebook platform and create more awareness about your brand.

I am also going to be offering you suggestions on some of the best Facebook marketing practices that are guaranteed to deliver good results. One thing you should bear in mind as we go forward is that, because of the evolutionary state of the market, it is essential that you stay updated. There are tools and applications that are designed around these updates. What they do for you is that every time you want to put up an advert, they ensure that the ad stays within the rules of Facebook marketing, and I will talk about this too much later. Just as Mark Zuckerberg said in the quote that I used earlier, Facebook essentially is there to connect you to the world. If you are able to do it right, setting up shop on Facebook will open you to a market that is just brimming with excitement for what you have to offer.

Essential Rules of Facebook Advertising

Facebook is currently under a lot of scrutiny globally and given the volume of traffic that the platform gets on a daily basis, this is expected. For this reason, Facebook is employing new guidelines consistently and this is in a bid to ensure that they are more deliberate in regulating the kind of content that is displayed on their platform. Normally, this would only affect people who put up posts that are insensitive and promoting violent content, however, because of the nature of the world we are in today, that scrutiny has extended into the kinds of adverts that Facebook permits on its platform. And to ensure that your ads become approved, here are some of the things you should be paying attention to now.

1. Certain content is blacklisted on Facebook

The category that your business falls under plays a major role in getting your advert content approved. It goes without saying that adverts that promote illegal practices will not be approved. But it is not just illegal businesses that you need to worry about. There are business categories that may compromise the values that Facebook is trying to promote and may fall under adult content. Ads that contain sexually explicit inferences are not acceptable by Facebook community standards. Other categories that may be affected by this rule include posts related to the smoking industry, adverts that promote gambling, and content that sells alcohol and drugs of any kind are not permitted to be sold on the platform. However, certain pharmaceutical companies are allowed to promote their products as long as they have been pre-approved by Facebook.

2. Follow the image specifications on Facebook

First of all, the image file must either be a png or jpg and it must have a minimum of 600 pixels in height and width with a ratio of 9:16 to 16:9. If you are going to add text in your ad image, you have to ensure that it does not exceed 125 characters. If you are going to include a hyperlink in your Facebook adverts, then this will affect the figures I just gave you. The ratios will now be come 1.91:1 to 1:1 and the text will come down to a limit of 25 characters. Now, the image itself should in no way promote nudity, sexually suggestive or explicit content, or focus on too much skin. Violent content or material that is considered too sensational might also prevent your ads from getting approved on Facebook. One tricky area that a lot of people don't know about is the inclusion of non-functional elements in your image. So, if you are going to include things like a checkbox or a play button that is not clickable, there is a chance that your ad will not be approved.

3. Keep your write-up focused

When you create an advert on Facebook, it is important to ensure that the copy for the advert is as compelling as possible. However, in trying to create a compelling narrative, you should ensure that you stick to the truth about your brand or company. Be as realistic as possible in the portrayal of your brand; in other words, try not to sell lies. In a bid to convince potential customers to buy into your product or service, do not exaggerate its performances. The copy should also contain information that is relevant to the ad, especially the landing page where you are going to be directing people to. Everything that you write should be relevant to the advert you are putting up as well as the people you are advertising to. And speaking of a landing page, ensure that the page you are directing people to is free of malware and is actually relevant to the advert. You cannot be talking about makeup and be sending people to a fashion store. Your landing page should have the following elements for it to be approved by Facebook:

1. Privacy policy
2. Price and bill in where necessary
3. An unchecked opt-in box
4. Information on how to cancel

4. Follow the targeting guidelines

In trying to find the right audience to market your products to, you will need to use the Facebook custom audience tool which helps you navigate the different demographics on Facebook and decide on the one you feel is the best for you. However, for your advert to be approved for the selected target demography, you have to ensure that it contains information that is relevant to them. Don't be lured by the volume of a particular demographic. Maybe you have a lot of people in that group, but the number of people who would be interested in the kind of product you offer may be very, very low. As part of the measures to ensure that the Facebook platform is inclusive, you cannot put up ads that are discriminatory. When you start targeting people based on their race, status, religion, or even disability, Facebook will classify your advert as predatory and therefore unfit to be approved. So, do try as much as possible to read the targeting guidelines on Facebook.

How to Engage Your Customers Through Your Page

Facebook engagement essentially refers to the interaction that people have on your page or post. This could include comments, likes, and shares. Just like the Instagram algorithm, the more engagement you have with your posts, the greater your chances of being featured on the Facebook feed. More than that, when people engage more with your post, you increase your chances of reaching a wider following. That is because the interaction on your page is able to reach a secondary audience through the primary contact that people have with your post initially. The primary goal of any business Facebook page is to ensure that your customers, or potential customers, can have a platform where they can interact directly with your brand. With that in mind, let us look at some of the things we can do to keep people engaged on our pages.

1. Avoid sounding like a sales pitch

Most people that I know do not like the idea of being sold to, and this kind of thinking is also present on digital platforms like your Facebook page. People do not come to your platform because they feel like listening to a marketer reel out the benefits of your product. They come because more often than not, you possess information that they cannot find anywhere else or you create content that they can relate with. Anything outside of this will most likely fall on deaf ears—or at the very least, prove to be ineffective as a strategy. Let your focus be on creating content that will appeal to your Facebook demography.

2. Avoid lengthy content

The vast majority of people who use Facebook access it from their mobile phones and when scrolling through their news feed, these people spend an average of 1.25 seconds to glance at a post. That is exactly how long you have to get the attention of people on Facebook. People who use computers spend a little longer but don't think that you have more time with them either, as it is just 2.5 seconds. Now, it may seem impossible to grab the attention of a person in that time frame let alone get your message across in 1.25 seconds. However, the realistic objective here is to get people to pause their scrolling and take a look at what you have written. One way to ensure that people stop scrolling and engage with your page is to keep it short. When people see a very lengthy post, they immediately skip ahead and just keep scrolling unless it is on a topic that they are particularly interested in. But if you keep it short with a catchy headline, you increase the chances of them stopping to engage with your page.

3. Always include a great image

A picture, they say, is worth a thousand words, and Facebook has taught us that this is so true. A post that has a beautiful image has more chances of attracting the attention of people on Facebook than one that doesn't. It doesn't matter how articulate the article is or how well written and thought out the post is. Without an image, there is a very strong possibility that people will just scroll through and move on. Remember, you only have 2.25 seconds or less to get most people's attention and so you want to ensure that you do it right. A great picture could be a flashing neon sign for your page. Before you even say anything in your post, a picture can initiate the talking for you.

4. Make them curious

One way to create a buzz in your comment section on Facebook is to ask a question. Questions get Facebook users to engage with your post in the most amazing ways. You can start the headline of your post (no matter lengthy it is) with a simple question. When people see a question, especially if you phrase it in a way that piques their interest, they immediately get curious and want to know the outcome depending on the kind of question you asked. And they would even go as far as wanting to contribute their opinions by commenting on the post. However, in your bid to make them curious and elicit solidarity with your content, avoid what Facebook has tagged as engagement bait. What this means essentially is putting up a question or comment that does not necessarily require them to engage with your post. Rather, it comes off as you trying to get people to like or share your post. An example of an engagement bait is, "Like this post if you are really into ice cream on Sundays." Or "Share this post for a chance to win this $1,000 makeup kit." Posts like these would get you the "likes" that you want temporarily, but your ranking on the Facebook algorithm will drop so low very quickly and it is usually difficult to recover from that.

5. Don't be stagnant with your strategy. Experiment.

On Facebook, it has been established that <u>videos give you the best engagement</u> across the board. And with this information, it might be tempting to ensure that all the posts you put up on your page are videos. However, because of the updates that are being done on Facebook consistently, it would be very redundant to simply stick to this strategy. It doesn't matter if you are doing regular posts with an image or using videos, you have to fine-tune your strategy consistently to find what clicks with your audience. Also bear in mind that the audience might be evolving. It is important that the way you post and the kind of content you put up on the platform evolves with them. That way, you are able to retain their attention and maintain consistent engagement with your post. Until you get to the point where you are fairly certain of the kind of content that will get you the engagement you need for your brand on the platform, I would say alternate between the kind of content that you put up.

The Facebook Algorithm that Can Change Everything

The Facebook algorithm essentially impacts your presence as a brand of the platform and while this sounds scary, it doesn't necessarily mean doom and gloom. By taking the time to understand how this algorithm works, you can navigate to those murky waters and utilize the platform to get to the results that you want. The reality is, despite the fears and worries surrounding Facebook's algorithm, Facebook remains the premium marketing platform on social media. Facebook's return on investment remains impressive when compared with other social media platforms. What you need to do is make some adjustments to your content strategy so as to boost your organic reach on Facebook, and this list will get you started.

1. Put a lot more effort into your audience targeting on Facebook

One of Facebook's updates in 2019 was the "Why am I seeing this post?" update. This was to ensure that users are only given content that they are interested in. One of Facebook's goals is to ensure that when users get on the platform, they enjoy their time there regardless of how long it is. Now with more than one billion users per day, you can imagine the volume of content that is being thrown at Facebook users. It would make it difficult for them to actually see and access what they are interested in. And so, it makes sense that Facebook would create this update to ensure that people see what they want to see. As a brand, to take advantage of this update, you need to target an audience that is absolutely interested in your niche. Trying to be vague about your audience demography because you want to reach more people is going to take you farther away from the people that actually matter to your brand.

2. Be transparent about your practices

There is a clampdown on misinformation and sensationalistic content on Facebook. People are typically drawn to sensational headlines and because of this, some devious parties use this as an opportunity to promote content that is violent and sensitive at the same time. To prevent this kind of information from being passed around on the platform to unsuspecting victims, Facebook takes measures to keep posts with contents of this nature from being published. Now, as a brand, this may not affect you directly because you are more concerned about your products and image. However, you need to bear this in mind when you are putting out information. Do not try to use sensational headlines to get attention. Focus on growing your brand organically and ensuring that the information you put on your platform is reliable, accurate, and relevant to the audience that will be viewing it.

3. Prioritize the timing of your post

If you do a little research online, you will find that there are specific times that people are most active on Facebook. These times are usually the best times to put out your post or content in order to drive engagement. The goal of this is to ensure that people are interacting daily with your page. We have already established that Facebook gives priority to pages that have engagement. Having more people interact with your page is how your post gets featured on the "Why am I seeing this post?" update. If you feel like it might be demanding to keep up with this kind of schedule (it does get tedious), you can sign up on apps that help you manage your posts. These applications and tools are basically linked to your account on Facebook so that you can schedule a post ahead. That way, even if you are not available to put up the content online because you have synced your Facebook account with these tools, the post automatically is put up during those prime times. My personal favorite for apps in this category would be Hootsuite or Sprout Social.

4. Make videos the pillar of your marketing strategy

Since we are all about ensuring that our pages have the requisite engagements needed to put us on the feed of our audience, why not utilize the most engaging type of post, which is video? You can alternate between image posts and any other kind of posts, other than videos, to keep things fresh and different from time to time. But having videos as part of your marketing strategy will increase your chances of driving up engagement. You do not need to set aside a hefty budget for massive commercials. Simple "how-to" videos can do the trick. Another interesting and not so common tip for getting your videos to work for you is to make it very short, but create a loop so that it keeps playing. You can also embrace the Facebook Live feature which allows you to deliver content in real-time via videos. When creating your videos, you have to bear two things in mind, which is to drive discussions on your platform and hold the attention of your audience. If you are able to achieve both, you will be rewarded with an organic reach thanks to the Facebook algorithm.

5. Push out your content through employees and brand advocates

Apart from Facebook adverts, your reach on the platform is limited to the number of followers that you have. So, if you are trying to grow organically, the post that you put out can only be reached by these people who are already following you. However, if you are able to get members of your team to share these contents with their own network, you can then amplify that reach. And the more this happens, the higher you rank on Facebook algorithm. This is a very simple trick that not many people are aware of but it is so effective in helping you overcome some of the challenges that are associated with Facebook algorithm. So, encourage your team members to share your posts with their network. You can also get brand advocates to do the same and as they do so, they can also encourage people in their network to share as well. It is like a ripple effect, one drop on the surface and the outreach is amplified to distances away from the initial contact point.

Things You Should Do Right Now on Facebook

Now, we know what audiences are looking for when they get on Facebook and we also know how to get their attention and drive interaction with our pages without compromising the rules and regulations of the platform. We have also learned about certain practices that we should avoid if we want to keep our ranking on the Facebook algorithm high. The next step is to integrate those little details that will go on to make a lot of difference in how people experience our brands on Facebook. These are details that are often neglected because they seem so minute, but the impact is immense. I should know because I experienced a lot of this firsthand. And so, you can learn from my experiences and build a brand on Facebook from ground up without having to make the mistakes that I did.

1. Have an interesting brand presence

Your brand presence on Facebook basically focuses on your brand offering. It gives people more information about you and if you set it up right, this could become an extended version of your "about you" page. That said, a lot of companies make the mistake of keeping this platform bare. This is because they feel that apart from the promotional content that they put out, the information they put on this page is not necessarily going to pop up on anyone's feed. However, when people want to patronize a brand or company, what they usually do is conduct a quick search to get more details about the company. If you keep your posts interesting, engaging, and as genuinely reflective of your brand as you can, people tend to trust you more. You can make a sale by selling not just the product itself, but your brand essence. And when people buy into your brand essence, you get their loyalty.

2. Personalize your brand

Social media is basically for people to connect with you and no other platform pushes for this kind of one-on-one interaction than Facebook itself. People want to feel like they are not just talking to a corporate entity or a wall. They want to feel like they are connecting with the human behind the brand. It doesn't matter how antisocial a person is, they still don't want to be serviced by robots. We already have this image in our heads that feeds our perception of what businesses and corporate entities look like. And when you remove the human element, you come across as cold and calculating. Nobody wants to buy from the guy who seems to be only interested in taking money from them. They want to buy from that guy who seems genuinely interested in their experiences, what they are going through, and what they have to say. So, try to ensure that your personality on Facebook has a human element that people can connect with. Humor is a great place to start.

3. Become a member of a Facebook group

Facebook is a universe on its own and Facebook groups are like the LinkedIn version of that universe. In Facebook groups, you are able to connect with people who have shared interests with you. As a brand, this is fantastic because you are given an entryway that leads directly to the doorstep of the audience you are looking for. However, rather than automatically launching into a sales pitch every time you make a comment in these groups, it is important that you offer opinions and tips that will then go on to establish you as a voice of authority in that niche. This is important because in turn, it will drive up engagement on your own platform. Your strategic comments in those groups will make people become curious about you and the services that you offer. And for this reason, they will come to your platform. So, it is not just about joining any old-fashioned Facebook group. You have to look for groups that are in alignment with your goals, as well as brand essence, and when you join them, endeavor to be an active participant there. If you can't find a group that matches your interests, create one.

4. Sync your blog with your Facebook page

There is a very strong possibility that Facebook is not the only social media platform that you are utilizing to promote your brand and business. And so, it only makes sense that you would become exhausted from trying to ensure that posts go up on the different platforms that you are using. That said, you can make your life easier by syncing your blog with your Facebook page, so that the moment you put up a new post on your blog, it is automatically put up on your Facebook page. This eliminates the problem of having to sit down and draft the posts from scratch. It also gives you the added benefit of exposing your contents to more people and when more people see your post, you get more engagement. Depending on the platform you are using there are plugins that are available to help make the integration of Facebook into your blog seamless and effortless.

5. Create a community

It is human nature to want to connect with others. This is why there is a popular saying that "no man is an island." When people come on Facebook, they want to reach out. You can give them what they want by creating a community of people with shared interests. You do this by ensuring that you interact with the people that come on your page not just through the posts that you put out, but you can also comment on the comments that they make. I would even recommend you going as far as commenting on their own pages and platforms. When you get notifications about birthdays, it wouldn't hurt to encourage the community to celebrate the person who is marking the occasion. Little details like this go on to solidify the connection that you have created on this platform. However, you should note that this kind of connection does not happen overnight. It is something that you are going to have to build over time, but if you are consistent and committed to the process, the result will be a powerful community that you can influence.

Once again, we have covered so much ground in such a short time, and to help you retain all this information that you have just absorbed, here's a quick recap.

- There is so much information on Facebook and to ensure that people are not overwhelmed by the content on their news feed, Facebook has introduced a new update that gives people only content they are interested in.
- To increase your chances of being featured on the news feed of your audience, you need to ensure that your post is engaging, relevant, and abiding by the rules of Facebook.
- Facebook is constantly evolving and so your marketing strategy has to be flexible enough to adapt to these changes as they come.
- The Facebook platform is centered around building connections. As a brand, you need to integrate human elements into your online persona in order to connect with the people on this platform.

Task

List out five pages that you connect with on Facebook. If the number of pages are not up to five, look for brands that are similar to the pages that you like to complete the list. When this is done, write out five striking things you noticed on these pages that attracted you to them in the first place. Do any of these practices correlate with the things that we have talked about here? Finally, what is that one thing you learned here that you weren't aware of previously, and how do you plan to implement this going forward? Let the answers you get guide your marketing strategy on Facebook.

Chapter Six

Twitter

"Generally, the view that I've had on Twitter is if you're on Twitter, you're in, like, the meme—you're in meme war land. If you're on Twitter, you're in the arena. And so, essentially, if you attack me, it is therefore OK for me to attack back."

Elon Musk

Twitter is one of the most engaging platforms on social media. Brands who are looking for a more direct interaction with their customers look to Twitter to achieve this goal. However, while the interface of Twitter is basically very simple and can be set up for any user regardless of their digital experience, it still requires an effective social media marketing strategy to get the most out of the platform. When Twitter first started out, the limit for the number of characters used in each tweet was 140. That still did not stop the power behind the voices of those tweets, as there are brands that were built on a single tweet that went viral. In the same vein, there are businesses that crumbled overnight because of the flip side effect of a viral tweet. There is a general assumption that viral tweets are coincidences or unplanned events. But expert social media marketers will tell you different. This is because they know that it is possible to carefully orchestrate a tweet that becomes a movement if you know what you are doing.

One of the beautiful things about Twitter is that if you are able to embed the basic elements of an effective Twitter marketing campaign in your tweet, it can reach your desired audience in a matter of minutes. It is important to note here that starting a viral tweet is one thing, sustaining a tweet that has become a trend is another. However, the potential virality of Twitter posts is one of the things that makes it an essential platform for promoting your business. If you want to create awareness about your brand or a specific product you are launching, Twitter is an excellent platform for it. At the same time, if you want to address consumer complaints using Twitter, it is important that you have a Twitter strategy so that you don't get caught unawares by the anticipated backlash. Let us not forget the case of Kylie's tweet about Snapchat. It was a classic example of how one wrong tweet can change the game for you.

How to Create a Viral Twitter Campaign

Decades ago, if you wanted to get a message across country, the options you had for getting this done were very limited. You either relied on relatives who were traveling to carry your message across physically, or you used smoke signals (which were utilized in cases of emergencies), and even then you did not enjoy the freedom of expression that social media has brought us today; the colors of the smoke were meant to connote specific messages. But today, in a matter of seconds, your message can leave your tweet in the morning, circle the globe, and come back to you long before you are even done with breakfast. This is one of the powerful effects of social media platforms like Twitter. Making a deliberate effort to get your Twitter post to go viral would require you having a network of people who can ensure that the post is spread person-to-person until it expands well beyond your reach.

In the early Twitter days, viral posts appear to happen without any effort on the part of the people who put them out there and we assumed it was a coincidence because we didn't understand Twitter metrics as well as those other elements that you can include to ensure that your post gets to where you want it to get to. Now, there are so many resources available to enable a post to go viral and the inclusion of certain features on Twitter makes the process easier. In the next few steps, I am going to break down the process to help you achieve this.

1. Decide on the content that you want to go viral

Before you set about creating a Twitter campaign, decide on the content that you want to go viral. Is it an image or post that you made on your blog? Are you trying to direct people to your store, or do you want to highlight a specific problem? The answers that you get will guide you on how to implement the first step in your campaign. For instance, if it is a site you want to promote, what you should do is go to a URL shortener (bitly is a great option). This would condense the link to the site you are trying to get people on and make it easier to include it in a single tweet without having to compromise on the messages that will precede it.

2. Create a hashtag for the campaign

If you are trying to create awareness about a product or service, or perhaps you want to drive a movement, it makes sense that you would create a hashtag that is unique to that movement. That way, anyone who connects with the message you are trying to pass across or empathizes with the content of that message can add their voices to your campaign using a customized hashtag. However, if you are just a generic brand trying to sell a product using the Twitter platform, and you want the message to reach as many people as possible, look for hashtags that are in the same field as in your brand or product. One way to do this is by going on the Twitter search engine and looking at what is trending. Oftentimes, you will find them with a hashtag in front. Now, find a way to include the topic that is trending and is relevant to the product you are selling in the same tweet. This will ensure that anyone who clicked on that tag would see the message you have posted. The hashtag takes your message beyond the people who are following you and brings it to an audience who are interested in things that are related, or similar, to what you do.

3. Craft an attention-grabbing message

Now, this is the part where you need to unleash all of your creative juices, as you want to grab the attention of your audience right away. If you thought the attention span of people on Instagram and Facebook was very short, you should check out that of Twitter users. I have been a part of trends that were so viral and gathered so much momentum that you would think the change was going to happen right away. First you have the raging bulls in the China shop and then overnight, everything becomes crickets. The movement dies just as quickly as it started. I should point out here that you cannot plan the future of your brand based on what goes viral. However, you can create awareness about your brand and you only get a shot at it. So, ensure that the post you want to go viral has a message that brings positive attention to your brand. Capitalize on the elements that you need to put into this message in order to get the best results from it and then move on. Because again, a post going viral today does not necessarily guarantee that tomorrow the business is going to be doomed or worth billions. Keep your attention focused on what happens now.

4. Include a call to action in your message

Calls to action drives your audience to meet your expectations when it comes to your social marketing strategy. If you want to make a sale, a call to action basically suggests that your audience makes a purchase via a certain platform that you would then go on to include in the post. Now, a lot of us are not comfortable using the words "buy my product." Personally, it irks me because I immediately think of those cold-calling marketers who seem bent on making your life miserable if you do not sign up to whatever it is they are offering you. You don't necessarily have to say those exact words but by including an incentive for that action, you are directing the customer to do just that. An example would be "Get a pair of sneakers at 50% off if you buy today." You have told your audience what you want them to do. I am hoping that preceding that message, you included details about your brand as well as a high-quality image that would steer your audience into action.

5. Tag the right people before you upload your tweet

Here is one truth you need to come to terms with straight away. It is not your content that makes a post go viral. It is people that make this happen. This does not mean you shouldn't put effort into creating the right content, but we have already discussed this. So, let us get back into connecting with the right people. If you tag the right people in your tweet, it is only a matter of time before you find your post reaching an audience of millions. One of the factors a lot of brands look at is people who already have a high volume of engagement on their Twitter page, also known as Twitter influencers. These people also have a lot of following. For maximum results it is expected that, as part of your Twitter marketing strategy, you will find two or three people who are in your niche and have an influence on the Twitter platform to ensure that your tweet gets out to the audience. These persons should also include a call to action that allows the audience to share that supposed tweet. This will continue until you reach the number of people you want to reach. Most Twitter influencers are paid to help with your post and oftentimes, they do not come cheap. If you connect with the right Twitter influencer, you should be able to get good returns on your investment.

Building and Engaging a Vibrant Twitter Community

If you are not a part of an active Twitter community, it will be impossible for people to engage with your page. The concept of community could differ but when it comes to social media platforms, the focus is on the volume of your following. Your Twitter community could consist of five people or 500,000 people. But before you look at the numbers, you should look at how engaged those people are with your posts. If you find that the 50 people who are following you are constantly commenting, liking, and retweeting your posts, you have a better engagement than the guy who has 500,000 followers with less than 1% doing anything at all on his page. What this means is that if you have a good engagement, the impact of this could be amplified by the number of people you are following.

That said, it is not just about having a large followership base on Twitter. It is also important to create and drive engagement with content that is relatable. These are just some of the few things you can do to improve the Twitter experience for your brand. In this segment, I am going to list out a few more things that would give the community you are creating on Twitter a voice. And not just that, it would empower their voice to help you push your campaigns.

1. Be consistent

Putting out content on an epileptic time schedule can make you seem unreliable. Beyond that, it reduces the engagement of people with your page. Again, I did mention earlier that Twitter has a very short attention span and this is not just related to the post that you put out there. It also has something to do with your platform as a whole. If you are not the kind of person who put up posts frequently, whenever the contents that you actually put up pops up on their timeline, there is a very high chance that they would simply glance through and move on without interacting with that post in any way.

2. Speak the language fluently

If you are not aware of this by now, then I am happy to inform you that Twitter has a language that is unique to its platform. It is important that you speak this language fluently, as Twitter users can be very snobby if you don't know the lingo, and even when you find a handful of people who are very tolerant of your ignorance, you may find yourself missing out on opportunities or making terrible social media faux pas simply because you do not understand the words that have been branded as unique Twitter phrases and knowing what context to use them. For example, the word mention on Twitter is used to mean adding someone in a Twitter post via their Twitter handle. There are many others like this that you need to learn. Do a quick online search to discover those phrases and words. Some of them are even acronyms. Learn and evolve.

3. Do your best to respond to all replies

It is bad manners to ignore people who try to engage you directly by mentioning you in your tweets. Whether it is as a reply to a post that you put up or simply making an enquiry, endeavor to reply within 24 hours—unless the comment that they made is very hurtful, and even then, I feel that you should have a strategy to address that. It is respectful to respond to those messages. In cases where it feels like a comment made on your post does not necessarily require a direct response from you, rather than type out a message, you can simply use cute emojis to acknowledge their reply and keep things light.

4. Build a strong brand

The premise for building a strong brand on Twitter is having a strong personality and to create a personality that is strong for your brand, you need to be very specific in defining what you think your Twitter voice should be. So, imagine that your brand becomes a person. What kind of person would they be on Twitter? That is the answer you need to get for yourself. For corporate entities or brands that deal with corporate businesses, it would be important to ensure that you have a professional voice on Twitter. This would mean that certain slangs and phrases will not be used on your platform and your tone of communication would be as though you were in a formal setting. For brands that are not in this category, you could try to introduce certain elements and be consistent with the inclusion of those elements in every single one of your tweets. It is kind of like your signature on those two. That way, when people see those tweets, they know that this is coming from you.

5. Promote the content of other people

On Twitter, one way to get people to feel invested in your brand is by retweeting their content. When you retweet the content of other people, you are essentially endorsing them indirectly. On this platform, a retweet is as good as an unofficial introduction of a person's content to your followers. This would encourage them to interact more with your followership base, and in the process, drive up engagement. In turn, this kind of engagement will make your audience or followers feel connected to your brand. To make the most out of this, ensure that the content you are promoting on your platform is related to your brand essence. Because, when you go too far out, it may cause a disruption or distort your current strategy on Twitter.

Twitter for Business

Up to this point, we have focused on the use of Twitter from a generic perspective. Right now, I want to break it down from a business angle. If you are a business entity and you are signing up for Twitter, I am going to list out a few ways that Twitter can serve your business as well as how to go about it.

1. Use Twitter to get real-time information on what people are thinking and saying about your business, or other businesses in the same industry as you. Getting the people's perception of your business can help you create a marketing strategy that will appeal to your consumer base. This is not about setting yourself up to be the perfect business model. It is more about ensuring that your customers are happy.

2. Create PR initiatives for your business and set up a crisis management protocol that is prompt and effective. In business, you are always going to encounter people who are not satisfied by the products or services that you offer. This is inevitable, however, having a crisis management process can help prevent a bad situation from turning worse. And in the absence of a crisis, the PR initiatives that you set up work towards keeping your business image away from scandal and protecting your reputation.

3. Twitter is a great way to increase awareness about the products and services that you offer through your posts. You can amplify the outreach of those tweets through paid adverts on the platform or you can collaborate with key influencers within your sector to get your tweets to

reach a wider audience. Whatever you choose at the end of the day, the main objective is ensuring that you create a reliable voice for your Twitter handle that will work at putting your products or services and the eye of the public.

4. Twitter comes in very handy if you want to monitor the performance of all the businesses that are in the same industry as you as well as get direct feedback on how people are experiencing your product and services. Simply look for the businesses you have in mind on the platform and follow them to keep up with what they are up to. Then search for your own business product or services using the hashtag and then join in on the conversation that is probably going on.

5. One of the many beautiful things about Twitter is that it gives you access to people that you normally wouldn't have access to on a regular day. And I am not just talking about high-profile individuals. I am also talking about potential employees. When you see people with potential and you feel will do very well in your company, you can chat them up and get that ball rolling.

Twitter for Individuals

Businesses are not the only ones who can benefit from the vibrant community on Twitter. As an individual, you can use the platform to create a brand that showcases yourself personally and professionally. With the right kind of marketing strategy, you can create and drive engagement in your Twitter community to the point that you are able to influence them. There are a lot of benefits that come with being a Twitter influencer but let us focus on what you stand to gain from signing up on the platform in the first place.

1. As with any other social media platform, Twitter gives you the opportunity to connect with other users. More than that, you can also reach out to brands that you want to work with. This can set the scene for collaborations.

2. Twitter gives you a voice and you can use this voice to talk about issues that are important to you. If you want to create awareness about a cause that is very dear to your heart, a single tweet can set that ball in motion.

3. Outside the career opportunities that are available on Twitter, you can build strong relationships with people that extend beyond the virtual world; there are so many testimonials of relationships that were built on Twitter.

And that is a wrap on this segment on Twitter. My own personal experiences with the platform have been fantastic. Mostly because I was able to build a lot of personal relationships with individuals even though I was running a business account. From my experience, I believe that at least one out of every ten people you connect with on Twitter form genuine connections with your brand and as long as you continue to drive engagement with the tips that I have listed out here, you should be able to build a brand that has a strong voice and is sustainable. That said, let us do a quick recap:

- Twitter gives you direct engagement with your followers.
- A single tweet is powerful enough to either make or break your business. Be deliberate about the content that you put out there and also have a crisis management plan.
- You can create a tweet that will go viral by including the following elements: a specific purpose, a hashtag, a mention of the right

people, and most importantly—a call to action that will ensure the tweet keeps going from person to person.

Task

Build your Twitter lingo. Get online and look for a site that has a list of at least 30 different words and phrases that are unique to the Twitter platform. Start from there and keep building on that.

Chapter Seven

YouTube

"The joy of YouTube is that you can create content about anything you feel passionate about, however silly the subject matter."

Zoe Sugg

YouTube essentially is a video diary of anything you are passionate about. It could be something that is focused on your life or something that is centered around specific issues that you know people are interested in. As you probably know by now, there are different formats to hosting a YouTube video. In this chapter, we are going to build on your foundational knowledge of YouTube and then explore different ways that you can use the platform to build your brand, grow an audience, and all the while make an earning from it.

Impress and Engage Your Viewers in 30 Seconds or Less

This is the part where I repeat the anthem I have been singing throughout this book: people have a very short attention span. It is your job to ensure that you are able to gain their attention, retain their interest, and make a conversion. Thirty seconds may seem like a very short time to get it done, but if you include the right elements in your campaign, it is not impossible. So, here is what you do.

1. Go for quality

When a video pops up on the feed of YouTube users, the quality of the image can determine if that person is going to continue watching or they're going to skip and move ahead. The skip button was put there for a reason. While not all of us are videographers or have expertise with the camera, there are tons of tools out there to help you sharpen the image and give you the quality required to grab and retain the attention of people.

2. Be the friend in their head

Start up your YouTube videos by having a mindset that you are in an actual conversation with people as opposed to you talking to your camera. This detail helps you stimulate and engage in conversation which in turn makes your viewers feel as though you are talking to them. People get turned off when you sound too mechanical or unapproachable. Imagine that you are the friend of this person in their head and the monologue you are having is not necessarily that but a simulation of a version of what the conversation would be like if you were in it.

3. Be consistent

One thing we have learned from all the other social media platforms we have discussed so far is that consistency drives engagement. YouTube is no different. If you want to have more engagement on your platform, you have to establish yourself as a voice of authority or knowledge in the area you are focused on. It doesn't matter if you are a professional brand or if it's a personal brand. Consistency is key. Note here that when I am talking about consistency, I don't mean you should flood people's video feed with your videos. Creating a schedule and sticking to that schedule is enough to get people engaged. A lot of my favorite YouTubers put up their posts once a week, but they ensure that on that day of the week, a post is always going up.

4. Create a simple but beautiful thumbnail

A little-known secret about YouTube is that the best-performing videos on the platform often have their own customized thumbnail. When uploading your video choose the option to customize your thumbnail. The thumbnail should include a little explanation in a text that basically tells the viewer what they will see when they click; try to make this text as appealing as possible. The title, however, is where the magic happens as this is what we encourage them to click on, so be as creative as possible here. Finally, choose a high-resolution image.

5. Keep your videos happy and short

Again, the problem of attention span comes into play here. If you put up lengthy videos on your channel, there is a very strong chance that you will lose your audience long before that video is done. So, the best thing to do is to get straight to the point in the most creative way possible. What most YouTubers are doing is centering their content around an engaging story that keeps the viewer glued to their screens. Try to adapt this method and you will find that people are engaging with your content more.

Creative Calls to Action to Increase Your Subscriber Base

If you are running a video marketing campaign on your YouTube channel and you want to get results from your viewer base, the best way to achieve that result is to ask outrightly. It really is that simple. Failure to include calls-to-action in your posts might result in a lot of views without any tangible outcome. A lot of YouTubers do not feel comfortable doing this, but then again, that is marketing for you. If you want something, you may have to be very outspoken about it and this video platform lets you do that.

However, there are ways you can creatively get your customers or viewers to do what you want them to do without seeming too direct.

1. Use Annotations

If you have ever watched a YouTube video, you might recall seeing those cute little boxes that appear sometime during or after the video to tell you what to do. Sometimes, those boxes tell you to subscribe. Sometimes, they tell you to click on a link. These are annotations and according to experts, using annotations can increase engagement by as much as 3,000%. I think people like them because they are not as intrusive as an outright call to action and for the most part, I would say it's the creative way people use these annotations.

2. Creative Skits

Another way to drive a call to action is with the use of creative skits. These are short dramatized videos where the YouTuber tells their audience what they want them to do. These videos are usually not longer than five seconds and I think they are most successful for this reason. They act as short reminders that people actually like.

How to Create YouTube Content with Just Your Phone

Creating a video channel with consistent posts requires you to follow a lengthy process that begins with the conception of the idea before bringing together all the elements required to make that idea a reality. Then you have the shooting of the video, which is quickly followed by editing and then the actual posting. When I first started using this platform, I thought to myself the people who are able to do this consistently more than once a week deserve an award for just efforts alone, because it can be tedious.

However, having a mobile phone can make this process a little more seamless, especially if you are just starting out as a personal brand as opposed to accompanying a brand where you probably have more than three to four people working together on one video. With your mobile phone you can bring an idea to life wherever you are; we just need to be a little more creative, a little more resourceful, and a little more knowledgeable about mobile technology and applications. So, here's my personal experience on how to shoot a YouTube video straight from the camera phone.

1. Hold it steady

One way to clearly distinguish between a video that was shot on a camera phone and a video that was shot with a camera is the steadiness of the video. I don't know about you, but I have shaky hands which means nine times out of ten, the video will be wonky. So, what I do is I get a mobile stand and then use props to position the stand in a way that it stays in a fixed place and still gets the content that I want to give out.

2. Pay attention to the audio

Not many smartphones are equipped with a microphone that can pick up sounds distinctively, so you need to be creative in this department. What I used to do back then was have an MP3 player in my pocket that would record the audio and then during the editing I found a way to merge the both of them. You can also get an external microphone and then insert the audio jack into the phone to get things rolling.

3. Get an excellent video editing app

Imagine that I said this yelling at the top of my voice because that is just how important it is to your work. Video editing apps these days do not require you to be a mad genius. Just focus on the lighting and the angles as well as the merging of the audios (if you did what I did in the previous point). You can also go as far as including creative concepts that add more of a wow factor to your video. Don't forget to include creative text and images to compliment what you have just recorded.

Promoting Your Brand with YouTube Marketing

YouTube is a massive platform to market on and if you didn't know this, I would like to recommend you to start a beginner class in social media marketing. The platform has a total of at least 30 million visits on a daily basis and if you do it right, your video clip is one of the places that people will visit when they come on YouTube.

1. True View Ads.

This is the most common type of ad on YouTube and in my opinion, I feel like this is the most tolerable type of YouTube advert and that's because people have an option to skip it at the end of the video. You may be asking yourself, why would it be a great option if people can skip it all? This is what happens when people have a choice in marketing. They are more likely to be favorable to your brand, especially if you ensure that in the first three seconds leading up to the point where they skip the video, you are able to create content that appeals to them. They are a great option for businesses and brands that are just starting out because they are cost-effective. They take you to the doorstep of your relevant audience and they are more likely to generate returns on investments

2. Non-Skippable Adverts

As the name implies, these adverts are not skippable and you can bet that a lot of people would find these kinds of ads annoying. However, it doesn't mean that the ads do not generate good returns on investment. As a matter of fact, if you target the relevant people to showcase these ads to, you can generate just as much engagement on your platform as those who use the true view adverts. This kind of advert is best if you are trying to generate awareness on a specific subject. I would advise that you take your time to find the right target market to showcase this to, as the key to the success of this campaign depends on the results that you get.

3. Bumper Adverts

In my opinion, bumper adverts give you the best of both worlds in that they utilize the non-skippable feature of the previous advert and then ensure that the content that is displayed is very short. That way, consumers do not get offended by the fact that they cannot pause the video. In the same way, it also combines the benefits of both platforms where you are able to deliver the message you want to pass across to your specific audience, without being cut off, before your message is effectively delivered. And if you do it right, you can make a conversion in six seconds, which is the allotted time frame. Use this to drive marketing campaigns that are time sensitive.

Chapter Eight

The Other Platforms That You Could be on

"Social media is the ultimate equalizer.
It gives a voice and a platform to anyone willing to engage."
Amy Jo Martin

Facebook, Twitter, and Instagram are one of the biggest social media platforms right now. However, there are other social media outlets that can be used to generate the same kind of engagement for your brand that you are seeking in these popular places. Just because these brands do not have the volume of followership that the top three I just mentioned have, it doesn't mean that they cannot drive your brand to a global platform. The key is understanding where your audiences are and developing a strategy that will get you to their doorstep.

No matter how popular these other platforms are, there are certain features they may not possess that you need to build your brand. If you have been carrying out the tasks assigned to you from the beginning of this book, by now, you should have more than a fair idea of where you think your brand should be featured. Going forward, all we are doing is highlighting the steps to utilize various social media platforms. We are done with the top three and now, we will enter into the second tier of the social media ladder.

LinkedIn

LinkedIn was initially thought to be the platform where job seekers and employees put up their virtual resume in a bid to secure better deals and better jobs. However, that platform has evolved into a marketing brand-to-brand powerhouse. Yes, the focus is still on the young professionals, but if you key into certain features, your brand can generate the awareness you are seeking. Especially if your services or products are tailored to the kind of market that is available on LinkedIn.

The key to promoting your brand of business on LinkedIn is subtle marketing. In this sphere, you cannot do the kind of direct marketing that you find on other platforms, as people do not like to be bombarded with information about your business. However, you could create a strong company page that will generate enough curiosity that will make people want to find out more about you. The content that you put up on LinkedIn should be more about offering value as opposed to creating humor or pushing social sensational headlines.

Finally, when you try to drive engagement on LinkedIn, it is important that you are deliberate and incorporate strategy in every single detail. From the kind of content you share, to the kind of people who you share those content with, your decisions should be intentional. The other bigger platforms have the volume of users that LinkedIn does not have. However, the users on this platform are a lot more concise when it comes to their demography. Therefore, when you share content, bear this in mind.

Pinterest

Pinterest is an image-focused brand that not a lot of people understand how to use, but the interesting thing is that the groups of people who use Pinterest are the kinds of people a lot of brands are sticking to, according to the platform. Pinterest has the highest number of spenders across the board on all social media platforms. If you go to their business page and look through their insights, you will be amazed by the wealth of information that is available there. While their interface does not operate the way Twitter, Instagram, and the like do, there are still things you can do to drive engagement on your platform—and by so doing generate the leads you need to achieve your social media marketing goals.

For starters, beyond setting up a profile on the platform, you need to ensure that you maximize the features by adding a few custom touches to set you apart. The next step is to become descriptive in your profile so that people who search for you can find you easily. This is where SEO research comes in, however, you should try as much as possible not to sound too robotic just because you want to integrate the keywords into your profile; it is best to sound as authentic and realistic as possible for genuine engagement. In order to optimize your profile on the platform, you need to optimize your website. This is because when people click on the images on Pinterest, it takes them to your website; if your website is not matching what you have on your Pinterest profile, there will be an automatic disconnect.

If you are a product-based company, one quick thing you can do to make the most of your time on Pinterest is to sync your web store with your Pinterest page. That way, when people click on your pins, they can buy the products right away if they feel so compelled. Just ensure that the images that you put up are of high quality. Finally, stay active. The more consistent you are on the platform, the more proactive you become in driving up engagement.

Snapchat

Snapchat is a perfect example of a business brand that turned itself around using a social media platform and in this case, it was the social media platform they created that became their saving grace. When Snapchat was first launched, it was regarded as a platform for teenage miscreants and parents were warned to keep their children off the platform. Today, it has become a very engaging platform for personal brands and businesses alike. Snapchat is still light years from becoming the cornerstone in any social media marketing strategy. However, they have some unique features that drive innovation and create awareness.

If you would like to create awareness about your brand without going overboard in terms of budget and planning, or perhaps you just want to showcase your company culture, Snapchat is the perfect platform to do that. It allows you to create lightweight content that is educational and fun at the same time. Because Snapchat is about connecting with your audience in a fun and exciting way, the main focus here becomes creativity. After taking the necessary steps to set up your page, explore the various features that Snapchat has included such as face filters, emojis, and so on. This will give a unique feel to the content that you put out and with your resourcefulness, it can stand you out from the crowd...which is a very good thing on this platform.

From my experience, I would say that the most important thing to do on the Snapchat platform is to have fun with it. Here you don't have to worry about being perfect all the time and it is this imperfection that endears you to your audience. People want to see what is really going on inside, not the perfect picture that a lot of brands and businesses tend to paint on other platforms. Here you are real, and you can manage that real content in such a way that it becomes the focal point of your marketing strategy on Snapchat.

Yelp

When I was compiling this list, I was a little hesitant about including this platform. Largely because it doesn't fit into the same format as the others I have listed here. However, I finally conceded to the idea because Yelp has a large following and like every other social media platform, it also has its unique selling point. For now, Yelp is mostly used by American. So, people outside the US may not benefit from its platform as much. If your audience is American and your business is based in America, this may be the right platform for you. Everything that happens on Yelp revolves around reviews, which is essentially how consumers rate their experience of your brand.

Even if you meet all of the criteria listed above, not every kind of business can utilize this platform. The top kinds of business that stand to gain a lot from this platform are those in the hospitality industry, entertainment industry, as well as the service-based industry. Businesses that are strictly operating online may not be able to gain much traction on this platform. One of the features in the registration of your business profile is the inclusion of a physical address. It is the address that you put up that Yelp will then showcase on its map to pinpoint your location. Businesses that do not have a physical address will not be able to enjoy this feature. And customers who are looking for a secondhand review before going for their own personal experience may be reluctant to buy into your product or service.

If you are able to overcome all of these hurdles, one of the many benefits you would enjoy on this platform is the option provided by Yelp to utilize their metrics to create future campaigns. The data available allows you determine the time that customers are most active on your platform or physical space, how they interact with your brand, as well as the things that you are doing right (and wrong) for your customers. If you put all of this information together, you can create a social media marketing strategy that is aimed at maximizing your current efforts while building on the new insights you have gained.

I feel like all of the information included in this chapter has been condensed, so much so that you can skim it and get the all you need. With that, I am still going to go ahead and do a quick summary.

- LinkedIn is for brands looking to connect with a concise demography.
- Pinterest has the highest number of buyers for products.
- Snapchat is good for promoting company culture.
- Yelp is good for generating reviews about your services.

Task

Make an attempt to summarize your company's product offering in two lines. When you have done that, look closely at all of the platforms we have discussed here and then ask yourself, "Where do I think my brand would fit in the most?" You are allowed to pick at least three platforms.

PART THREE

CRISIS MANAGEMENT VIA SOCIAL MEDIA

Chapter Nine

A Social Media Crisis Plan

"Faced with crisis, the man of character falls back on himself. He imposes his own stamp of action, takes responsibility for it, makes it his own."

Charles de Gaulle

The virality of social media posts gives its users the power to create changes overnight. Some of those changes can be good for business and sometimes, those changes can spell doom for a brand. In previous chapters, we talked about how certain comments on social media were able to bring a brand to its knees. And it is with this context in mind that we look to explore this topic. For starters, a social media crisis management plan essentially communicates how the social media team of that company is going to manage crisis when it arises.

Crises are those unexpected things that happen to us in business and while we hope to never experience one, we plan for them anyway. As a social media user, I would assume that even on a minor scale, you may have experienced some form of antagonism on social media. While we cannot call that a full-blown crisis, these are incidents that may have called your person into question. For brands and businesses, those minor incidents are blown out of proportion and therefore it is important to have a crisis management plan in place.

Why it is Important for Your Business

1. It is crucial for the development of prompt response in case of emergencies

When you have a crisis management plan in place you are rarely caught off guard, as you have already prepped yourself and the members of your team for a likely scenario. Because of the viral nature of social media, speed is essential in creating responses, as this will help to curb the situation before it gets out of hand.

2. It keeps you calm and focused on the problem at hand

In the middle of a crisis, emotions are usually all over the place and tempers are running high. A crisis management plan will help you keep a clear and calm head above proverbial rising waters. This way you are able to disseminate information without further compromising your situation.

3. It helps you take back control of the situation

This day's news spreads like wildfire and this is largely due to the influence of social media. Without a contingency plan, that fire can burn and raze down all the hard work you have put into building your brand. A proper crisis management plan will give you back control of the situation because usually, one of the first steps is taking control of the narrative that is being peddled.

4. It distributes the burden of bearing the crisis alone

A proper crisis management plan disseminates information across management. One single unit or person is not left to carry the burden. In this scenario, the viable plan when it comes to effectively managing the crisis is to delegate, communicate, and resolve, and all of this will happen in different phases.

Setting Up a Social Media Crisis Plan

The first step is to create a communications plan and to create a proper communications plan, you need to fill out the following information:

1. Define what your company will consider a crisis

Depending on your level in business and your volume of engagement on the platform, a crisis could be anything from a very bad review to inappropriate content being put on your platform. Determine what you will need to address right away and what kind of incident can be ignored temporarily. As you do this you should also draught business or company policy when it comes to crisis management. This would be the guideline that will direct all your activities when you are in crisis management mode.

2. Break down the chain of command

Essentially what you're trying to do here is define who handles what. People who are given strategic positions in this process should be made aware of the company policy when it comes to crisis management. At this point you should also delegate the company's spokesperson. This is because information dissemination has to come from a single source for clarity and authenticity.

3. Determine what information will be going where

As a brand or a business, your influence will be felt by your customers, business partners, stakeholders, and employees before you get to your following on social media. Create and design the kind of information that will be going out to each of those people.

Now that you have created a crisis management policy and have intimated members of your team on what to do, the next step is to ensure that people do not take advantage of the situation and further tarnish your brand. You begin that process by ensuring that you have taken control of all your social media accounts and secured them. This will prevent a cybersecurity breach, which could further complicate the situation.

Next, stop all scheduled posts for the time being so that it doesn't appear as though you have taken on a nonchalant attitude towards the crisis. When you come online, ensure that your voice is reflective of the one you have set up in your crisis management policy. Engage with people who are trying to communicate with your brand during this time but do not argue with them.

Finally, it is important that you learn from these experiences so that you can prevent future occurrences. I believe that each crisis makes you better as a brand if you are able to manage it effectively.

5 Elements of an Effective Social Media Crisis Management Plan

There are a few things you can do at this point to let you know that you are on the right track. You may not be able to direct how the storm blows, or the duration for which the storm will last, but you can resolve to ensure that your brand is able to weather it. Here are the five ingredients to ensuring that that happens:

1. Your social media crisis management policy

A clear and detailed management policy is an essential ingredient for managing a crisis effectively. Update this annually.

2. Your social media management team

Your team is the backbone that will provide the support for your brand to lean on during times of crisis. If you have a weak team, the support that they will provide will be weak. And this will impact your chances of surviving a crisis.

3. Your speedy response to the crisis at hand

During a crisis, especially on social media, silence is never the best answer. The more time you give for viral posts to continue spreading, the more damage it will cause your brand. Respond as soon as possible.

4. Your crisis prevention plan

There are tools that are available online to help you monitor activities that may pose a threat to your business. An example of this would be Zenfox, which alerts you to potential crises on social media by alerting you to dangerous messages or content that is targeting your brand.

5. Your ability to maintain communications internally

Internal communications are what helps you to present a cohesive unit when you have to face social media. If you are unable to present a united front, social media will pray on this fact and this will hurt your brand even more.

In summary:

- A crisis management plan is a lifeline for when things get out of hand for your brand.

- You need a social media policy to determine your protocol in times of crisis.
- Guard the passcodes to your social media accounts to prevent a security breach.
- Develop a crisis response that is fast.

Task

Read up how Johnson and Johnson handled the allegations that their products were harmful on social media. Compare that with how Lockheed Martin handled their #WorldPhotoDay Tweet fail. What are the lessons you learned and how would that impact your strategy going forward?

Chapter Ten

Taking Stock and the Lessons Learned

"Creating a Backup Plan, There is no better teacher than adversity. Every defeat, every heartbreak, every loss, contains its own seed, its own lesson on how to improve your performance the next time."

Malcolm X

In life and in business, the best thing we can do for ourselves is to ensure that we are set up for success. I would like to think that you reading this book is one of those things that can ensure that this happens. However, just as Malcolm X said in the above quote, experience is the best teacher. So, this chapter is dedicated to some of my experiences as a business owner. And I will be sharing some of the most important lessons I have learned along the way.

Creating a Backup Plan

Whatever you do, always have a backup plan. No matter how perfect, detailed, and well-orchestrated your strategy is, there are a lot of factors that can influence the outcome. The best you can do is ensure that you are fully prepared for it and one of those things, especially when it comes to social media, is to ensure that your Plan A has a Plan B and that your Plan B has a Plan C.

As you set up your primary account on different social media platforms, do ensure that you have a secondary account somewhere with your brand name on it. This is just in case something happens. You could end up getting hacked or someone else forcefully takes over your account.

Basically, you never really know until it happens to you. Don't wait. Set up a secondary account today.

Managing Your Social Media Data

The wealth of information available at your fingertips is amazing. All you have to do to access it is just...look. Twitter, Instagram, Facebook, Pinterest, Snapchat, and so on...all of these platforms have their own individual metrics designed to offer you insight into how your posts and brand is performing online. The people that reach out and connect with you also form a part of this data. If you do not find a way to utilize the information that is coming to you, you will end up losing out big-time on these platforms.

Mine that data, as they say, and use it to your advantage. Leverage the information that you have in creating a marketing strategy that would change the outlook of your brand.

Assessing Your Marketing Performance

Having a continuous assessment of your brand is one way of being very practical with what Malcolm X told us in the beginning of this chapter. You are allowing your experiences to be your teacher. It doesn't matter how successful the campaign is or how much you failed in terms of meeting your goals and objectives. The point is there are lessons in all of these, and it is important to pinpoint those lessons and put them into practice.

This is how you evolve into becoming a better version of yourself. Another reason for assessing your marketing performance is to ensure that your practices are up to date. From the beginning of this book, I established that social media is constantly evolving. These platforms that we have today may seem like the pillars of digital marketing. There is a possibility (albeit very slim) that they might become obsolete tomorrow. You need to ensure that you are ahead of that curve.

Rebranding and Rebuilding

Personally, I don't believe that anything is over until you accept that it is. You may have experienced some harsh failures along the way and perhaps lived through losses that were just too difficult to bear. However, it doesn't have to be the end of your brand or business. All it takes is a change in attitude, a little fire born from resilience, and the determination to succeed.

Like the legend of the Phoenix that was supposed to announce your finality, it could become the birthplace of your greatness. The important thing is to ensure that you learned the lessons you needed to learn on this journey and taken the tips that this book has provided you. Use that information to rebrand and rebuild yourself.

Conclusion

"If you want a happy ending, that depends, of course,

on where you stop your story."

Orson Welles

Social media is such a powerful platform today and you are right to want to utilize it to your advantage. But more than seeking what you would gain from the platform as a businessperson, my advice for you is to think of what you can offer to the platform. People will come to you when you have something of value to give to them. I learned from an old friend that marketing is essential for the survival of every business, but integrity and service is what keeps that business going. Don't mistake the wealth that comes from having so many people support and follow your brand as the be all and end all for your brand.

I believe that you can be so much more than your following on social media. Buy into the ideology that you can change the world and with each step that you take on this journey, you will find that the vision you have for your business will adapt to this new that idea you have. And it is only when you allow that process to happen that you will find yourself doing truly great things and influencing the world. I hope that the information that I have provided in this book is able to help you at least find your way on this journey. I wish nothing more than for you to succeed to the volume that you would measure it. And even more than that, I wish that your brand will join the leagues of brands that are working towards making the world a better place one step at a time.

Whether you're growing a business entity or working on establishing a personal brand that will eventually become a global icon, take the knowledge that you have gained here and make it work for you. Closing this book does not necessarily mean that the journey ends here. As I said when we were closing the last chapter of the book, it only ends when you say it does. Social media will continue to evolve; you should learn to evolve with it. But every time you hit a glitch along the way, feel free to come back to these pages and start the process again. No knowledge is ever truly lost. You only get deeper insight and perspective.

I wish you all the best.

Book #2

Social Media Marketing 2020

How to Crush it With Instagram Marketing

Proven Strategies to Build Your Brand, Reach Millions of Customers, and Grow Your Business Without Wasting Time and Money

Introduction

The goal of marketing has always been to push target audience members into making a conscious choice to purchase a product, subscribe to a service, or to even change their perspective on a certain issue or topic. As such, we cannot rally fault old-time marketing strategies in being pushy with their messaging. After all, how else are you going to do something if it is not hammered to your head that whatever they want you to do is of great importance?

But here is the problem with the market today: *Things Have Changed.*

With the dawn of the Age of the Internet, a stronger focus has been put on consumer agency and choice. Now, the consumer is less of a drone who is susceptible to overt coercion to do or purchase something and more of a thinking buyer who puts a lot of thought and care into every purchasing decision they make.

There is also fact that the Internet right now is divided into many communities, each with their own language, culture, and overall philosophy. A person who uses Facebook tends to display certain expected behaviors while using the site and another who frequents YouTube will do so differently at that platform.

The point is that marketers need to know how people think and feel on each known site in order to craft a message that they will respond positively when exposed to. This is where Instagram comes into play as it is one of the easiest platforms to overlook, underestimate, and disregard as marketing tool.

What many are not aware of is that the platform can actually be used to expand the reach of any brand for a fraction of the cost and effort one typically spends in other social media sites.

Think of it this way: imagine that you are an experienced baseball player who suddenly has to make a career shift into cricket. The two ball games might be different but the skills you learned in the former will still be essential in the latter.

This is the same when venturing into a new kind of platform for marketing such as Instagram. The rules might be different there but the concepts that bind the whole thing together are the same.

To put it in other words, survival and success in your venture into Instagram depend greatly on your ability to adapt to the culture there without forgetting about the basics of online marketing.

The only question, however, is *how you are supposed to do that.* In this book, you will go through the different conceptual differences that make Instagram stand out as a platform and a viable marketing channel. You will also learn how to craft your message there and create content that will get that message across to your target audience.

Of course, you will also be acquainted with the most successful brands on the site right now and how they managed to establish themselves in it.

Just do remember that Instagram is just like any other site out there. You have to know what makes it tick in order to make your stay there as successful and profitable as possible. If done right, you might just be on your way to creating marketing campaigns that will definitely turn heads on the platform – and for the right reasons, of course.

Chapter 1. Instagram: An Introduction

So what makes Instagram, well, different?

The most basic description of Instagram is that is an image sharing platform in the vein of older forums like 4Chan and 9gag. However, the way it presents its content can be seen as something a bit more elaborate or, for the lack of any other word, flashy.

But as for the viability of the platform as a marketing channel, there are a few facts about the site that you need to be aware of.

User Population

Instagram has over a billion active users (which are users who have logged in in the past month. Over 60% of these people login on a daily basis. Half of the user population follow brands.

80% of its population is comprised of private individuals while the rest is are small time businesses, large corporations, non-profit organizations, and any other entity made by laws and incorporation.

The biggest segment that makes up Instagram's entire population belongs to the Teenager Young Adult crowd. These are people aged 14 to 30 and have one of the most active spending behavior in the Internet in recent years.

In addition, 32 of teens in the US reported that this platform is the most important social network for them.

Frequency

An estimate of 51% of Instagram's users log in to their accounts at least once per day. Also, 37.5% of these users use Instagram's Stories feature on a daily basis while a third of the population come from businesses.

Also, visual content in the form of photos happened to be the most engaged type of content in the site at 58%. Aside from that, images that pertain to Fashion, Lifestyle, and Inspiration tend to be consumed the most.

As for peak engagement at the site, it spans at 4 to 5pm, regardless of the time zone. This means that there could always be a spike in Instagram activity at any time in any place across the world.

Other Metrics

Surprisingly, people tend to consume Instagram photos with the least bit amount of edits and filtering. This means that there is no popular photo type or filter that Instagram users prefer sharing and engaging at the site.

As far as advertising is concerned, the site is home to more than 2 million advertisements and other marketing campaigns on a monthly basis. For profiles, they have the potential to gather no less than 600 followers in their lifetime while also being connected to an average of 350 active accounts.

All in all, these data shows that Instagram makes for a rather robust network and a fairly effective marketing tool to add to your list of online marketing channels.

Unique Features

But what exactly makes Instagram unique? Generally speaking, Instagram offers three unique features that no other site has replicated yet.

1. Mobile Optimization from the Ground Up

Technically speaking, Instagram is not mobile optimized. However, this is only so as the phrase "mobile optimization" connotes that the site was made to adapt to mobile devices as far as their screen sizes and navigation systems are concerned. The truth is that Instagram has been designed for mobile users right from the very start.

This is quite important as mobile users already take up a third of the world's population of Internet users in recent years. In Instagram, everything from content creation to marketing can be down in one hand. If connected to the right accounts, a single person can be exposed to a near-infinite scroll of new content every time that they are logged in to the site.

2. A Highly Visual Medium

As will be discussed later on, visuals happen to be a fairly effective medium with which to do your marketing. The impact that they can generate with a fraction of the effort needed to set up other marketing mediums is something that no marketer should ever underestimate.

Fortunately, Instagram is a platform that encourages that use of visual media. In fact, the most engaged kind of content on the site right now are pictures and the best ones tend to net in comments, shares, and likes by the hundreds of thousands to even millions. That is the kind of engagement that one cannot purchase through paid advertising.

Also, Instagram can automatically adjust the sizing of photos so that they are uniform on the platform. This way, your marketing campaigns can look coherent and do not break immersion from one image to another.

3. Simplicity

However, what gives Instagram its strong staying power in recent years is the sheer simplicity of using it. Its interface is not as cumbersome as the ones found in, say, YouTube or Facebook which makes it a hit for younger demographics. For marketers, this means that they can also easily monitor the engagements for their content without having to sift through pages of charts and readings.

Also, the simplicity of the site means that businesses can leverage their presence without having to understand the more technical and finnicky stuff that runs the entire platform. Lastly, the community on the site right now has an energy and willingness to consume all kinds of content that no other site has managed to compete with.

4. Re-Using Content

In some ways, Instagram provides marketers with the ability to repurpose their content. You have a long article that you want to share on Instagram? Turn it into an infographic. If you have a video on YouTube, take a memorable still from that and post it on the platform.

The point is that even old marketing campaigns can find a place on Instagram and still be effective in funneling traffic there. This should save you a lot of time from having to plan content specifically for the platform.

5. Cross-Channel Marketing

More often than not, Instagram can make for a perfect fit to your already existing marketing campaigns. In fact, by adding one more site to your list marketing channels, you can increase the amount of traffic to your site and expand the reach of your brand in new markets.

For example, you may display your Instagram photos on your website. When a customer browses through the site, there is a chance that they may not have been following your Instagram profile.

But if they see a link to your gallery in Instagram at your own site, they would click to see your account, start following you, and get a constant stream of new content from it every time they log in to their own IG account.

Alternatively, a follower on Instagram might not have known of your site. With the Shoppable Instagram version, they can go to the shop version of your IG account, click through the products on offer there and be taken to your website.

Either way, Instagram provides another point of entry for potential customers in learning more about your business. And, aside from that, they can get to know your business more from every site that your account can take them to.

Some Caveats

So, marketing in Instagram should be easy with all these advantages, right? Wrong.

Just as with any other website out there, Instagram has a few quirks that make it far from the perfect social media platform to market in.

1. Linking is Next to Impossible

Unless you include them on your main profile or creatively include them in each post, you cannot directly include links to outside pages for your marketing campaigns on the website. The reason for this is that Instagram wants to discourage businesses from flooding their target audience's feed with their content and maintain a balance between user-generated and promotional content.

However, as was stated, there is a way to include links to your marketing content. You only have to do so in a way that is not as direct and blatant as in other social media sites.

2. Text Content is Near Ineffective

Instagram, as a highly visual medium, is not exactly the best place to do purely text-based marketing. People come to Instagram for cool and inspirational images that they can share in other sites. This means that you have to master the art of delivering your marketing message using only a few words or a few short sentences. If you have to use text in your content, you have to find a way to incorporate it in more engaging forms of media in order to gain some traction for your campaigns.

3. No Conversations

Again due to the fact that Instagram is a highly visual medium, starting a direct conversation with your target audience and customers in the site is rather difficult, if not impossible. The platform just wasn't designed for that.

If that is the main concept behind your marketing campaigns, it is best that you adjust to the limitations of Instagram so that you can still generate engagements for your brand. If not, then you might have to use those marketing campaigns for other platforms.

Native Advertising: What is It and How Can You Use It?

The goal of content marketing in any social media site has always been rather simple: go to where people congregate and then provide them with something that they are looking for (or, at the very least, are aware of). If they like what you have to offer, then engagement with your brand will increase.

However, there is one term that content marketers have been using frequent in recent years and it is called Native Advertising. In more ways than one, this is what should help you establish your foothold in Instagram given its rather unique concept. Or, generally speaking, it should help you improve the way you push your content in any social media platform that you wish to operate on.

1. **What is It?**

In the simplest terms possible, native advertising is simply the marketing strategies that you use that is native to the platform that you promote on. To make this easier for you, let's have an example:

In Instagram, the most engaged kind of content are images and the most popular theme are Fashion, Lifestyle, and Inspiration. As such, native advertising for Instagram involves the use of images that are aimed to brighten one's mood or uplift their spirits. For Twitter, the native form of advertising will be Tweets. For YouTube, that would be videos. And so and so forth.

2. **Why Should You Use It?**

As with any other marketing strategy out there, the reason you should be considering using native advertising in Instagram is for the advantages that it offers. Here are some of them:

a. **Increased Brand Awareness**

If you produce content that is native to the platform you are advertising on, you can attract the attention of your audience at a more efficient rate. You have to consider that performance metrics are essential to your campaigns as they can immediately tell you if your strategies are working in real time.

In this regard, native advertising, tends to offer better engagement rates, quicker conversions, and a generally higher level of brand awareness and loyalty. As an added bonus, the chances of audiences creating their own marketing efforts such as comments, shares, reviews, and testimonials for you is higher if you shift to native advertising.

b. **Better Content Relevance**

If you produce content that is compatible to Instagram, especially in the language it uses and through the tools that the site offers, it would be easier for your audience to share and engage with it. You have to remember that the best kind of advertising is those that encourage trust and loyalty in the brand.

As such, creating content that not only fits the format but also the culture of Instagram, makes any topic that you raise or any solution you propose through your marketing all the more consumable. If there's plenty of engagement, there is even a chance that your content is going to become viral. And that is always something that a lot of online marketers would prefer.

c. **Customer Agency**

The updates in Google's algorithms have shown that customer behavior in recent years have shifted from a fact-finding approach to a more problem-solving orientation. In essence, they just don't find stuff online for knowledge's sake. They need to find ways to make that knowledge applicable in practical and real-world scenarios.

Native advertising, in this regard, helps marketers push content that provides value to their audiences. The core concept of the strategy is not to only present ideas and themes that would make people convert into customers but to present such in a manner that relates to them on a personal level and gives a solution to a problem that they constantly deal with.

For instance, you might be a seller of countertops and you use your IG profile to showcase what you offer to the market. If you are only showing good countertops without even an explanation why or just for purely marketing purposes, you are not going to attain a lot of traction on the site.

However, if you present your offerings by showcasing them as part of a lifestyle or even highlight some eco-friendly options here and there, you are at the very least tapping into a need that people have in relation to the kind of products that you are offering. After all, who does not want a countertop today that is nice to look at, durable, germ-resistant, and made with environmentally conscious materials?

Simply put, native advertising can help you convince your audience that you may be in the market not only for profit but also to offering something that is valuable, real, and sustainable. If you show that you care more than the money that you could earn from these people, your audiences would tend to reward you more with their loyalty.

Setting Up Your Instagram Account

Getting your own Instagram account activated is a fairly straightforward process. In fact, you can do this within a few short minutes if you want to.

Step 1. Download the App

Although the desktop version can be accessed through an Internet Browser and integrates well with your existing PC setup, the mobile version would actually play a more crucial role for your marketing.

With the app, you can immediately publish any image that you have taken and interact with your audiences on the go. It would really help you do your Instagram marketing while you are doing other tasks.

Step 2. Sign Up

Of course, you'd have to let Instagram know who you are by filling up an information sheet. This includes your name (or the business's name), e-mail address, other basic information like age, gender, and physical address, and your password.

Alternatively, since Instagram is linked with Facebook, you can choose to log in with your Facebook account which duplicates all your basic information from the latter to the former.

Step 3. Switch to a Business Account

Within Instagram's setting is an option that says Switch to Business Profile. This is a rather crucial step to take as Business Profiles have some inherent advantages over normal profiles which would really help you in your marketing campaigns.

In fact, here are some of the advantages that you could expect if you set up a Business Profile.

- **Advanced Analytics**

Instagram will provide you real-time data to help you determine whether or not your marketing campaign was successful there. It will tally up any kind of engagement your content gets from likes, shares, and comments and then present them in a format that is easy to process and interpret.

- **Extra Business Information**

With a business profile, you have the added advantage of letting your audience know other pertinent business information like the physical address, store hours, main webpage, and other contact information.

Remember that although online marketing is needed, it is on-foot traffic (where people actually show up to your business to make a transaction) where things matter the most. You have to let people know where you are setting up shop so they can part with their money as soon as they are converted.

- **Marked for Marketing**

With a business profile, every content you published is immediately tagged as an ad. This means that Instagram's algorithms will automatically push your posts up which increases their visibility in the news feed of every Instagram user.

The only disadvantage to this is that your content is immediately identified as an ad by users as well. This means that they can ignore it even more if they feel that whatever your publishing does not interest them.

A. Linking

By switching to a business profile, the No Linking limitation mentioned a few paragraphs before is immediately done away with. Now, as a business profile, you can add links to your content and your Stories which should drive traffic to whatever page you currently have in the Internet.

A Word of Advice

The Switch to Business Profile is only available at the very first instance that you set up your profile. Once you have chosen to have a private or business profile, you can't switch from either later on.

Once you feel confident with your choices, select Done and your profile is ready.

To Wrap Things Up....

The essence is that Instagram is a fairly easy platform to get yourself familiarized with. After setting up an account and getting to know the different content creation options being offered there, you should have your own official Instagram account for the business.

But this does leave a question: just exactly WHAT are you going to publish there. Yes, we know that it's going to be images. But what kind of images should you publish there that would resonate the most with your target audience?

Chapter 2: The Content Creation Process

It's an oft-repeated phrase in the world of online marketing that "Content is King". From the blogs that you read to the images that you share and post, content is always the primary way of getting your point across the Internet. This also means that most of your strategies online will deal with the creation and publishing of such content.

But what exactly is content and how do you create good ones? To answer those questions, there are a few things that you need to understand first.

Why Original Content Matters

There is this idea that content creation is a rather daunting task. After all, you would be creating something that may or may not be liked by everybody else in the market, and this affects the success of your brand in the Internet.

That pressure alone is enough to scare a lot of people from creating otherwise unique and engaging content. However, there are a few benefits as to why you'd rather deal with content creation anyway. Here are some of them:

1. Becoming Credible

Consumers nowadays are more fickle and discerning as ever. They are not so easy today to convince to be loyal to your brand as things were in the past. No amount of expensive marketing campaigns will ever be enough to compel a person to always part with their hard earned cash whenever they encounter your brand in the market.

Unless, however, if you can convince them to do such by earning their trust first. This, in turn, requires you to provide them with something valuable like information that they can use in practical situations through your content. The more value you provide and the more consistent you are with such, the easier it will be for people to trust you.

2. Response to Change

It is no secret that industries change especially in the online world. Changes in government regulations and even the climate can affect how people regard certain businesses and brands. The best strategy that any content creator can use, then, is to push content that would tackle and address such changes to get their name across the market.

For example, the US Government might start imposing huge tariffs on other countries like China. Or what if a new law is passed that is life changing for many people, such as same sex marriage? What you could do in this regard is to start talking about that issue on your content and find a way to incorporate it into your marketing campaigns. Note, however, that it's best to be careful about this as well. It has to be relevant to your audience as much as possible.

If you can even talk and predict how such changes can affect the market, you are putting your brand at an advantageous position as "the business who called it" when such changes do take effect.

It takes a bit of inspiration from Journalism, in actuality. If you are the first to publish content that covers new changes in the market or the world, the more valuable your brand will be to the rest of the market.

3. The SEO Process

Content Creation and the Search Engine Optimization process have always gone hand in hand. In fact, the visibility of your content to your audiences will be determined by the search results pages by way of their algorithms.

Back then, list-type articles were all the rage as Google's previous algorithm deemed it so. However, when the Panda algorithm was implemented, the focus shifted to problem-solving information.

How search engines rank content is fairly straightforward. Whenever a query was put in, the search bots would scour the entire Internet to find key words and phrases that would match what was being asked. The more that bots find those words, the more visible that page or content will be in the results pages. Search engines do not reveal the specific algorithms but there are other factors as well including whether or not your content is deemed reliable or valuable.

This can be a double-edged sword on your part. If the kind of content that you produce does not meet the standard of search engine bots, you will find that its rankings will drop in the results pages within an instant. However, this is not the end to that content's usefulness which conveniently leads to the next point which is...

4. Potential for Re-purposing

The most seasoned of content creators know that there is more than one way to use content. Let us say that you have created an article about the best cleaning solutions for, say, wooden countertops. That's one way of conveying your message.

But there are other ways to do it. You can make an infographic out of your article and post it on Instagram. You can take still from a video and post it there while inviting others to visit your YouTube page.

There are even entire Podcasts made using only one article as a script while the rest of the people there add on to what has already been addressed in the primary content. The point is that the possibilities for saying the same thing over and over again without being redundant is endless if you are that creative.

5. Better Conversion Rates

The ultimate goal of content has always been to compel people to purchase a product or service that you might be offering. However, this can't be done if they (a) don't know you or (b) don't trust you at all.

Content that is made well can make your brand even more visible to end users which increases traffic to your site. The more value you provide for each content you make, the easier it is for a person to convert from an audience member to a paying and loyal customer to the business.

In essence, once a person thinks that you are trustworthy source of practical knowledge, they would hesitate less to consume what you have to offer. Even if they have to constantly part with their money just to get what you are promising to them.

The Pillars of Content Creation

So how does one go about creating content that is unique and effective for any sort of online campaign? The process can actually differ from one content type to another and from site to site but they cover the same aspects. In fact, every good content out there passes through five pillars.

1. Planning

After all, you can't create what you have never visualized. To plan content, you need to do several things:

a. **Identify the Target Market** - Naturally, you have to know who you are going to expose your marketing content to and this would include learning what topics, problems, and issues would resonate with these people the most.

b. **Your Goals -** What are you hoping to achieve from your marketing campaign? Do you want your brand's awareness to increase? Or do you want to expand and tap into new markets? Or perhaps your content is there to drive traffic and online sales for the business? Whatever your goals, you have to write them in paper.

c. **Know the Platform and Tools -** As was stated, the best kind of content are those that are native to platform. Take the time to familiarize yourself with the language and culture of Instagram and master every tool that the site gives to your disposal.

2. Creation/Production

This is where the bulk of the content creation process will be focused at. Once you have identified your target market and ideal marketing channel, you should now identify the kinds of topics that you want to talk about.

Whatever topic that you should choose, make it sure that it is highly relevant to the market or, at the very least, something that they are familiar with. This is also where things like keyword searches will become important for the SEO process.

You should also identify the purpose of your content. Does it inform or entertain? Does it want to inspire or convert people into customers? The goal you have for that content will affect its overall tone.

You should also consider where you are going to source your content with. Curating and crowdfunding are good alternatives if you are not that good in creating your own content. However, for the best results, it is best that you create your own content.

3. Optimization

Once content has been created, you should then make it a point to make it as highly engaging and consumable as possible. The first check it has to pass is on Factuality. Everything contained there must be true and accurate as readers might also be verifying what you are saying from outside sources. Errors in fact might even affect your brand's reputation especially if you do it more than once.

The next check is on Grammar and Structure. Does it follow a strong and clear narrative from start to finish? Does everything inside that content work in proving (or disproving) a certain issue?

Does every paragraph follow basic subject-verb agreements? Can anyone go through what you just made without getting lost in between the beginning and the end? These are just some of the things that you have to check to prevent issues later on.

This is also why it is better that you would invest on an expert editor to check on the quality of your content as they are the counterpart of creators. You may even do it yourself provided that you have the time and skills to do so. Either way, you have to make sure that whatever you publish has gone through stringent checks in quality.

4. Marketing

Aside from creating content, you should also build interest for it. Think of it as something similar to what videogame developers and publishers do every June with the E3 Show. There, they would release trailers and demos for their upcoming products to generate buzz prior to their respective releases.

For content, there are multiple ways to do this. The most common method is through social media where you post updates regarding upcoming content. Everyone that has been linked to your profile will see the update and would theoretically be interested in whatever will come out.

Another method is through e-mail where you send an email to all those subscribed to your mailing list to notify them that something is about to be released.

Either strategy is way more effective than traditional marketing as you are already targeting people who already have an experience with your brand or are exposed to it on a regular basis. This means that they would show less hesitation in consuming whatever you are trying to offer to them.

5. Publishing and Measuring Results

Once enough hype has been built for your business, all that is left to do is to publish it. However, this is not the end of the process.

Once you have published your content, the next thing to do is to measure how it is being engaged in the market. What many content creators forget to do is to constantly interact with their target audience.

Due to the level of interaction provided on the Internet, they may want you to clarify on an issue you raised in your content or correct you with certain facts if they think that what you were presenting was not truly accurate.

Either way, this provides an opportunity to interact with your audience which further drives traffic to your pages and makes your content even more relevant.

After a few days or weeks, you must then take note of the actual level of engagement generated by your content from the likes, shares, and even comments. You should take note of any issue that your audience pointed out regarding your work and the subtopics that they were engaged with the most. This will give you an idea as to what to publish next and help you improve your skills as a creator.

What Makes Great Content?

Content may come in all shapes and sizes in marketing. However, what can make content be considered as good? There is no definitive answer to that but the best ones always seemingly follow a scheme.

Content Classification

To make this easier, what you will have to remember is that content can come in three major categories which are:

A. Product - this is basically the types of content that offer something tangible to your audiences be it products or services.

B. Role - Content of this type assumes a role of sorts in relation to the life of every audience member. What is that content trying to do for the audience? What goal is it trying to achieve for them? What are the questions that it is trying to answer? Identifying the role that the ad will take will determine the narrative that it is going to tell to its audience.

C. Emotion - A content of this classification is designed to connect with audiences at a personal, intimate, and emotional level. The point of this content type's existence is to evoke some sort of emotional response in its viewers. Or, at least, it does provide them with another perspective on how things should be viewed at.

So, which then of these three types is the content that you should be publishing in Instagram?

The answer is all of them. Each type has its own strengths and weaknesses which means that a diverse portfolio of marketing content that focuses on one or another is going to help you in the long run.

The point is that you don't favor one over the other. Focusing too much on pushing your product or services prevents you from making a personal connection with your audiences, thereby ruining the opportunity to make them convert. On the other hand, if you focus too much on triggering emotions, you run the risk of confusing your audience as to exactly what you want for them to do.

Thinking Like a Journalist

The best kind of content out there, if you think about, serves a purpose. If a person goes to your Instagram page, they are most likely not there just to ogle at your pictures. They might be there to seek information, confirm their biases, be entertained, or get the persuasion that they need to complete the sales process.

Whatever the reason, the point is that you should put out content that should be able to convince your audience that you have something worthwhile to offer. Remember that making people convert is hard these days without you offering something tangible to them first.

And there is no other profession out there that can convince people to think and act differently than a Journalist. So why not copy their style for your marketing content? Here's how:

1. Identify Your Angle

Journalists always write their story from an angle or a perspective of sorts. Think of it this way: there is always more than one way to view things which means that no two people viewing the same thing can ever share the same exact point of view. As such, the best journalists create their content using an angle that their readers can relate to.

For instance, if you are a cleaning product supplier, you may produce content that shows how your products are being used for practical purposes. The angle of the narrative that your content conveys will actually serve as a point of entry to your audience towards the customer conversion process. This is because you are giving them an idea as to how to process the information that you are about to give to them.

2. Start Right

The impression that your introductory lines will affect the overall reception of your content. If the angle defines the narrative, then the introduction will start the process of turning your ideas into actionable responses.

More often than not, it is in the introduction where you will spend a lot of time of as this will dictate the mood of your overall story. To make it easier on your part, make the introduction answer the 5 Ws:

- Who
- What
- When
- Why
- Where

This should start your story within just the first sentence if done right.

3. Give Your Content Humanity

Emotions play a vital role to the reception of your content which is why you should give your content a "human" factor. For instance, a quote from a popular person gives credence to any point or argument that you might raise.

On a more direct note, you can always use user-generated content like testimonials and reviews to get the point of your Instagram content across. And speaking of getting to the point...

4. Do Not Waste Words

Given the image-heavy format of Instagram, it is best that you directly convey your message to your target audience. Introduce the problem, offer the solution, and then make a call to action.

Never, in any case, go off into long tangents or digress from the point. You should keep your audience's interest for the story at a high so they won't scroll down to the next content on their food. Say what needs to be said but do not leave out any important detail.

The Call to Action

As was mentioned, it is your content that would do all the convincing your audience that your offer is great. However, it is at the CTA where the final push towards conversion occurs.

So what does a good Call to Action look like? Here are a few qualities that you should include in yours.

1. Value

Always remember that people rarely buy these days just for the sake of it. If you want them to do something for you, make sure that you offer something of equal value in return. As such, the CTA should summarize the main points of your content to give your viewers the idea that what they are about to do is ultimately beneficial for them.

2. Visibility

Your CTA should be placed somewhere in the content where it is easily seen and distinguished. You can do this by putting them on a separate paragraph if your content is text-based or as a caption for images. The goal is to get the viewer's attention long enough to decide whether or not they want to complete the sales process.

3. Personality

One quality that the normal, everyday person has that no company could ever compete with is the ability to be trusted more. CTAs that offer an intimate and unique twist can connect with people more than those that are just blatant with their marketing. After all, there is a huge difference between saying "buy our stuff!" with "come and have a wonderful experience with us!".

4. Clarity

Being clear is always recommended as the overall goal of marketing is to compel people to do something. Your CTA must let the viewers know EXACTLY what you want from them and what it is they will be signing up for. Also, you have to highlight and summarize all the properties that make your offering stand out from the competition.

5. Shortness

CTAs don't have the luxury of a space big enough for you explain everything to the viewers. Instead, they only say a few words that convey what has already been established in your primary content.

And if you think one paragraph is too short for that, remember that you can now link your content to your webpages since your profile is a Business type. Your viewers can complete the conversion process to wherever your links take them to.

The Caption

In Instagram, the picture might be the one doing all the selling but it is the caption that eases in your audiences for what is to come. That is why you need to make it as catchy as possible.

As such, here are a few tips to remember when creating your title.

1. Be Emotional

Do you know who appreciates adjectives like "state of the art", "cutting edge", and "top of the line"? Robots.

If you want to get your audience's attention, look for words that would definitely trigger an emotional response. Instead of "Best", why not use "essential"? After all, consumers are looking for something that they need, not a symbol of perfection. If you can make that human connection, you should have your viewer's attention hooked right from the start.

2. Tap into Logic

Again, a bit of word play will help you in getting your reader's attention. Once you have made that emotional connection, you can start on appealing to the rational part of the brain. So words like "act", "do", "think", and "reason" will be effective in this next part.

Also, you should adopt a more authoritative tone at this part of your headline. Words like "Facts" and "secrets" give off an air of credibility which gives a subliminal clue for the brain to pay attention to whatever you are going to say next.

If possible, never use vague or generic words like "thing". Most readers would find that rather mundane which ruins their engagement to the content to follow.

3. Be Bold

Your caption should offer something interesting to readers without giving away too much of the message. Will the image or link teach them something new? Will they get a new piece of information that will finally answer the most pressing questions of their life? Will it tell them about where to get the best Thin-Crust Pizzas in (insert city here)?

Whatever the case, make sure that the caption actually challenges your viewers to go through the content and to links being provided. Once you have their attention, all that is left to do is to hope that whatever your image is saying will actually live up to the promise set in the caption.

To Conclude

There is a certain art to content creation, undoubtedly. You can't just approach this aspect of advertising with a purely mechanical disposition. Being knowledgeable about certain topics is good but you have to also be passionate with them. Passion is the one final element that will ultimately push your content to convert people into customers loyal to the brand.

Do it right and you will not only produce content that is well created and highly engaging but ones that consistently make a connection with whatever target audience you have in mind.

Chapter 3: The Power of Images

Can a Picture really say a thousand words?

The short answer is yes.

In fact, the success of social media sites like Facebook and Instagram are proof that image-based content maintains a strong presence in the online world nowadays.

But why should you even consider using them aside from the fact that they are the primary commodity in Instagram? The reason for this is that it has always been a rather potent medium when it comes to conveying marketing messages.

Why Do Consumers Prefer Visuals?

Compared to text-based and sound-based interactions, image-based content tends to be more preferred by the average online audience member. The primary reason for this is that imagery as a communication tool is easier to process and is more visually arresting.

Of course, this means that visuals can spike online engagement to a considerable degree. In fact, in a report by Buffer, it has been found out that in the twitter platform, content with images tend to receive 18% more click-throughs and 89% more favorites compared to those with no images at all.

In addition, content with images to enjoy as much as 150% more shares and comments compared to other forms of content save for videos. And not only are consumers engaging with visuals more, they tend to remember the messages better with the aid of visuals.

An infographic shared by Adweek shows that 80% people remember marketing messages more versus the 20% who do so through text. In short, images make a more lasting impression on its own compared to any other available format out there.

All in all, visual content can be used effectively for various marketing content. If done right, they might pose a number of advantages which include:

- Easy customer retention

- Immediate impact in customers

- Ease of presentation and processing of information

- Faster mental stimulation

- Grabs customer attention better

- Help customers in making a purchasing decision

The Anatomy of a Good Instagram Post

So, if visuals are a fairly effective marketing medium, how should you include it as part of your Instagram campaign? A good Instagram post, regardless of purpose, always contains several qualities which are as follows:

1. Visual Quality

This is the most basic concept that you need to master in Instagram. People only flock to your account if you provide them with high-quality visual content.

Of course, high quality visuals can be made possible by investing in state of the art equipment. But there is more to visual quality than using the most modern DLSR camera model.

The skills of the photographer itself will also matter in taking that perfect shot. This will be discussed later on.

2. A Compelling Caption

As was mentioned a chapter ago, your caption can draw in people to your image. As such, you need something that should be compelling.

The tone of the caption must match with the message you are trying to convey. If you are not sure with what you want to do with your caption, then at the very least make it inviting.

However, the caption must always include a link that directs people to whatever webpage you have, preferably the main page or the sales page. This is also where a good CTA will be included as it will direct people to do something to get something in return.

3. The Hashtag

They may look like unnecessary additions to your image but hashtags actually make them more visible and engaging to the community. How this works is quite simple: when people search for something like #fashion on Instagram, the site's algorithms will scour the entire site for content that contains that hashtag.

In essence, it is like a miniature version of Search Engine Optimization. The more relevant your hashtags are, the quicker it will be for people to find your content amidst the veritable sea of images on the platform.

4. Engaging with the Community

This is not exactly an inherent feature of Instagram posts but a direct result of good ones. Instagrammers who know the trends of the platform know it is essential to constantly engage with their audience.

How this is done is actually quite simple. When you post something, people are typically going to comment especially if they are interested with the topic. You can engage with your community by replying to these comments which, in turn, generates more replies.

In essence, setting up a conversation with your customers is a good way of establishing rapport with your audience. And, of course, the more people find you trustworthy, the easier it is for them to convert into paying customers.

5. Sizing, Specs, and Dimensions

Instagram may automatically resize large images but the people behind the platform would rather that you follow certain specifications when uploading images to the site.

For images, the dimensions should follow the basic shape of the square. The reason for this is that the shape allows it to easily readjust for different screen sizes and orientations.

For videos, they should be no more than 15 seconds, the wordings must be at 20 words per frame, and is optimized for sound-off viewing. If you follow these rules, you should be able to create Instagram posts that would be interesting at the very least and highly engaged with at the most.

The Types of Visual Content that Would (Most Likely) Go Viral

What kind of visual content should you use for your Instagram campaigns? What you will use depends greatly on what purpose you want to achieve.

When it comes to online campaigns, there are several visual contents that you can use which are:

1. Infographics

The perfect marriage between visual and text-based content, Infographics are best described as articles in image form as they contain a lot of information presented in a highly visual manner. It is a far less intimidating option as to purely text articles and the information is easier to process and understand.

The only problem with this, however, is that they are rarely compatible in Instagram due to their size. At best, you can only link to such infographics which will take your viewers to a separate page.

Also, they are quite dependent on statistical data. Unless you have a lot of those on hand, there is no point to create one yourself.

2. Photos

Conventional photos are important for several reasons. For businesses, they allow viewers to make a personal connection with the brand as they are quite eye-catching and relatable. Also, this gives businesses the chance to let people take a peek behind the scenes and learn more of the people running the business.

Also, photos are great for showcasing your products and services. In fact, you can display your entire product catalogue in Instagram and link it to your main website. This takes off a huge data load from your site (which makes it load faster) while still increasing traffic in between it and your Instagram profile.

3. Videos

If infographics mix text and images, then videos mix text, images, sound, and motion. It is the perfect blend of every known content format out there and it can help you convey your message at a far easier and faster rate.

The only disadvantage with videos is the demanding production value behind them. It takes quite a lot of effort to capture videos, edit them, and then publish them on the page. Also, remember that Instagram allows only for no more than a minute of video footage so you need to make a video that says what you need to say within that time frame.

But videos do have other benefits offered which include:

- Improved customer retention

- Better SEO ranking

- Higher rate of engagement in customers and audience members; and

- A stronger personal connection between businesses and their customers.

4. The Inspirational Quote

For pure emotional appeal, there is no other visual format out there that can beat inspirational quotes. Why they are highly engaged with is quite simple. Everybody needs that pep talk, regardless of where they get it.

Also, there is no strong motivator towards completing the sales conversion process than, well, being Motivated. If you can get people the emotional fix that they need, they are more susceptible towards any marketing message that you might want to convey.

One neat advantage of inspirational images is that they are quite easy to create. You only need that quote and find an appropriate image such as a relaxing view of the sunset or, better yet, the picture of the person who said it.

5. Screenshots

Content of this type is usually made when you want to highlight a specific part that would otherwise not be noticed by everybody else. For instance, there might be this memorable (or, in recent times, meme-able) moment in your video.

You can immediately create a screen shot through the Print Screen option on your keyboard, the screenshot feature on your mobile phone, or any third party image capturing device.

As such, screenshots can be used for a number of content including instructionals, commentaries, and even product reviews and testimonials.

6. Quizzes and Other Gamified Content

One great way to drive up engagement for your content is to ask a question. After all, nothing can illicit responses more than something that is quizzical by design.

Also, quizzes can give this impression that your brand is hip, smart, and creative. Creating quizzes is also fairly easy and straightforward. One variant of gamified content you could use is also trivia as it turns information regarding your product or service into something interesting or, better yet, useful.

Puzzles are also a great image content for you to use as it taps into the more logical part of the human brain. By encouraging them to answer the puzzle, you increase the click-through rates for your content to a considerable degree.

7. Memes

A fairly new trend, memes are a great way to increase your brand's engagement with younger demographics. It also helps that memes are mostly visual based content and, for most of the time, illicit laughs.

Memes like Grumpy Cat and the Condescending Willy Wonka are examples of memes that advertisers have used for their visual marketing. If you do insist on using memes, it is best that you understand the joke behind the image. There have been far too many times when marketers used memes incorrectly, resulting in a tone-deaf or way-too-trying-hard marketing message.

How to Capture an Instagram-Worthy Picture

As was stated, there are some benefits to be had from creating your own visual content. Marketing photos are perhaps the easiest to create as you already have one when you push that button on your camera.

But, of course, only good photos have the highest rate of engagement in the platform. To truly capture moments that are worthy of being "Instagrammed", there are a few principles that you have to master first.

1. Lighting

This is the foundation of all good photos as even the best-looking subjects out there won't evoke any response from your audience if they can't see it. If possible, only use natural light as they create photos that are brighter and richer in color.

Flash photos, on the other hand, might be bright but the glare of the flash might obscure some important details in your picture. This results in a bright but washed out picture.

If shooting outdoors is not an option, you must take photos near windows or in a well-lit room. If you have to take the photo at evening, find a good source of ambient light like a street lamp or a nearby store window.

2. Exposure

Sure, you can always brighten up a photo with some good editing tools. However, an image that was overexposed to begin with is not worth saving.

Phone cameras have an advantage over professional cameras as you can adjust the exposure by tapping the screen up or down before taking the picture.

The rule of thumb in exposure is that the subject itself must be clearly visible but its contours and details must not fade out from the image.

3. Timing

There is this term among photographers called the "Golden Hour". this is the time when the sun is at its lowest point in the horizon, resulting in truly breathtaking pictures.

As such, you need to find the right time to capture your images. If you can, always take your picture during cloudy days. They diffuse a lot of the sun's light which results in a softer effect.

4. Composition

This refers to the arrangement of the photos which includes the shapes, textures, colors, and other elements that make up your image.

When balancing the composition of your image, always follow the Rule of Thirds. Divide your image into a 3x3 grid and align the subjects in a photo along the lines to create a balance. In this instance, your subject must be at the centermost box to balance the image.

Alternatively, you can employ what is called as balanced asymmetry where the subject is off-center. However, this should be balanced by another element to fill in the void left by the shift in alignments. For example, your subject of a flower might be placed to the left or the right but this should be counterbalanced by the sky or a near wall opposite to where it stands.

You can do the rule of Thirds by turning on the gridline option on your camera's setting. This should help you line up the elements better for taking the shot.

5. Angle

The most common thing that people do when taking a picture is hold the camera at eye level and click away. The end result is decent but nowhere near dynamic or interesting.

Try some weird angles to give your image new perspectives. You may view the subject from the bottom or you can climb up to something and take your pictures from above.

Some photographers would even lie on their stomachs or balance themselves between rocks just to take that perfectly angled shot. It's not necessary for you to make yourself uncomfortable to try new angles. Just don't settle for the usual angle if you want your images to look like they are in motion.

6. Framing

Instead of zooming in, you should leave space around the subject that you are focusing on. This allows outside elements to add more visual oomph to your image.

For instance, a picture of a glass at night is already great but you can make it even more interesting by giving space for the night sky above. This adds an air of "mystery" or "melancholy" to your image which makes it more memorable to the viewer.

For camera phones, you have to tap into the focal subject to make the camera focus on it. This is because they have an automatic zoom function which shrinks the field of view. This means that your image is already pre-cropped which limits your options for editing later on.

7. Leading

Leading lines are invisible marks on your image that draw the eye of the viewer and gives more depth or motion. Even natural elements like roads, waves, and buildings can make your image deeper than it really is, resulting in a semi-3D Effect.

8. Depth

The elements outside of the subject can also bring in a layer of depth to your image. As such, do not ever zoom in to your images before taking the picture.

There is no telling what other interesting things outside of your image's subject that could make things even more interesting to the final image. That tree in the distance or people on the background can add another layer to the image and prevents it from becoming flat.

This works well if there is a contrast between the subject and fore and backgrounds. For instance, if the object is motion, everything around it must stand still. Or if everything is in motion, the subject must lay still.

This clash of movement between the subject and the elements surrounding it will make your image stand out even more when you publish it on Instagram.

To Conclude

Making or capturing images for your Instagram marketing efforts might take some getting used to. After all, nobody became an expert photographer or graphic artist overnight.

However, practice is the key to making it right with your visual content. If done right, you should be able to make some interesting photos which will draw in a lot of viewers to your account.

Chapter 4: Understanding Your Instagram Audience

The end goal of your Instagram marketing is always Visibility. But who should you be visible to? The site is home to more than 1 billion active users per month and surely there should be a fraction of that population who is going to take you up on your offer.

Fortunately, every kind of person and business has an audience in any social media platform they use. It is up to them to find out who these people are and what to do to get a hold of them.

What Are Analytics?

By the end of this decade, Instagram is not only becoming an important marketing tool but also a viable place to build a community in. In short, everyone who wants to survive in the world of Social Media should consider venturing into Instagram before it gets too big.

But this does pose a question: How could anyone tell that Instagram is the best place for them to be? Or, to be more technical about it, how would you know that your marketing strategies are working there?

The answer is Analytics.

In Instagram, there are analytics being provided that help you understand how each of your posts are performing and the overall trend for your account. This is a bit different from metrics as analytics show your account's marketing potential as a whole. Metrics, on the other hand, show

To make this simpler to understand, here's a distinction. The number of followers you have is considered a Metric. The rate of how your follower base in the platform is growing at a certain period of time is an Analytic rate.

But let's not get ahead of ourselves. Here are the 5 Metrics that you should be aware of in order to do Analytics right.

Follower Growth

This may be the simplest metric but it is undoubtedly one of the most important ones. The number of people who follow you on the site will affect the overall performance of your marketing there in a number of ways.

Think of it this way: In order to target people on the platform, you need to have Reach. Through the people that follow you, your brand gets exactly that. The more people engage with your account, the more clicks you will get. And the stronger your traffic is in between your channels, the more visible your brand will be online.

Follower Count vs. Follower Growth: What's the Difference?

But, as was stated, having a large number of followers is no longer enough. You also need to track how quickly your follower base is growing over time.

For instance, if your follower base increased by 1% on March, another 2% on April, and another 1% on May, it is a telltale sign that your brand's reach is steadily yet constantly expanding.

On the flip side, if it grows by 8% on May, then 2% on June, and then 1% on July, it might imply that your base is not as growing steadily as you would like. Perhaps there is something in your strategy that is no longer working.

Worse is when your follower base grows by the negatives every month. This is a telltale sign that you are losing subscribers to your account.

Sadly, the growth rate of your Follower base is not something that is readily provided in Instagram's Insights feature. To get this you have the option of counting your followers each month on a spreadsheet and calculate the change in percentage yourself or have a separate Instagram analytics program do the recording and analysis for you.

Demographics

Aside from knowing the size of your follower base, you'd also have to know its composition: just *who* are your followers? Regardless of what you have set as a goal for your marketing campaign, a crucial understand on the profile of your follower/potential customer will help you hone your content to match what they need or expect from you.

For instance, you might think that your brand is catering towards young American teens but find out that most of your Instagram follower base are middle-aged adults in Europe.

This was the same predicament that befell on Mattel in the mid-2000s when they were marketing their show My Little Pony towards kids only to find out that a larger portion of their fanbase belongs to the Adult demographic; and are males for a reason. Thankfully, they managed to find a balance between the two groups and the MLP brand remains strong even up to 2019.

The point is that knowing what composes your audience demographics, whether or not they fit the persona of what you think is your primary audience, can tip you off on how to better mold your marketing messages. You might even discover new niches in the market that your brand has yet to tap or, to that effect, nobody else has.

Fortunately, the Insights feature can give you good analytics of the composition of your audience. You can even tell which gender your brand caters to the most and from what regions across the world.

How to Make the Most of Your Audience Demographics

Before anything else, you need to have a customer persona set up for your marketing. These are a list of qualities that your ideal customers would display which helps you create your marketing content. A guide on identifying your personas can be found in the following section.

You must use this persona, then, as a benchmark to check if what you think your audiences are would match the profile of the people that do actually compose your audience in real time.

Is there any difference between your personas and your actual audience? What similarities do they share? In what way can you tap these new niches without alienating your primary audience?

Alternatively, if you think that your marketing is a bid too broad, you can use the Analytics to identify the actual profile of most of your customers. This will help you laser-focus your efforts into targeting these specific individuals in the market.

Website Clicks

Here is one bitter pill that anyone on Social Media should swallow: Followers and Fans are not automatically Customers. Just because someone has shown interest for the brand, it does not mean that there is a potential for income there.

This is what happened to the Star Wars brand who saw a dip in box office returns for their last two films despite seemingly strong followings in Social Media. On a lesser scale, this is what happened to a young

Instagrammer named Arianne Renee who failed to sell 36 T-Shirts of her own making despite having 2 million followers on the site.

What you should be looking for is the number of times that people were so convinced by your marketing that they actually visited your other channels or, to that effect, your main web page. This is where click through rates come into play and they happen to tell you accurately whether or not your Instagram marketing is driving up traffic to your pages.

For instance, if your marketing campaign contains a link to your main webpage and people click it, they would be taken to that page. This counts as one click-through and is a strong indicator that your web traffic is not stagnating.

This metric is quite crucial if your marketing campaign's overall goal is to drive traffic to your webpages. Alternatively, it might be not as important if your overall goal is brand awareness.

Of course, a lot of click-throughs means that your website is hosting a lot of visitors every day. That won't give you the assurance that each visitor is converting into a customer but it does tell that your campaign has the potential to eventually compel people to do so.

Also, if your site's traffic is unchanged, then perhaps you should consider changing the tone of your CTA. Perhaps it is not too forceful or effective in making people visit your other channels.

How to Track Web Traffic at Instagram

Fortunately, the Insights section can help you get an idea as to your page's outgoing traffic. It is at the Activity Section under the Interactions tab. This should tell you how many people clicked to your bio over the past few days or weeks.

This is a good start for measuring your traffic but it's not the only method. You can also use Google's Analytics program or add a UTM Code to the link in your Bio. The latter will tell you how many of those click-throughs actually led to a sales conversion.

Lastly, you can use Facebook's Pixels feature. It is also effective in tracking outgoing traffic from your Social Media pages and tallying up all conversions that were not only started but actually finished.

Reach

Although this is not a key indicator of performance for online marketing campaigns, it does tell you how much of a buzz your brand is generating in the market. Reach is the metric that measures how many people have seen your posts. This includes the people who saw your picture/video/any other content and those that watched your Story.

You might be thinking, *Isn't this like Impressions, though?* Not really.

Impressions is counted every time your content is seen. Reach, on the other hand, is counted, every time a unique user does something with your content. As such, it is better to look at the Reach than the Impressions that your content makes.

In fact, Impressions is more like a vanity metric as it doesn't tell you how many times that person ignored your content before actually interacting with it. Reach will tell you that and also how many people have seen your content, leading to a more accurate measurement.

Why Reach Really Matters

In essence, Reach is important as it tells you one of the most important things in Instagram for marketers: whether or not your posts are showing up in the feeds of the people that you are targeting. There are a lot of factors that could affect reach such as the level of engagement for your account, the time people spend perusing your content, and even the time when you published it.

As such, reach can tell you in general terms how popular your content is as well as if it has good timing and an interesting hook for engagement. For example, a high percentage of reach could tell you that a lot of people are spending time looking at your photos as opposed to merely glancing at them from the feed.

Alternatively, it could mean that your content schedule is working for you as people are engaging at it immediately after publishing it. Or perhaps it is a bit of both which tells you that your marketing is effective even if only at a technical standpoint.

But what if your reach is getting lower? You could consider reorganizing the timing of your content. Or you could look at the next most important metric which is...

Engagement

If Content is the King on the Internet, then Engagement is Instagram's very own feudal lord. To put it less creatively, engagement is the most crucial metric that you could ever refer to when it comes to your marketing campaigns on the site.

Engagement can tell you how much of a connection you are making with your followers and potential customers as well as other influential people and brands. In fact, when it comes to Engagement, Instagram has the highest levels of such compared to other social media sites.

Why is Engagement really important on Instagram? The reason is that the algorithms bump up those posts that get a lot of engagement. In essence, the more engagement each posts you have gets, the more visible it will be on the site.

For Instagram, engagement comes in the form of the number of likes, comments, and shares that your posts get. And you can see this by adjusting the settings of your Content tab found at the Insights panel.

What is Engagement Rate?

Although engagement is a good metric, there is an even better metric in the form of engagement rate. It tells you the percentage of the people that actually engaged with your content and compare it to the reach that it enjoyed from.

For instance, one post might have a high reach but a low engagement rate. This means a lot of people saw it but not a lot interacted with it.

Alternatively, if a post has a low reach but a high enough engagement level, it could tell you that whatever message that post contained reached the right people and caused them to respond.

So what is a good engagement rate? There is no hard and fast rule for that but experts do encourage that they reach at least 1.75% as of the most recent months. So, if a post has 5000 in reach, then it should strive to at least get 87.5 in engagements.

The Ultimate Takeaway: When all is said and done, these metrics will tell you how much your content is being treated at in Instagram's market. That is something that you absolutely have no control over in the same way that you have no control over how people perceive your brand in the real world.

What it does great, however, is giving you clues and hints as to how to better approach your market. The metrics can help you predict how people are going to react when exposed to the same message or a variant of it. This way, you can carefully improve on your message until you reach that point when you can target your audiences confidently in the platform.

Finding (And Reaching) Your Target Audience

Now that you know how people behave statistics-wise on Instagram, the next part will involve finding the people who will most likely consume what you have to offer. Remember that you don't have to target every Instagrammer out there for your campaigns, just the right ones.

With that in mind, there are few things that you have to remember when finding your audience and then reaching out the them. They are as follows:

1. Define Your Audience

You may ask "what's the point of even having an idea as to who my target audience is?" After all, whoever they are, they will come to your profile if they like what you offer, right?

You would actually have to do this for two reasons:

a. It will Challenge Your Assumptions - There is a great chance that the actual target audience for your brand is bigger and more diverse than what you thought of. You might even discover new niches in the market that your brand has not put in the effort of targeting in the post.

But, of course, with knowledge comes the need to adjust. Now that you know that there are more people out there that have an interest for your brand, would like you to adjust your marketing efforts to also include their needs and expectations.

Going back to the My Little Pony problem, did Mattel choose to ignore that older demographic? No. That is because these individuals had a stronger purchasing agency and can even influence their children to consume Mattel's products.

So what they did is change their marketing to include these people and even made some tweaks on their product to make them more appealing to the new demographic.

In Instagram, you will discover a lot of new niches that might show an interest for your brand. By identifying these people, you can come up with strategies that better target them which increases engagement for your brand.

b. It Will Make Things Easier for You - For marketers, there is nothing more frustrating than the Unknown. This is for the reason that the unknown is hard to predict and even harder to adapt to.

By identifying the various profiles of your potential customers, you have a more solid foundation to stand on when it comes to promoting your brand at Instagram. In essence, you are giving Method to the Madness that is online marketing.

2. Identify Your Personas

First of all, what is a Persona? It is basically a set of qualities and characteristics shared by your assumed consumers that will tell you how they are going to react to your marketing.

It's a bit different from Demographics as your Personas are based on your assumptions while Demographics are based on cold, hard, statistical facts. They may share some similarities but rarely do you get a demographic that perfectly fits your marketing personas.

Setting up one is fairly easy. All you have to do is to come up with a list of behaviors that people display when exposed to your brand in other channels. Perhaps your Facebook community liked that one marketing campaign of yours. You could use that data to form a sequence of response of sorts to every marketing strategy that you have used.

Next, you will then give them a face by categorizing all these qualities into different sets of "identities". These identities can then be based on basic classifiers like age, sex, social status, income level, and region. Perhaps people in Age Group A would react differently compared to Age Group B. Or perhaps Income Level A would be more recipient to your marketing than Income Level B.

Doing so gives you some rudimentary customer personas that you could refer to when creating your marketing strategies. Of course, you could use these personas as a benchmark when identifying your actual audience in Instagram.

3. Reach Out

Once you have segmented your target audiences and know what they care about, it is time to start reaching out to those audiences. Just remember that each persona will require a different approach. However, just keep in mind a few things when trying to reach out to your different potential segments.

Mind the Timing

Using your Instagram's analytics, you should find out in what time of the day (your time zone, of course) when people interact with your content the most. The norm is that activity peaks just in between 5pm to 9pm, where people get off their work or school.

However, that is not exactly applicable in all instances as some demographics are active on other parts of the day or exclusively on a few days of the week. Whatever the case, Instagram's analytics tool will tell you when and where people interact with your content the most.

Find the Right Content

You should also identify what type of Instagram content people have engaged with your brand the most and what campaigns have worked well in the past few months, if any. This will tell you how the most on how to approach your target audience the best.

But a word of warning: just because something worked in the past, that does not mean it should work now. For instance, using a Meme might generate a lot of engagement in your past campaign but using the same meme for this new campaign might be detrimental. It's like telling a joke: it is only funny if you do it once.

Also, there might be some tweaks in Instagram's algorithms which causes the in-site search bots to push certain types of content more today than others in the past. As such, it is highly important that you do your research on current trends on social media and even Instagram's own policy changes. This way, changes won't surprise you and severely hurt your campaign's chance of success.

Study the Competition

Perhaps the most cost effective way of doing your research is just to observe what everybody else is doing. What are other brands similar to yours doing in Instagram? Are they succeeding there or do you think you can add a more effective twist to their strategies?

Whatever the case, the content published by your competitors can serve as a major source of inspiration; from a certain point of view. Perhaps one of their campaigns worked so well and it wouldn't hurt to do the same for your brand.

But, of course, there is a fine line between inspiration and downright being a copycat. Just take inspiration from what worked with your competitors but don't copy things point by point.

Leverage Instagram Stories

There are more than 500 thousand people around the world that use Instagram's Stories feature on a daily basis. There are quite a lot of features on offer which allow you to interact better with your audiences and enjoy from a more direct from of engagement with them.

Much of what you can do with the Stories feature will be discussed in detail on a later chapter but the point is that you should take advantage of this feature as much as you can. Find content that you can use to post there and keep track of your level of engagement there.

Use Hashtags Properly

Use the Follow feature to keep track of what niches in your target market care about the most in recent times. Of course, this means that the proper use of hashtags will make you more visible to Instagram as users and search bots can see your content quickly and consume the ones that they care about the most.

Of course, this is dependent on the fact that you have already identified your niche in the market. The more niches you can tap into, the more potential buyers you can attract to your brand.

4. Application

With these information, you can set up a rudimentary targeting scheme which may look like as follows:

Business Type: Finance

Product: Savings Program

Demographic: Males

Sub-Class: Late Teens to Adult, College-Level

Target With: Instagram Stories Re: Saving for the Future

Best Times to Post: 6-9PM

Competitors: Other Banks and Financial Institutions

Here's another example

Business Type: Bar

Product: Food and Drinks

Demographics; Adults, Working Class

Target With: Visual Campaigns that highlight bar's customer experience, food, and signature drinks.

Best Times to Post: 3-10PM

Competitors: Other bars and restaurants

Just remember, however, that just because one strategy hasn't been used in your industry or niche in the market that has not been tapped, that you should use them. For example, Adidas might have published an excellent Instagram campaign that extended their reach in the platform while also yielding in tons of engagement. It might even be featured by the media and hailed as one of the best Instagram campaigns of (insert year here).

Of course, you might be tempted to use that strategy for your brand. But here's the problem: Adidas is a clothing brand but you are not. Perhaps you are in banking in finance or perhaps you run a small bar. Using the same strategy might yield different results for your case, results that you may or may not like.

But this goes the other way, too. Just because you are not selling exactly the same products as other successful brands does not mean that you can't use the same tactics that they have employed. All that is needed here is a bit of common sense on your part. If you think it's going to work for your brand or not, take the time to do your research and run up some predictions here and there.

It pays to be extra careful with your campaigns right now given social media's current climate (which shall be tackled later on).

Using Influencers

In some cases, a lot of brands (especially the old-fashioned, brick and mortar types) are a "hard sell" in the online world. The reason for this is that things that made them relevant way back when the Internet was not a thing is no longer working these days.

You can't just tell people that your offerings are great and expect them to eat it all up. More often than not, the high degree of agency and access to information provided by the Internet will make these people highly doubtful of all that hyperbole that you've just told them.

The point is that conventional marketing strategies are not going to work on the newer demographics today, which are made up of the ones that we call "Millennials". But that does not mean that they won't listen to these marketing messages. It's just that they typically only do so if delivered by certain messengers. And this is where Influencers come into play.

It goes without saying that collaborating with an influencer can make for a sound marketing strategy regardless of what platform you choose to operate in. And luckily for you, Instagram is the home to many effective influencers like the Kardashians, Beyoncé, Dwayne "The Rock" Johnson, and Jay Alvarrez.

As such, here are a few things to remember when using Influencers to optimize their effects.

A. Match the Niche

Just because influencers have something called "clout", that does not mean that they have mass market appeal. Rather than finding the most popular people on Instagram to help your brand expand its reach, the more prudent tactic is to find the influencer that resonates most with your target market.

Make a list of speakers, industry authorities, celebrities, thought leaders, and other people that your target demographics are following on the platform. You can do this by doing a simple search on Google and determine which topics brands like yours tend to deal with. Then, make a list of names of the people that have tackled the same issues as these will be the most suitable influencers for your campaigns.

B. Assess, Assess, Assess

Once you have a list of potential influencers to tap, you must then determine how effective they are in regards to your brand. You can do this by looking at three factors which are:

● **Relevance** - Does everybody in the industry know who that influencer is? Does their style match the type of strategies that you usually employ?

You can determine this by taking a look at the type of content that they usually produce as their manner of speaking and style will tell you who they tend to reach out the most. After all, why use an influencer like the Paul Brothers or the Kardashians if you are not a) a fashion brand or b) marketing to teens?

- **Resonance** - Some influencers tend to create content that does not elicit the proper response with their audience. This is what is called being "tone deaf" and it can hurt your brand if they do this frequently.

Whenever an influencer does this, do they get a lot of dislikes compared to their likes? How about the number of shares and the quality of comments that such content generates? Also, you have to be careful as to how that influencer pushes their opinions around or weigh in on discussions especially in topics that you usually tackle.

- **Reach** - Take a look at the size of their audience. This will include the traffic that comes in and out of their Instagram accounts and their other pages. What you want is an influencer that not only commands a large audience but targets roughly the same demographics as you.

C. **Always Scrutinize**

The last thing you would want to take a look at is the general manner of which these people conduct themselves online. As such, there are several aspects that you need to take a look at which include:

1. **Frequency** - What is the volume of content that this influencer makes over a period of time? Are they always online or show up at the right time? Do they have a consistent content creation schedule?

There are a number of content creators and influencers out there that can post more than 20 Instagram status updates per day and then there are those that post only once a day or a week. Of course, it's not just the quantity of their content but quality. Some that post content once a day might net engagements by the millions of likes and comments per post.

2. **Focus -** Some influencers do well covering one certain topic while others can get all over the place but still generate a lot of traffic. The requirement on this part is rather simple: make sure that that influencer covers more than 30% of the topics that your brand also covers, at the very least.

3. **Tone -** This will cover their overall style as an influencer. Some are upbeat and perky. Others are cynical and abrasive. Some revel in being diplomatic and philosophical while others embrace controversy and are in your face with their demeanor.

4. **Language -** This does not exactly cover their preferred language I.e. English, French, or German, etc. What this does cover, however, is how they communicate with their audience. Influencers who cuss a lot, for instance, might generate a following with younger and brasher folk but might be off-putting for older demographics.

Also, this might be due to generational gaps. There are a lot of Gen-Xers and Baby Boomers out there that do not know who Ariane Grande is and those that do might or might not find her personality appealing.

In addition, find out if their style of language matches yours. Your brand might be comfortable with talking to your audience in a polite and professional way. As such, look for an influencer that does the same for your audience.

What you have to remember is that dealing with other people in the Internet is a hit-or-miss affair. Even the best collaborations can fall apart unless you know how to deal with your collaborators in a way that both of you can benefit from the relationship.

Also, influencers can only do so much. It you that has to do the heavy lifting as far as your native advertising is concerned. This means that you also have to engage with people regularly if you want to be as visible in your market as possible.

To Conclude

Social media marketing, as a whole, is a never-ending process. When looking at the success of your Instagram account's efforts to reach your target audience, there are two things that you need to consider.

First, is your brand listening to the larger conversation? The things that the Instagram community cares for as a whole do change from time to time. What may be relevant to your business now may not be appreciated that well by the rest of the Instagrammers.

That is, of course, if you insist on saying things the way that you want them to be said. There are ways of conveying messages that you care about while making sure that they are relevant to the rest of your audience. Just keep in mind that you pay attention to what other niches in your ever-growing audience cares for to keep your content relevant on the platform.

Second, what is quality of the content that you make? How well does it stack up against your competitors? Do your target audience even engage with it the moment that you post it?

The questions are answered if you take the time to understand what your analytics are saying to you. You need to know the trends that your content is following and compare them to how your competitors are faring. Perhaps the path to improvement lies in you understanding the strengths and weaknesses of your marketing, and that of others.

Chapter 5: Using Instagram Stories to Build Your Brand

The Stories feature is one of the more recent additions to Instagram and it has undoubtedly added a new twist to how things are being shared on the site. Initially released to compete with Snapchat, Instagram stories now has a lot of features which makes Instagram less of a glorified photo album and more of a viable marketing tool.

Integrating Instagram Stories for your marketing campaigns, then, could help instill loyalty to your customer base while also keeping the brand engaged with them.

Why Bother With Stories In The First Place?

As with all new features out there, the first thing that you might ask is why you should even consider Instagram Stories for your marketing efforts. The short answer is that stories offer a quick and engaging format, which makes it perfect for mobile users.

Also, there is the fact that popular brands have taken notice of the feature and a third of Instagram Stories now are generated by businesses and other large entities.

To put it in even simpler terms, Instagram stories are fun to go through or create and provides an unintimidating method for customers to reach out to the brands that they like the most. It offers a unique sense of authenticity that would otherwise take years and thousands of dollars to build in conventional online marketing strategies.

If that was not enough, here are several more facts that would make Instagram Stories a viable marketing tool:

1. **User Base -** As of now, Instagram Stories is reportedly use by 400 million users on a daily basis. That is 400 million opportunities for authentic engagement.

2. **Minimal Effort -** Stores have a short lifespan of 24 hours. Once that time has elapsed, whatever you post will be gone.

As such, you don't have to exert maximum mental effort to create stories and still get tons of engagement for your posts.

3. **Experimentation -** Typically, Instagram Stories are not segregated with the rest of the content being produced on the site. This means that you have the opportunity to test new campaigns here to see how well they can get engaged with in their 24-hour lifespan.

If something you post there receives a ton of likes and shares, then you can always migrate it to the more permanent form of your regular Instagram content. If it does not, well, it will be forgotten in a mere few hours with no costs on your part.

4. **Traffic -** Stories are quite integrated to Instagram's basic features which allows you to drive even more traffic to your main page and other marketing channels. You can add links to your Stories or advertise products that you may have on offer on Instagram's shop.

And then there is Instagram's Explore feature which allows your products to be easily discovered. If you are creative enough, you can even find ways to promote your other content from other social media accounts through the Stories feature.

How To Use Stories

So it's settled that the Stories feature has quite a lot to offer to marketers. The question is how you can use it to maximize your results? Again, its up to you how you can use Stories for your marketing but there are several surefire ways to integrate the feature to your campaign. Here are some of them:

1. **Tutorials**

This is the simplest and most direct method that you can use to take advantage of the stories feature. Tutorials can be short how-to videos or articles regarding the use of your products or services. Alternatively, you can use Stories for in-depth, multi-post content like product demonstrations and comparisons.

Either way, there is something about Stories that makes it the perfect place to put you more informational content in. For example, Delish dedicated their entire Stories page for posting of recipes on a daily basis. Also, Sephora used theirs to teach their customers how to make good use of the products that they offer.

Perhaps you are a tourism business. You can use the Stories feature to provide daily tips on travelling or feature some of the hotspots for certain cities and countries that you offer travel packages at. Or perhaps you own a restaurant or bar. You can use the stories feature to highlight the history of your signature dishes or give recipes so people can replicate the dishes themselves (without giving away your trade secrets, of course).

2. **User Generated Content**

There is nothing more persuasive and authentic as marketing content out there than the ones that are made by your own customers. The reason for this is that User-Generated Content accurately reflect the feelings and opinions that customers have regarding what you offer.

And since it is authentic and made by people who have direct experience with what you have to offer, they offer a more compelling sales pitch than whatever marketing strategy that you can come up with. This is why reviews on Yelp can make or break a restaurant's reputation. This is why movies can make a killing or fail spectacularly based on their ratings at sites like Rotten Tomatoes.

For Instagram, you can use content made by your customers to sell your own business in a number of ways. For instance, gyms can use the before and after pics of their members to convince people that their fitness regimes work.

For clothing brands, they can share pics of their customers wearing the products that they offer. And it makes for a far more convincing selling point for average folk than if a runway model does it.

And, for restaurants, they can always share the pictures of people dining into their dishes or having a good time at the place.

Aside from visual content, you can also share screenshots of reviews and testimonials made by people on review sites like Yelp or on Facebook on your Instagram account.

3. Behind-the-Scenes Looks

After that major plot twist in The Wizard of Oz, people have developed a seeming interest for what goes behind the public image that celebrities and businesses project in the market. You can use this to your advantage by giving people a peek behind the people that make up your business.

Use the Stories feature to let viewers see what a day in the life of your business looks like. Perhaps it could be you doing something on your desk or your staff creating the products or managing the services that your brand offers.

Either way, this well help in "humanizing" your brand as people now have a face to make an emotional connection with in regards to your business.

Movie studios often do this on Instagram by posting pictures of launch events or the goings-on in their movie sets. Even celebrities do this by posting pics of them relaxing with their families or staying at home doing nothing.

By showing that there are regular people that compose your business, you give the impression to your audience that your brand knows what it feels like to be human and thus can provide for basic human needs.

4. Polls and Quizzes

One neat feature in Instagram Stories is the ability to put up polls for your audience to interact with. Aside from the fact that polls are interactive by design, they also give you an insight as to what people care about the most which you could use for your marketing campaigns in the future. So it's an interactive campaign and market research scheme all rolled into one.

Putting up a quiz or poll is generally easy. You could use general information from the market or even trivia coming from your own brand. However, do not forget to add one last element which is the CTA at the end of the poll. Something like "Swipe to Finish" which leads to a separate business page is bound to increase conversions coming from this kind of content.

5. Special Announcements

If you want to add an element of prestige in your promotions, you can always use Stories to get your announcements across. For example, you may announce a special sale on Stories or announce a new set of products there.

As people go through the story, they may encounter an option like "Swipe to Link" or "Swipe to Shop". This will then take them to a separate page where they can get discounts for their purchases or better yet, get a hold of whatever you are trying to launch days in advance.

It brings a sense of belongingness and accomplishment to your customers, knowing that they got hold of something sweet since they made the effort to interact with your story.

6. Customer Feedback

Aside from polls and quizzes, you can also host live Question and Answer sessions on Instagram Stories. This should provide your audience the opportunity to directly interact with you while having their questions answered. It is something similar to Reddit's Ask Me Anything feature but a bit less text-based.

However, do keep in mind that how you answer questions will ultimately determine whether or not this tactic works for you in Instagram's stories.

When the videogame company Electronic Arts launched an Ask Me Anything session on Reddit regarding issues about their game Star Wars: Battlefront II, they botch every question by giving every answer a Public Relations and Marketing tone. And then there was their answer to lootboxes which they claim gives players a "sense of Pride and Accomplishment".

Needless to say, an opportunity to fix their relations with their customer base further drove the wedge while the Pride and Accomplishment answer was entered into the Guinness World Book of Records as the most downvoted Internet comment in History.

7. Limited Time Offers

There is nothing that make people convert faster than being on a sense of Urgency. This is why limited offers worked so much in conventional advertising and still does even in Social Media today. Instagram stories have a 24-hour lifespan which makes them the perfect home for your limited offers.

For instance, you can make an announcement there about a sale which leads to a separate page where people can get a discount code. As such, only those that have interacted with the story while it is still posted can get a hold of the discount.

How to Improve Your Stories' Performance

There is a difference between posting stories and making them actually effective. Anybody can post a story on Instagram but it takes a lot of care to create one that not only engages with your audience but would actually compel them to do something mutually beneficial for the brand and the person.

To do this, there are a few tips to keep in mind when creating your Story.

1. Put Interaction at the Forefront Always

The kind of story you put up determines the level of interaction it will generate. For instance, Q and A sessions are designed to be highly interactive along with polls, swipe to link schemes, and even overlay text.

Of course, there are the challenges which directly tap into a person's primal competitiveness. Use hashtag challenges along with swipe to links, limited offers, and other gamified content to make your content even more engaging to your audience.

2. Highlight

The 24-hour lifespan of Stories can be both a problem and a benefit for your business. It's good that you don't have to exert a lot of effort in pushing your content in stories but you run the risk of losing what is a practically good Story in just a day.

By using the Highlight feature, you can extend the life of your best-engaged stories by a few days or more. Not only will this extend their lifespan but would also neatly categorize your content. Now, you can know which of your stories are generating a lot of engagement and which are not.

3. Run a Story Ad

It's often been told that Instagram Stories get 5 times more engagement than regular Instagram content. As such, the feature makes for a good place to run your advertisements on. And keep in mind that not a lot of brands are not doing this (yet) which means you can still take advantage of the small population of advertisements there.

4. Work with Influencers

As was previously stated, working with the right collaborator can be beneficial to your Instagram campaign. For stories, working with a collaborator gives you access to certain perks like product reviews, cost-effective promotions, and a smaller rate of customer acquisition cost.

And with Stories, the exposure is beneficial to both you and your influencer of choice. They get to closely interact with their fans while naturally pointing the same fans to your products which should increase conversion rates while also expanding your presence in the market.

5. Get Creative

There are a lot of features on offer in Stories that would make your stories even more attractive. Things like emojis, moving graphics, filter, and video editing features can enhance your text and visuals.

But, of course, there is a fine line between adding enhancements to your text and visuals and flooding your stories with too many distractions. Just use the right enhancements to get your point across so you don't lose your audiences in the confusion.

6. Never Underestimate the Power of Tagging

Tags are there to make your content even easier to discover by potential audiences. For example, Geotags help audiences discover where you are mainly operating at or where you are currently located. This will also link your brand to nearby tourist attractions, major events and hotspots, driving traffic to your page.

Hashtags, on the other hand, can make your content relevant to whatever is currently happening across the world. When the Duke and Duchess of Cambridge tied the knot, Lego did a series of campaigns based on the Royal Wedding with the appropriate tags. This enabled their campaign to be part of the conversation; more importantly, it was linked to an event that everybody else is talking about.

The Main Takeaway

When all is said and done, what you have to understand is that there are many ways to push a story. The strategy that you will use depends greatly on the type of business that you have and the customers you are trying to target.

As such, it is best that you try out a few approaches and experiment with your content if the budget allows for it. Over time, you should be able to find a content that is highly interactive that your brand can use repeatedly in the future.

Lead Generation With Stories

In all of these campaigns, what you have to remember is that your end goal is to generate leads which subsequently generates sales. If your campaigns are not impacting the bottom line of the brand, then there's no point doing it in the first place.

So how do all these campaigns lead to sales? If you include links to your web content, of course.

The new Swipe Up feature should take your audiences from the story to a page of yours which should nudge people one step further into completing the conversion process.

To generate sales and leads for your Instagram Stories, there are a few things that you need to keep in mind.

1. Share Your Web Content

As was stated, Content is the King of online marketing strategies. Good content is essential for a good SEO ranking and in generating and nurturing leads.

With Instagram stories, you can share a relevant photo or other similar content and then add a link to that which takes audiences to various pages that you own. That page may be a blog, or an ebook, or even your YouTube channel.

The point is that Instagram Stories can consolidate the traffic coming through your different web channels which, in theory, should increase the chances of people converting into paying customers.

Also, you can use stories to promote sales and special events as more than 30% of Instagram users have been known to purchase a product based on what they saw on their IG feeds. Keep in mind that social media can influence the purchasing decisions of people today so it makes sense to do a lot of visual-based marketing there.

Target, for example, uses their Instagram account to specifically target impulse buyers. By constantly showcasing whatever is new in their product line at Instagram and then following that with the Swipe Up button that leads to a sales page, Target has hastened the purchasing decisions of these kinds of buyers.

Of course, this results in faster conversions in an already fast-paced buyer base.

2. Make Influencers Your Ambassadors

Going back to influencers, we have already talked about how effective they are in pushing your products and services without being too "pushy" with their own audiences. Also, they already have sizeable followings which may become your potential customers with the right kind of messages.

But there is one more element that you have to consider with influencers as far as Instagram Stories and concerned and that is how you treat them. In other marketing, it is enough that they are your collaborators. In Instagram Stories, however, they become your Ambassadors.

What's the difference, then? A normal messenger may push the product and service but an Ambassador does way more than that.

More often than not, they can sell the brand to their audience and that includes everything from the products, services, and even the lifestyle associated with your business. They may even come up with ways to how make better use of your offerings which adds another dimension to the way your business is being treated by the rest of the market.

If people see that a person that they can interact with is doing great using your products, then they are less hesitant to make the conversion themselves. And consider the fact that Influencer-sourced leads often have higher chances of becoming customers themselves.

3. Respond Directly

One of the direct results of becoming more active in Instagram Stories is the increase of direct messages coming your way. If a story of yours does not include a link, users will be able to see a message bar. Using this, they can directly message your account for all sorts of queries and concerns.

While this is a feature that can easily bridge the gap between a brand and its audience/followers, it can be detrimental to your business if you choose to ignore DMS entirely. If you are not quick enough to answer a question, that potential audience may get tired and look elsewhere for someone to meet their needs.

This is why it is important for marketers to not just focus on sticking to the script that they have planned for the campaign. They must be quick enough to address any issue raised by their audience, legitimate or otherwise.

To Wrap Things Up...

Understanding how Instagram Stories work and what you can gain from it is just the first half of a rather elaborate solution. With a rather unique storytelling concept and a strong potential for conversion, how you actually use the Stories feature as a marketing tool will determine how your campaign in that page will be effective.

What you must not forget is to constantly engage with your fans there and be consistent enough in providing them with something to consume. The more you give value to your audience there, the quicker conversion rates will be for your brand on the platform as a whole.

But entertaining people is not just your end goal in marketing. You have to give them something tangible in order to give them that final push towards conversion. And, luckily enough for you, Instagram does have a page dedicated to everything related to products.

Chapter 6: Shopping in Instagram

In recent years, Instagram has been slowly veering away from its purely Social Media concept. In fact, the site has been trying its luck with ecommerce with its new Shop feature.

Again, with all things, you can choose to ignore this feature entirely for your marketing campaigns. But, if you think about it more, why would you?

Instagram has been relentless in updating the feature and a standalone app is already in the works. What is clear that ecommerce is becoming an important part of Instagram and, as far as you are concerned, a viable marketing tool for your business.

What's an Instagram Shop, Exactly?

The best way to describe the Shop page is that it combines your Instagram profile with a standard product catalogue. As such, the Shop allows you to directly promote your products to your audiences through posts, Stories, and every other page on Instagram.

In essence, you are setting up a mini version of your main website at Instagram where people can go into and hopefully complete the customer conversion process. The page is also quite helpful as it provides potential buyers with a lot of information including:

- Product Name

- Images

- Description of the Product

- Price

- A link that leads to your main website for further details (or to complete the ordering process there)

- Other products related or similar to it

Benefits

Instagram's venture into ecommerce has been lauded by industry experts and small online businesses alike. But what does choosing to set up shop on Instagram bring to you compared to, say, Amazon? Here are some 3 distinct advantages.

1. It Reduces Noise

With a lot of businesses vying the attention of the same group of people, it can get difficult at times to even compel potential buyers to drop whatever they are currently doing and visit your store.

So, if you can't get them to go to your store, what's the alternative? YOU take your store to THEM. On Instagram Shop, casual viewers can go to your shop and check on the prices without being taken away from the main site. Plus, if they think that they are ready to make a purchase, they can start a transaction with just one push of the button.

This non-intimidating and simple concept can be enough to encourage people to take a look at what you have to offer while casually scrolling through the main Instagram feed.

2. Direct Promotion

One of the major drawbacks to Instagram has always been its linking feature. In fact, to this day, you are only allowed one link at your main profile and you can't add clickable links to any of the content that you post.

As such, it was such a chore to directly promote products on the platform especially if you already have a sizeable catalog of things to sell. This one-link-only scheme can even hurt conversion rates as you are only allowed to direct your potential buyers to one page which could be lost if ever you update your bio.

This is where the Instagram Shop comes into play as it allows you to integrate all of your Instagram marketing campaigns with the store itself. So, if you have something to promote, you can directly lead your audiences to the Shop page which speeds up the conversion process. It also reduces the chances of people tuning off your marketing since they now have somewhere to go to in order to check the things that you have to offer.

Lastly, navigating from the main Instagram feed to Shop page and back is quite simple and easy to understand.

3. Massive Exposure

Every product that you post on Instagram's Shop would be included in the new Shopping Explore tab. On paper, this should increase engagement with your brand provided that you optimize the hashtags of each of your entries.

Also, the Explore tab is unique for each and every user as it is put up based on their activity on the site as well as their interests. As such, the things that would appear on every person's Explore tab is bound to be made up of things that they may take a liking to.

The end result is that your products will be exposed to an audience with an already high purchase intent insofar as the type of products you are selling are concerned. To put it in other words, customer conversion rates are higher on the shop as the target audience there are likely going to buy whatever you have to offer.

To put it even simpler terms, the Shop is a powerful tool that can boost sales for your products quickly. That is, of course, if you set things up properly.

How to Set Up Shop

Before anything else, you have to understand that the Shop option is only available for now if you set up your profile as a Business. As such, if your profile is Private for now, you may have to set up a separate account for your business and shop.

There are also other ways to set the shop up via Syncing with pages like a Facebook Shop page or a Shopify account. If you have either, you can automatically sync your Instagram Shop with them which copies and migrates all your data from there to your new page. As for the Facebook page sync, Instagram will ask an extra requirement of you being the admin of that page before they allow the link.

But whether or not you have an existing Shop page or not, there are three steps that you must take in putting up an Instagram Shopping tab.

1. Read the Rules

Instagram has a handful of requirements that would be shopkeepers should meet before they are allowed to promote their business at the page. First, the Shop page is not for the selling of services, only products i.e. physical goods.

Next, Instagram has set up a list of commerce policies that shop owners should adhere to. Violations of one or multiple stipulations on a frequent basis might lead to the termination of your Shop page or, worse, your entire account.

Third, your business must be located in a country with access to the feature. Instagram has a list of countries where the Instagram Shop feature is currently available. You better hope that your country is included there if you want to set the shop up.

Finally, you must make sure that your version of Instagram is up to date. Fortunately, updating the site or the app will take only a few minutes, downloading and installation included.

2. Building the Catalog

It is here that having a Facebook Shop would come in handy as Instagram tends to pull off information from its sister site when creating your catalog. There are several options on the catalog page of which sites you can link up to such as Facebook and Shopify. Just click on those two options and your Instagram catalog should be set up in a few minutes.

Once you are confident that your product catalog is decently organized, the last thing you want to click is the "Make Products Available" option. This should allow Instagram to start promoting your products at the Explore pages of your target demographics.

3. Setting up the Sales Channel

This part is dependent on the fact that you have a Shopify account. To set up the channel, all you have to do is to go to your Shopify Dashboard and click on the available sales channels there.

You should see your Instagram profile as one of the options there. Just click on the + icon which directly connects your IG profile to the Shopify page. This means that any person who wishes to purchase a product of their liking will be taken there.

Of course, you can also link your IG profile to the sales channel in your main website. This should increase the traffic from your IG profile and main website and consolidate all of your transactions.

4. Wait for Approval

At this point, you should have done the following:

- Set up an Instagram Business profile

- Linked the profile to Facebook Shop and Shopify

- Synced your product catalogs in other sites with your Instagram page.

- Linked your main website to the Instagram shop.

Once you have done all of this, Instagram's administrators will then review your account which could take a few hours or a few days.

If you do get approved, you will get a notification that tells you of such.

5. Get Started

Upon receiving that notification, what you will have to do next is to confirm which of your shops that you would want to connect with your Instagram profile. You should click on the Get Started option at the Business settings and select the Shopping option.

Next, you will then have to select the different shops you have currently available. Doing so will sync all your product catalogs into one.

However, there may be an off-chance that your product would not be neatly organize upon assembly or there will be duplicate entries for the same product. This happens regularly if you source your info from multiple sources. Fortunately, you can sort and take out the entries that you do not like and create subcategories for similar products.

Either way, Your Instagram Shop is now good to go.

All that is left to do is to tag your products in each of your posts as well as your content on the Stories page. In fact, you can tag as much as 20 products in multi-image posts or at least 5 for singular image posts.

However, just keep in mind that your Shop page can only be fully activated upon the posting of your first Shop post.

The Main Takeaway:

At a glance, you could already get the notion that setting up your Shop at Instagram can get a hassle especially if you are not that tech-savvy. You are not exactly creating an independent shop page but one that syncs itself to whatever existing shop page you have on other sites.

But if you do this right, you should be able to put up a page that is easy to navigate through and is automatically promoted on Instagram's Shopping Explore feature. All that is left to do now is to make sure that you have enough products to sell in your different sales channels.

Remarketing and How It is Done

The word "remarketing" might sound like an intimidating marketing term but it's actually quite a simple concept.

Let us assume that you have over 50,000 followers after several months on Instagram. That size is something considerable for a mid-sized business. However, would you believe that the number of people who follow you and actually find your products to be interesting does not even reach 10%? Most of them just find your marketing campaigns neat and not much else, while others just stumbled on your profile by accident.

With that volume of people going to your Shop page, main profile, and main website, wouldn't it make sense to retarget them with your offers? That is the very concept of remarketing and, to do this, you have to identify the kind of people that interact with your brand. They usually fall under 3 categories.

- **Buyers** - These people are the ones that need the least convincing as they already had purchased your products before. The best thing that you can do with the people is to entice with the another, better offer and hope that they would take you up on your offer.

For example, you might be a clothing store and a lot of people purchased a certain item from your Shop a few months ago. You can retarget those people with an offer for a "version 2" of that shirt or something that goes along well with it. The point is that   you should give them a good reason to buy something from you again.

- **Cart Bailers** - These are the people that actually went through the effort of converting into customers but just missed the final part: parting with their money. These people have already placed something on their carts or their favorites list but did not actually purchase them for one reason or another.

You can place these people on a separate list but are actually easy enough to remarket. After all, they already have shown interest for your product. They only failed to take action on those interest or even follow through with their purchases.

- **Browsers** - These are the people that actually went through your Shop but did not do anything particularly noteworthy there. They didn't like any of your offers and did not do anything remotely close to starting a transaction with the page.

Remarketing these people can a bit more effort as you still have to convince them that whatever you are offering is something of value. However, you can make this easier on your part by putting these browsers into one group and creating a more labor-intensive marketing campaign that exclusively targets them in the future.

So once you have identified the kind of people going through your Shop page, how do you actually go about remarketing them? There are a number of strategies that you can use, depending on the kind of people that you want to retarget. However, in order to make any of your strategies effective, there are several things that you have to remember.

1. Start with Top Performers

Are you familiar with the term "low hanging fruit"? This is a kind of marketing where you do minimal effort for maximum effect. In the case of remarketing, this involves going back to the campaigns that net you a lot of engagements and reintroducing them to the market, with updates of course.

The reason for this simple: that campaign had a lot of potential to convert more people. What if it can yield you more if you reintroduce it in the market? This strategy is not exactly frowned upon in marketing as remarketing does get expensive especially with Google's AdWords feature.

Once you are sure that you have wrung out every extra bit of conversion you can get from these campaigns, you can then move on to newer ones.

2. Maximum Effort Counts, Too

Although click-through rates tend to drop in time with remarketing, studies do show that conversion is more certain with these ads especially in shoppers who are familiar with the brand.

As such, it is recommended that you do not hesitate to spend a bit more or get a bit more creative when it comes to your remarketing schemes. Think of it this way: the people you are marketing already know what your products are and have already expressed their interest for the brand. As such, the chances of experiencing better conversions from these people are higher as well as reduced marketing costs for every successful sale.

3. Be Careful with Your Keywords and Tags

Anyone who has ever done SEO that broad keywords are generally avoided. This is because they only work well in funneling a lot of traffic and not much else.

However, conversion has already occurred partly or totally in remarketing. As such, broader keywords and tags will help you on this matter. Also, it helps that broad keywords and tags are cheaper too which means that you can get a ton of conversion for a fraction of your initial marketing costs.

4. Special Offers are the Key

This strategy works well with those that bailed on their purchases. The reason is that these people already displayed interest for the brand but did not follow through the sales process for one reason or another.

With remarketing, you can target these people by offering something even better than what they initially planned to purchase a while ago. Be it a bundle, a special discount for returning audiences, or an entirely new item, whatever could sweeten the deal can help in bringing these potential customers back to the fold.

5. Be Frequent but Don't be Annoying

As with all things, remarketing only works well if you don't overdo it. A shopper will find it annoying if you bombard them with the same ad again and again to the point that they would tune you. This is regardless of how good your offers actually are.

If possible, do time your remarketing efforts so much so that they are evenly spaced one ad from the other. The duration of how long an ad should be followed with another should not be too long that people forget what you were offering them and not too short that it becomes a daily occurrence. And do remember that spamming messages has never worked well in the Internet.

To Wrap Things Up...

So, is Instagram's Shop page completely necessary to make your marketing campaigns there work? Not really. The feature still has a lot of kinks to work out and there is the fact that putting it up in the first place is quite tedious.

However, that does not mean that the feature does not pose some advantages to brands as far as their sales are concerned. Remember that the end goal of marketing is always the business's bottom line. And since the Shop feature does directly affect that, it is best that you take the time to learn what it can offer for your business and whether or not your staff can keep up with its rather strict demands.

Chapter 7: Appealing to Generation Z

As of now, the most relevant market to target are the Millennials. This is because they have the right combination of youth, activity, and purchasing power which makes them a potent segment to focus on, especially on Instagram. But, just as with any generation, they would soon be replaced with a far more potent generation to market to.

Born during the late 1990s, right at the formative years of the Internet Age, Generation Z is a highly cautious and tech-savvy generation. With almost all of them finally acquiring purchasing power, they are already playing a valuable role on how marketing is done especially in the online world.

However, there are challenges to face when marketing to these individuals. Their high affinity towards technology and access to a trove of information makes them difficult to market to if you insist on using traditional forms of marketing. In fact, many predict that Gen Z folk would require a different approach altogether compared to the generation that directly preceded them.

There is one thing that you should remember about this market and that is the fact that Social Media has a huge presence in their lives. As such, you have to learn how to use that dependence to your advantage in creating campaigns that they will engage with. Besides, many of the insights that apply to this group also apply to many millennials, so you might want to take note.

What Makes Gen Z a Challenge to Market To?

Since they were born right at the dawn of the Internet Age, Gen Z folk have a stronger connection to online technology than older age groups. This strong affinity, in turn, has brought about some distinct behaviors in them as far their treatment with marketing messages are concerned.

If you insist on making the Gen Z people a core group to market to, there are some notable behaviors that you should be aware of which include the following:

1. They Don't Give a Damn About Brand Loyalty

In traditional marketing, the way the message is form revolves around telling the rest of the world that your brand is the best out there for certain conditions or the best out there period. For Gen Z people, however, such kind of marketing is seen as pushy, abrasive, and noisy.

If you are used to the notion that you can drown the rest of the market by making a lot more noise through your marketing, you can be certain that Gen Z folk are going to tune you out. They won't convert and become loyal to you and they can access information on the Internet to stand by their convictions.

In essence, they won't take the bait if all that you are saying is that your products or services are good. However, what they do look for are businesses that can provide solutions to problems that they constantly face.

For example, Gen Zs don't shop at certain clothing brands because they offer cheap prices or they use high-end materials for their products. They do so because the designs are hip and cute which helps them with their image (a problem that they often deal with on a daily basis given their age range and how society functions in recent years).

To target these people to become paying customers, then, you have to offer ideas and solutions to whatever issue that resonates with Gen Z people the most. The more effective that solution is, the more recognizable that brand will be to this age group.

2. Marketing is in a Free For All Now

Back then, it was the norm that the competition you have to take seriously are the brands that offer the same products and services as you. Or, alternatively, it is those companies that target the same demographics as you.

However, given the higher level of consumer agency being afforded by Gen Z folk today, competition for any kind of business comes in various shapes, sizes, and business types.

In most cases, the competition that you have to seriously consider now comes not from big-time businesses and key industry players but from smaller businesses and brands. For instance, a deli today does not have to deal with other delis but also fusion cafes and bakeries that offer artisanal meal options for Gen Zers who want more quality for a fraction of the cost.

The reason why smaller companies are becoming a larger threat today is for the fact that they are closer in proximity to the markets that they operate in. By virtue of being closer, they can better engage with their target markets and Gen Z people are all about businesses that show their humanity nowadays.

Also, you should consider the fact that this group hates Information Overload. If they are exposed to the same kind of marketing message on a day to day basis, no matter how good it is, they will tune it out and ignore such brands for the rest of the foreseeable future.

3. They Care For More Things Than the Bottom Line

In a twist that would make every hardcore capitalist out there shake to their boots, marketing today has been forced to take an angle of selflessness. No, this does not mean that businesses have abandoned their purely capitalist roots since the name of the game is still about making money.

However, what this means is that businesses today are compelled by Generation Z people to consider other forms of capital to remain sustainable in their markets. Things like Altruism, care for the environment, community relations, and other feel-good ideas out there can make people gravitate towards your brand.

Remember that marketing today is all about giving value. So what better value is out there right now than signaling to the rest of the Gen Z market that you care for the same things that they care about?

Of course, this does pose some problems. Brands that opt to focus on social issues must not forget that they need to secure their bottom lines first. And keep in mind that Gen Z people are generally more wary of businesses attempting to reach out to them.

If your move towards becoming more socially aware is generally viewed as insincere and pandering, there is a chance that you will not only get the support of the Gen Z people but you will also alienate other generations who are not too keen with businesses suddenly becoming all too preachy with their marketing.

This is what happened when Gillette decided to make their official stance known in issues like Feminism and the #MeToo Movement. Although it can be seen that their goal was noble i.e. to reach out to a comparatively smaller demographic, the way they handled their messaging was botched as it looked like they were attacking their primary customer base which were men.

In the end, Proctor and Gamble had to deal with an $8 Billion write down for Gillette and had to do a major refocusing of their marketing in the latter half of 2019.

As the saying goes right now: if you choose to "Get Woke", you open yourself up to the risk of getting broke.

4. They Move Through Devices a Lot

Gen Z people are born at a generation when technological dependency was it its highest. They also are the generation with the strongest access to multiple technological devices that it is no surprise that they would move from one device to another.

If Gen X folk have a hard time moving from one screen to another, Gen Z people can do five. Due to these constant leapfrogging between devices and social media platforms, the challenge now for marketers is to be able to predict what devices they often use the most and what platforms they have a strong preference for.

5. They Are Bold with their Opinions

Here's the thing with Generation Z people: if they think that your brand sucks or your marketing sucks, they will not hesitate to tell you. In your virtual face.

The reason for this is simple: these people where raised in a time when Personalization become a norm in marketing. Everything has to be tailor made to suit their needs. Combine this with their access to social media and you have an entire generation of people who are not afraid to express their love and disappointment for the things that they are exposed to.

Older generations would call this trend "bellyaching" but, for marketers, it is something that they could take advantage of. Also, for marketers, it is important to remember that criticisms from this age group counts as a valid form of social interaction so it is best to take what they say with a purely objective standpoint.

Why Instagram Plays a Huge Role with This Group

As of now, Instagram is one of the strongest platforms to operate on as far as Visual Branding is concerned. In fact, it is the one that caters the most to the sensibilities of the Gen Z people compared to Facebook and Twitter.

Due to its highly visual nature, Instagram is a natural pairing for brands that thrive on offering highly visual content. This includes Food Service, Fashion, Lifestyle, Travel, and Self-Help.

But this does not mean other businesses can't use the site as well. Financial services used to veer away from Instagram as the nature of their product was seen as incompatible with the format provided on Instagram.

This all changed in 2013 when PayPal launched a campaign there that depicted the lives of its users with a strong focus on how the services it offers makes the lives of people easier. Things like showing the ability to pay for your bills remotely or purchase things through their program might look simple at a glance but they did tap into the Gen Z's need for mobility and simplicity in their transactions.

In essence, by showing the lifestyle that is eventually reached with their product, and not the product per se, PayPal managed to secure a foothold in younger demographics who were starting to acquire their purchasing powers at that point of time. As far as analytics are concerned, PayPal's simple but ingenious campaign led to a 327% increase in audience engagement for that year alone.

Sadly, not all businesses are that clever and commit a grave mistake on Instagram which old-school marketers would call as "Preaching to the Choir". They create posts that target themselves instead of their followers and potential customers. Things like offering discounts, coupons, and announcements of sales are great but they are not that effective in reaching out to Generation Z audiences.

If you want to know if your messaging would work on Gen Z people on Instagram, there are a few questions that you need to answer as honestly as you could.

- Do these people use my products or services on a daily basis?

- In what way does your offer improve the quality of their life?

- In what way does your brand lend a hand in making their world a better place?

The way you answer these questions might even lead you to improving your core marketing message which should aid in generating interest for your brand in your people and, of course, starting a conversation with them. Then you should consider refining the way you present your messages in a manner that makes it more personal and human to this young audience group.

Why Videos Matter More Now And How To Do Video Marketing On Instagram

The introduction of features like Instagram TV and Facebook Live only further cements the notion that video has a place in the years to come as a marketing tool. In fact, studies revealed that demographics coming from the younger generations can watch as much as 86 videos per day of varying lengths.

How can anyone take advantage of this rising trend? The answer is on investing on good video content and the right distribution channel. Videos, by themselves, can be used to create an entirely unique brand persona while entertaining or educating audiences. If done right, it could even yield a lot of engagement from a lot of demographics.

In order to set up a potent video content campaign on Instagram, there are a few steps that you need to follow.

1. Find the Right Messenger (and Message)

First and foremost, your brand has to invest in a person with a personality good enough to carry the marketing message in your video. This is quite important especially if you are going to use the TV feature for content like tutorials, webinars, and product demonstrations.

When it comes to targeting younger demographics, you also need to know a few things about your audience like:

- How do they talk?

- What interests them?

- What issues do they care about the most?

- What don't they like in general?

As for the message, you must remember that Gen Z people care a lot about social issues which you can use to your advantage. Ben and Jerry's video channels on YouTube and Instagram, for example, have videos that talk about things like gender equality, climate change, and freedom of speech.

By giving the impression that they want to start a conversation with social issues, the brand managed to establish a strong and loyal following in younger people in the recent years.

2. Be Authentic as Possible

Due to the constant connection to the internet and overexposure to all kinds of marketing, Gen Z people tend to a lot more skilled in detecting insincere marketing than older generations. If they feel that brands are approaching not because they want to establish a personal connection but to purely earn from their purchases, younger audiences can and will ignore that brand for as long as humanly possible.

Also, people nowadays don't like to be talked down to or being pandered to. For them, these can cheapen the value of the things that they care about if a blatant marketing tone is laid on top of it. Being transparent, on the other hand, tends to be more acceptable for these people.

If you can't muster an interest in social issues or choose to be neutral with certain issues, then the best that you can do is to be as honest as possible about it. It would be more effective to strive for a more authentic image than to shoehorn a political or social issue to your marketing.

If your brand wants to support a cause, on the other hand, it must be able to draw a parallel between that cause and its own values. For example, if a restaurant claims to support environmental issues, then it should be seen in its practices like how it sources food, to the kind of utensils they provide (e.g. straw, plastic spoons) to how it even disposes its waste.

The point is that being authentic as possible tends to make people care about your brand more. In Instagram, the ability to show that authenticity (as opposed to merely talking about it) should net you a lot of support from younger people.

3. Make it Mobile Friendly

There are three particular reasons why you should optimize your videos for mobile platforms. First, a third of the entire population of Internet users today access the online market through their mobile devices. Second, videos are one of the most shared contents out there at 92% more than text and images.

Third, and exclusive to Gen Z folk, almost all of them have a mobile device now. So how do you make your videos mobile optimized?

The first thing to do is to keep it short. Videos that have longer watch times are harder to share as younger demographics are often intimidated by anything that goes beyond the 20 minute mark. The 5 minute mark is good but you can also aim for 10 minutes depending on the subject you are tackling.

Next, pack every minute with actionable ideas. This is where a good messenger comes into play as they can turn otherwise boring ideas into something exciting and easy to process.

Other Important Strategies

As was previously mentioned, Gen Z people are a bit trickier to market to. However, that does not mean that they are next to impossible as potential marketing audiences. Here are several more strategies that you can use when interacting with this demographic.

1. Loyalty Through Interaction

Gen Z people might not be that particular with loyalty but they are actually more eager to interact with brands. Here are some specific data that you could use regarding Gen Z buying behavior:

- 42% would actually participate in online challenges and events that a brand might come up with.

- 38% are more likely to attend an event in the real world sponsored by an online brand.

- 44% have shown interest in helping brands improve on their products by submitting design ideas and propositions.

- 36% are more than willing to create user generated content that brands can use for their marketing provided that they ask for their consent first.

This means that you could use some older forms of online marketing for these people. This includes challenges, polls, quizzes, and even customer feedback. They are even less hesitant to brands whose Instagram profiles also reply to their comments.

The more you interact with these people, the more likely it is that they would consume whatever you have to offer. But the manner of your interactions would also matter which leads to the next point which is...

2. Understand How they Use Social Media

Even if Social Media sites are designed to cater to all people, the way that each person uses it is different from one another. As far as Gen Z people are concerned, Instagram is used for two things only: to express themselves and to discover the hippest and trendiest brands in the market.

Your marketing should focus on the latter by keeping up with what people care about these days. Whether they are the newest superfoods or the most recent progressive issues, your brand must find a way to incorporate these messages in order to tap into younger demographics.

For example, GoPro found out that its target demographics are into engaging or sharing videos of people extreme sports on social media. Thus, they came up with a brilliant marketing campaign that highlighted people engaging in dangerous and thrilling scenarios which includes firemen going through a burning building or thrill-seekers jumping off cliffs. It was so effective that engagement for GoPro's social media profiles rose up to 300% for that campaign's entire period.

3. Make Privacy a Point

Out of all the marketing generations, it is the Gen Z people that are most protective of their privacy. In essence, they want to make sure that whatever happens in the Internet, stays on the Internet. As such, they are less likely to share their personal information for brands especially the ones that they don't trust.

Also, Gen Z people are more likely to gravitate towards spaces where their identities can remain safely private like Facebook's Messenger app or Snapchat. As such, it is ideal that you put a bit of emphasis on marketing for these private channels as the people there are less likely to resist whatever marketing message that you are trying to convey.

But you have to gain their trust first. This can be done through the aforementioned focus on transparency. Give them the assurance that whatever information that they will provide will not be used for any purpose that they did not consent to. Or, better yet, you could try to come up with marketing campaigns that are not overly reliant on asking the audience to cough up private information.

To Conclude

As of writing, it is the Generation Z people that marketers have the most issues with. They are technically unpredictable, prone to sudden shifts in mood, and are the loudest when expressing their opinion.

It also is important to note that these individuals are starting to acquire stronger purchasing powers which means that the effects that they would have on the market would just become potent in the next decade.

But, fortunately enough, this age group is still receptive to marketing messages, just not through the usual strategies that marketers are most comfortable. The ability to adapt your Instagram strategies to address what these people are looking for can become vital if your overall goal there is to expand your brand's reach towards segments that you have yet to tap into.

Chapter 8: Public Relations on Instagram

The way brands market themselves in the field of social media is always evolving. This means that new strategies are always cooked up every year to make businesses and individuals stand out more in places like Instagram. On the flip side, this means that it is harder to make an impact if you are comfortable with using the same strategy over and over for years on end.

But the one strategy that has remained timeless ever since has been Public Relations. The ability to create goodwill with your brand and maintain that is a skill that many find hard to pull off but remains a necessary asset for many business.

And since Instagram has evolve past its filtered photo album days and is a viable marketing tool, a good PR strategy will not only be more than welcome here but it might just ensure the brand remains visible in the market, and for all the right reasons.

The "Nice Guy" Approach Still Works

We have all heard phrases of how marketing is supposed to be cutthroat and everyone doing it has to be precise, relentless, and assertive. But there is a fine line between being an effective marketer and being that Hollywood stereotype of businessmen being pushy jocks in fancy suits.

The truth is that being the "nice guy" in marketing does yield a lot of results and most of them are ultimately beneficial to the business. This is why Public Relations as a strategy is tantamount to being that "nice guy". So how does one do it especially on Instagram? Here's How.

1. **Collaborate, Not Compete**

As was previously mentioned, changes in consumer behavior have turned marketing into a Free for Fall. Everyone is a potential competitor and cross-promotional schemes means that any brand can vie for the same people as others in the market.

Of course, being competitive is part of human nature. It's what allowed the Business world to thrive even in the age of distrusting consumers. But an effective business person and marketer does not have to butt heads with every other person there that does not share their brand.

Instead of being competitors, a "nice guy" marketer sees every business as a potential addition to their network. As such, they can tap into these businesses to meet a common goal instead of undermining them in every step of their campaign.

2. **Being Diplomatic**

There's no arguing that a lot of conflict starts with miscommunication. A business may say something seemingly innocent about their competitor which the latter would take as an offense. Of course, this is not to discount the fact that businesses have not been engaging in typical corporate trash talking for years or the fact that some business owners take criticism too personally.

In Public Relations, one of the essential skills you must learn is knowing what to say, when to say it, and how to say it. An understanding that marketing networks are volatile is a key skill here so it really pays to be the least toxic person in the market.

For instance, you might put out content on Instagram with the intention of congratulating a competitor. Your staff must find a way to say your message as sincerely as possible so the other group does not take your compliment as thinly-veiled sarcasm.

Or what if you just want to put out an announcement that your business is about to unveil a new product or service? You can do that without taking jabs at your competitors by mocking their previous campaigns.

Conversely, this means that the brand itself must be able to accept negative customer feedback and criticisms and thoroughly consider how you respond to such. The less conflict every move your brand generates, the more opportunities for networking and business will pop up.

3. Transparency

Bluffing and bluster used to be effective strategies in closing deals or saving face. There was this seeming fear to appear weak in front of a potential partner so marketers then used to make bold claims in the hopes that they don't get called out for it. Problems arise, however, if people do call you out on your bluff and find out that you not much to offer.

One important skill to master in Public Relations is the ability to tell the truth without needlessly compromising yourself. Things like the actual capabilities of the business or the product to its policies.

This is not about giving out information that would unnecessarily expose your business to people who might take advantage of your brand's weak points. It is just that you are better off not dealing with expectations that your brand could not meet.

4. Being Empathetic

Every marketing effort that says that your business cares for something would mean nothing if you don't show it. This goes beyond saying things that people like or standing up for causes that people right now care for.

In PR, there is a strong emphasis to make people feel that your brand sees them as actual human beings with legitimate needs and concerns that must be addressed. This is where a lot of brands fail with their PR and marketing as their efforts end too short that everything feels forced.

What you have to always remember is that people nowadays are more discerning as consumers. They can tell when a business is just trying to connect with them without offering something meaningful. And if they smell insincerity, they will not hesitate to call brands out for it.

5. Consistency

One particular reason why businesses do not enjoy a lot of trust from the public is their tendency to say one thing and do another. It's like when a videogame company promises not to put microtransactions in their games and do exactly just that or when a company claims that they care about their customers but take every opportunity to antagonize them on social media.

And this concerns not only customers and outside elements. There are instances when companies project an image of a healthy workplace and yet we hear reports of toxic work environments, employee abuse, and worse. In both instances, the point is that being inconsistent can be detrimental to the reputation of a brand.

Good PR, then, is about practicing the old saying "practice what you preach". If you project an image of approachability on Instagram, then it must be seen in the way your staff deals with customers, suppliers, and even each other. If your brand has an environmentally conscious image, then it must be seen through implementing equally eco-friendly policies. And so on and so forth.

These are just some of the ways that a good PR strategy can help your business improve on its image. The point is that being altruistic, amicable, and an overall fun brand to be around with has never been at the expense of one's competitiveness in the market.

Generating Great Publicity

Do you remember the phrase "There is no such thing as bad publicity"? Well, in the age of social media where every action you take is magnified and archived for future references, that is no longer true.

In fact, people can take what you said and done badly (no matter how noble the intentions are) and make a lot of fuss about it online. So what chances do you have in the market when your marketing strategies are intentionally designed to vilify, antagonize, and jeer people?

Bringing in the right kind of social media attraction is an essential strategy that you could take. And there are a few ways that you could go about doing that.

1. Media Relations

Personalities like bloggers, journalists, columnists, and reporters command a certain sphere of influence in the online world nowadays. This is why you need to extend effort to get on their good terms.

First, take the time to know how these people conduct themselves from their overall style to the topics that they often talk about. Then, you should reach out to them and convince them that having a relationship with your brand will prove to be beneficial on their part.

However, this is not to say that you want them to write biased puff pieces to push your credibility up. At best, these media folk can turn to you as an authority of sorts when it comes to certain social issues.

Also, having the media at your "side" tends to help soften a lot of fallout in case the market partially or completely rejects what you have to offer.

Let's look at Disney's case especially with their handling of the Star Wars brand. Because George Lucas was able to establish goodwill with his target market for decades even before the rise of social media, the brand continues to command strong respect from authorities and is seen by many as a cultural icon.

This is why its Instagram campaigns are still generating a lot of engagement and why a lot of media folk are still willing to defend the franchise despite some current missteps. And such defense is even erected against some fans who feel that the brand is mishandled by the current management.

Fortunately, a lot of bloggers and media people frequent Instagram for a number of reasons. You can easily get a hold of them there or through their other social media channels.

2. Newsworthiness

Having friends in media is one thing. Generating enough buzz in that field is an entirely different challenge. What you may think is newsworthy content such as introducing new products or staff or even opening new branches may not exactly generate enough interest in the public.

Before releasing a story, you should consider how the public is going to react to that. You must ask yourself whether or not that story offers something that people will care about or find to be valuable. Instead of the usual announcements of new products/services/staff on Instagram, you can always use the platform to air out your brand's official stance on certain topics or show the world that your participating in charitable movements.

You can also become newsworthy by responding to breaking events. An official statement of sorts regarding certain incidents and how the brand stands with the community at large is often that effective in endearing your business to the public.

3. Damage Control

Although nobody should ever want to find themselves in having to deal with an emergency, the way you can handle such will have a strong impact than any planned publicity stunt. This is because an emergency forces you to handle things that you did not planned for, a sentiment that is shared by a lot of common folk today.

And in times of crisis, one good PR strategy is to immediately soften the fallout that could potentially occur from such event. Say, for example, a competitor leaked out competition about your company or a journalist wrote a scathing hit piece about your brand.

Naturally, outrage will be fanned which causes a lot of your customers to impulsively reject your products and services. So how is one supposed to react to all of that?

What any business should do is directly address the issue. Perhaps you could post something on Instagram that explains the rumors or denies them outright. Or, if the rumors are true, you can always issue a proper apology at the platform or through any of your major social media channels.

There is no assurance that the doubt implanted on your target markets is going to disappear. You might even have lost huge chunks of loyal customers for something that may be true or just blown out of proportion.

The point is that swift response is the key to proper damage control. The more you downplay things and not address legitimate concerns, the more damage that controversy can inflict to your brand.

To Conclude

Is public relations challenging? The answer is yes. There is so much effort that you have to make to establish goodwill and there is no assurance that people will ultimately see the brand in a positive light.

But is it worth it? The answer is still on the positive. Remember that being agreeable, amicable, and approachable as a business is never meant to dull one's competitive edge in the market. In fact, you can still go toe to toe with your more aggressive (and underhanded) competitors without becoming as cutthroat as them.

Public relations is all about maintaining that competitive edge and projecting such through solutions that benefit everyone, not just the company. If done right, you can establish a strong presence and command strong loyalty in your fanbase on the online world without having to step on other brands.

Chapter 9: Reaching the Online Marketing Plateau

Just like with any other field out there, online marketing can be like a ladder. As you learn new things and develop new strategies for platforms like Instagram, you slowly go through the ranks, get the hang of using what you learned, and proceed to the next big step on your venture.

But, as with any other field again, there comes a time when you reach a peak in marketing and, suddenly, there is no longer any growth or development. This is what is called as a plateau and it can be one of the most precarious places that any online marketer could find themselves in.

Why is this so? Because what follows after a plateau is a slope and, if you are not careful with your next steps, everything will go downhill from there.

Is there a way to get out of this lull? Yes, there is. It all boils down to what you can do to keep the momentum alive until the next big thing in marketing is announced.

What is the Plateau?

The "plateau" is actually a rather vague concept in marketing. You won't find it discussed thoroughly in an academic setting. Even industry experts have never even established a proper definition for it.

So what exactly is the plateau? To make things easier for you, here's a scenario.

Imagine that you are a fan of a certain movie franchise. After seeing the main character endure hardship after hardship in every past entry, you are now in the final movie where he is ready to face his ultimate adversary.

It is now the climax of the movie where both characters clash and the hero won. The ending is seen. The credits roll.

Suddenly, you are hit with this realization:

What Now?

This is a personal plateau for you and the same is true for marketers. Once every strategy has been learned, every trick of that channel mastered, and every trend identified, you feel that nothing can faze you now. There is no need for improvement anymore. Your place on social media is secured and your customer base is large and happy.

But, unlike natural plateaus, marketing plateaus are one of the most dangerous places to be in. In most cases, threats can come there in two forms.

1. Becoming Complacent

Picture yourself working so hard to master the features of Instagram while also making sure that your strategies there are well thought of. Luckily for you, they did which makes you happy.

Your success in one strategy gets you pumped up to create more strategies that eventually became successful themselves. But, with enough wins, you start losing that "fight" in you.

You and your brand feel that brand recognition is now enough to generate leads for the business so your staff start creating mediocre content. And, suddenly, a new standard in marketing pops up or Instagram made a massive change in their algorithms which affects businesses.

All of those strategies that you have learned and mastered are now deemed ineffective, bringing you back to square one. This is what exactly happened to those businesses at the dawn of the Internet age who did not bother to learn how to venture into the then-new market. By not learning how to do online marketing, they suddenly found out that all of their mastered skills and strategies were obsolete when social media started popping up.

2. Stagnating

Or what if you or your staff are not exactly reckless or that arrogant to think that your brand is untouchable. In fact, your business was paying attention closely to the changes in the market.

But, all of a sudden, your strategies are no longer yielding the engagements they once generated. Soon enough, your ventures in the online world start becoming expensive and ineffective for you.

This is what stagnation basically looks like. Your online venture, in its current form, has stopped performing well for your business. In most cases, the quality of your content has not changed. It is just that response for whatever your business is offering ranges from indifference to dislike.

Not addressing this problem has always proven to be a fatal move for marketers in the past. And it is important to note that online marketing is about to enter into a new age by the 2020s with a strong focus on personalized, intimate user experiences. Being at a plateau at this transition period will not do any business good.

What to Do, then?

The one thing that you have to understand with marketing plateaus is that everyone will eventually encounter them in their ventures. There will come a time when there will be no new developments on sight and a stagnation could be seen to last for a few months, depending on the platform.

And since plateaus are unavoidable, the best that any marketer could do is to make the most of their time there. Here's how:

1. Learn Where to Invest More

This strategy is hugely dependent on the assumption that your content had been warmly received in the past. To put it simply, if some of your content has not been generating the amount of engagement in Instagram but is otherwise good, then it is safe to assume that this kind of content needs a bit of an update.

This is a rather blunt strategy at this point since it requires you to do more than what you are currently doing. For instance, if you are posting on Instagram once per day, then increasing that number to 3 or 4 might do you favors. However, make sure that overall quality is not sacrificed with the increase in quantity.

2. Diversify

One other reason why reception for your content declines is the fact that you are offering the same thing over and over with little to no variation. Or perhaps you have been talking about the same topics over and over and people do get sick of hearing the same tune for months on end.

Even if the quality of your content can't be faulted, repetition does not encourage loyalty to the brand. Diversifying, however, keeps things fresh and entertaining which should drive up engagement for your business.

If you have been posting meme after meme on Instagram, for example, make sure that the next content is either a video or a quiz or a poll. The point is to never get stuck or be comfortable in doing the same thing again and again just to save effort on your part.

3. Look for a New Niche

If your current audience has been giving you the cold shoulder at worst or a lukewarm reception at best, then perhaps you could find better engagement from an entirely different market. Doing so opens your brand to new opportunities for marketing as well as new topics, issues, and strategies that you could learn and master.

To put it simply, venturing into new niches of the market not only helps in expanding the reach of your brand but it could also put you in a position to better hone your skills and diversify your content while in a rut.

Of course, the challenge here is to find that new niche. Catering to the same demographics might make it hard to find an alternative audience. To make this easier for you, try to watch what demographics your competitors are targeting or have yet to tap into. Either way, it is best not to limit one's reach to segments that the brand is most comfortable catering to.

4. Go Multimedia

If you had been providing too much image and text based content on Instagram, you run the risk of making people get tired of your content pretty quickly. Sure, pictures and text works great for retaining information but it does have the impact that videos and polls have.

Highly visual multimedia content tends to generate more engagement as it targets more senses while also adding a bit more diversity in your content lineup. And if you make that content interactive, you should drive engagements for your content to an even greater degree.

And if you think that going multimedia is going to run against the point of surviving a plateau, it doesn't. Memes, for example, are cheap to create but tend to be the most shareable media out there right now. You don't even have to change a lot just to keep things fresh. Of course, with memes, the trick is knowing when and how to deliver the punchline.

5. Consolidate Your Presence

Assuming that you are already implementing the ideas above, the next best thing is to try improving your online presence. For starters, you can revisit your defunct and often forgotten social media pages or even features in Instagram that you rarely use. You can even look at links in your content, bios, and pages to see if they still work in driving up traffic to your business.

Once you are assured that your presence is properly optimized, you can start on going back to your library of published content and retarget your niches, both old and new. Of course, there is the tried and tested method of collaborating with other creators and online influencers to attract even more audiences to your brand.

Surviving this plateau is going to be determined by your ability to adapt as well as mix and match effective marketing tools and strategies. Of course, it goes without saying that you must not lose sight of your overall goal as your business goes through the motions. Remember the priorities of the brand while trying out new things and the business should be able to stay afloat even if everything else in the market is stagnating.

Letting Go

One of the core rules in survival is to let go of the things that would weigh your down or prove to be unnecessary in the long term. If your resources are low and the chances of success are less than likely in your marketing ventures, there is even a risk to be had in insisting that your brand operates on the same scope or maintains the same number of channels and workforce.

This would be one of the hardest decisions you would have to make but it could be integral to your brand's survival in the online world. When downsizing your marketing operations, there are a few things that you need to consider.

1. Make a List

This is basic but essential to your survival of the Plateau. Make a list of all the channels currently employed by the brand, the tools at your disposal, and the strategies and campaigns that you are currently running. This is where analytics would also come into play as you need to know how your channels are performing in terms of engagement, web traffic, and search results page visibility.

Then, slowly arrange these channels and strategies according to how well they are performing. With a clearly set distinction between channels and campaigns that are working the best and the least, you will have a better idea as to which of them you should terminate.

2. Remain as Objective as Possible

Cleaning house can be hard. There might be campaigns or strategies that you and your staff have a sentimental connection to or there might be channels where you made your first steps in online marketing.

When you have to confront the fact that some things have to be let go, you should maintain an objective mindset. Try to establish the most logical reason why you are scrapping of this project so you at the very least don't devalue the efforts everybody has poured into it. Make sure that everybody else in the team knows why this is happening so they could shift their efforts elsewhere. And speaking of elsewhere...

3. **Take a Hit**

Aside from projects and strategies, there is also the chance that you would have to let go of some key people on your staff. At this point, you must prove to your people that this downsizing is also going to affect your business and yourself.

For example, if you are going to let go of a few people, then at the very least try to make them see that you are hurting economically. A pay cut here or reduced bonuses (or better yet, none at all) for you can do a lot in projecting solidarity with your team. And by assuring them that whatever you do will ultimately help the business in the long run, there is at the least the chance that morale for your staff is not severely hurt.

To Conclude

A plateau is not exactly the easiest thing to pass through for any marketing venture. More often than not, your brand will not be the same after passing here provided, of course, that you managed to survive through the ordeal.

However, what you have to understand is that plateaus are unavoidable things in marketing. If you don't hit one on your marketing, then good for you since you might be one of the lucky few out there.

If you do stumble on your own marketing campaign plateau, you must be able to find a creative workaround for your current predicament. This way, your stay there would be a bit more manageable.

Conclusion

After learning everything that you could ever possibly want to know on how to pull off a marketing campaign on Instagram, there is still one question that you need to answer:

Is marketing on Instagram all worth it?

This does not ask if the platform is the right fit for your business as that is something that you should answer yourself. What it does ask, however, is if there is a point to even trying to venture into Instagram.

When it comes to Instagram, there are always 4 points that you have to consider in determining if the platform is the right channel to do your marketing in.

1. **Stories Matter now More than Ever**

The launch of Instagram stories and other similar features in social media sites have proved one thing for marketers: you can no longer sell anything online just with pretty pictures or quotable text.

Stories have a highly interactive and multimedia nature in them which means that they can be consumed in various ways (even ways that you did not plan for) and encourage people to engage with the, driving traffic up to a considerable degree. And if people are engaged, they retain information at a far better rate.

And, of course, stories make your marketing content all the more personal and we have discussed thoroughly as to how people respond well if you engage with them on a personal, intimate level.

2. **Everyone Is Into Collaborating**

Influencers have played a hugely vital role in marketing during the latter half of the 2010s and their influence could not be felt more than in the Instagram community. Their ability to command a following while also compelling the same to do things that they ask for is something that modern-day marketers would wish they have right now.

But here is the thing that you need to understand about Influencers. In order for them to effectively become an ambassador of the brand, you have to successfully win them over as a customer themselves. In other words, they themselves must come to the conclusion that whatever you offer works so they could tell others the same.

Looking for the right influencer does pose some challenges for brands nowadays but rest assured that there is always the right influencer for any kind of business.

3. E-Commerce is the Key to Conversion

Online marketing in the last few years of the 2010s has seemingly shifted to a policy of "Show, Don't Tell". What this simply means is that they are slowly migrating a portion of their sales processes from their main web page to the wherever platform they do their marketing in and Instagram is no different with its inclusion of the shopping feature.

The reason for this is quite simple: conversation rates tend to speed up even more if the audience member does not have to sift through multiple websites just to complete a deal. The least likely they have to hop from page to page just to get what they want, the easier it will be to make them part with their hard-earned cash.

We are in a day and where one's own image can be made and unmade with just one status update. Customers that insist on doing things on a purely marketing-focused approach tend to find it hard to make a connection with their target markets who want something more.

In Instagram, businesses should offer more than their usual products and services. They should be selling lifestyles, ideas, and relationships as this is what makes people gravitate towards the site. And it is good to know that you can adapt to the culture of the site without having to forego what makes your brand unique or, on technical terms, what it is trying to do with its online marketing campaigns.

So, should you be on Instagram at all? The answer is a definite 'yes'. By creating campaigns that speaks to your audience on a personal level while still ticking the usual marketing check boxes, you should find a rather warm reception for whatever you have to offer to the site.

Thank you for taking the time and effort to go through every page of this book. Now that you have learned all that is to know about pulling off an effective marketing campaign on Instagram, all that is left to do is to apply everything that you have mastered.

Good Luck!

Book #3

Social Media Marketing 2019

How Great Marketers Stand Out from the Crowd, Reach Millions of People, and Grow Their Business with Facebook, Twitter, YouTube, and Instagram

and

How You Can Too

Introduction

The Age of the Internet is an exciting time to be in. With access to a wealth of information at the palm of the hand and the ability to interact with other people seamlessly across the globe, there is no better time to start a business or maintain one than now.

But with every new era of technology comes a new set of problems that businesses have to regularly face. In this era in particular, there is a strong demand to keep one's offerings relevant and responsive to the time without essentially straying from the business's core goals and vision.

Platforms like YouTube, Facebook, and Instagram offer individuals the opportunity to interact with one another through the creation and sharing of content. For advertisers, this presents an opportunity to directly interact with a new breed of consumers. However, this has its own set of demands as there have been changes in the patterns of consumer behavior brought about by exposure to these new forms of entertainment and communication.

And then there is the matter of how one's own reputation can easily affect the branding of the business online, whether for better or worse. In fact, the high level of interconnectivity and interaction in online communities means that it is easier to inadvertently hurt one's own reputation and harder to repair the same.

Lastly, there is the fact that the rules and standards on how one should create their content and observe proper decorum changes regularly in various social media platforms. What would work a few years ago would be rendered ineffective now and what was deemed acceptable long ago could be seen as offensive and inappropriate by many today.

In essence, managing a business's social media presence as well as extending its reach to new segments of the market is a tightrope walk. You have to balance different demands and standards coming from different social media platforms if you want to funnel quite a lot of traffic to your main webpages and enjoy high customer conversion rates.

But here is a secret: In as much as social media can be intimidating for newcomers, marketing a business here operates roughly on the same principles that make traditional marketing strategies effective. All that is required is to adapt those same principles in one's own social media marketing campaigns.

A deep understanding of the consumer today, with all of their quirks and demands, is necessary in crafting a message that resonates with them the most in every platform that they congregate in. Of course, there is the need to understand what makes each social media platform different from one another and the culture and language that they have adopted for their different communities.

If done right, your business's reputation in the social media world will not only remain favorable to you but will eventually flourish and remain strong for years to come. But, of course, we're getting ahead of ourselves.

It is time now to get acquainted with the intricacies in the field of Social Media Marketing.

Chapter 1: Preliminary Considerations

Before we go through the different social media marketing strategies, we have to address one thing first:

Why is Traditional Marketing Failing?

And to answer this question, we have to understand the basic concept of marketing. In essence, we create advertisements that say something about a business, have it shown in any of the channels we own or pay rent for, and then hope the advertisements draw in enough people willing to become paying customers to your brand.

And so the usual sequence for traditional marketing is always this:

A. Person watches or listens to something.

B. Advertisement butts in for thirty seconds or so to tell the person about what a business is offering.

C. Advertisement ends and the program resumes.

Think of traditional marketing as like a horror movie jump scare. It's something that people more or less do, not expecting to interrupt the mood, and minus the scares.

However, such form of advertising through the different online media right now is suffering from the lowest possible click-through rates and the reason is quite obvious: It's invasive, interruptive, and quite so unpredictable in its appearance that your modern potential customer gets more annoyed than intrigued.

And, given the level of control one person has with the kind of information being fed to them these days, it is not too uncommon for people to tune out from these advertisements as soon as they pop up.

According to surveys, traditional marketing has been rejected by potential audiences in a number of ways, including:

- Teenagers and young adults saying that they would unsubscribe from social media channels and websites if they feature too much forced and un-skippable advertisements.

- 86% of TV viewers immediately changing channels if advertisements start appearing.

- 91% of e-mail subscribers dropping out of their subscriptions in an e-mail list if they receive too many irrelevant notifications.

With such level of discomfort being attributed to traditional forms of advertising done in the online world, it is no surprise why they are not faring well recently.

This implies that you have to create something that would resonate well with your audience the most in any social media channel that you would wish to operate in. This means that you have to mold your message to fit the format and language of every social media site out there.

And to do that, you have to understand what makes for good marketing content.

The Anatomy of Good Advertising Content

Regardless of shape and format, advertising content would always follow the same scheme. In essence, content can come in three major categories which are:

A. **Product** - This is what the advertising is offering to the audience. It is tangible and comes in the form of a purchasable item, service, or other promotion.

B. **Role** - The advertisement basically assumes a role in your audience's life. What is it trying to do for that person? What kind of problems does it solve? What type of questions is it trying to answer? Answering these questions often determines the narrative being presented by your marketing strategies.

C. **Emotion** - An ad of this type is designed to connect to the audience on an emotional, if not personal, level. The point of this content is to evoke some kind of emotional response from your audience. Or, at the very least, it tries to introduce a new kind of perspective that could change the way they regard a certain issue or problem.

So which of these content types are the best for your business? Neither. Each has its own set of strengths and weaknesses which means that focusing on one while disregarding the others is not going to do you any favors in the long run.

For instance, focusing too much on product-based content can make your advertising feel out of touch with your audience, as they don't connect to your brand on a personal level. On the flip side, if you don't have a lot of product-based advertising and too much emotional advertising, then you are not giving your audiences something tangible to anchor their loyalty to your brand.

The anatomy of a highly effective marketing strategy in social media, then, is finding a balance between all three of these categories. Simply put, your marketing must offer something tangible, introduce something that is actionable, plays a relevant role in the lives of your target audience, and can connect to them on a personal level.

Organic and Paid Marketing: Which is Which?

A common misconception with marketing is that all types of marketing content can be lumped into a single category. The truth, however, is that marketing can fall into two categories: organic and paid.

A smart business owner would use both advertising types in tandem to reach their target market and even discover new segments in the process. However, in order to do that, you have to understand what makes both advertising types different from one another.

Organic Marketing

Marketing falling under this category is best for a number of functions including:

- Establishing the style and voice of your brand.
- Educating potential audiences.
- Driving traffic to landing pages.
- Making the business an authority in a certain topic or industry.

Simply put, organic marketing is there to increase the "awareness" for your business. The cycle of organic marketing often follows the same sequence which is:

A. The scheduled production and publishing of content like blog posts and articles for Search Engine Optimization (SEO) purposes. The articles must be aligned to what your target market cares for the most, the problems that they face, and even issues that are being tackled in the wider industry that your business is a part of.

B. Sharing of these posts on social media. Again, the way that this content is shared must be in line with the format and language of that platform.

C. Tagging influencers and other appropriate brands in your social media posts as well as using your content in regular newsletters for subscribers.

D. Monitoring how the content is being consumed by the market. Analytics and other monitoring tools will become crucial in this phase, as it tells you whether or not people are engaging with your content and if your content is funneling traffic from your social media accounts to your main web pages.

If it is not obvious to you, organic marketing is focused on tactics that produce authentic and value-based reactions. In essence, if you produce something of value to your audience, you are convincing them more to convert into paying customers. And if you already have converted them into paying customers, the content you further produce will help in ensuring that they remain loyal to your business.

Paid Marketing

On the other hand, paid marketing is designed to help businesses optimize the sales conversion process. If organic marketing is there to "establish" your presence, then paid marketing is there to "push" it. Due to this, paid marketing is much more focused on sales and generating a purchase-focused action among target audiences.

How the paid marketing cycle goes is as follows:

A. Commissioning for the Creation of "Advertising Content." This would also include creating a schedule of when these ads are going to be published and in what sets.

B. Once the initial results are in for every published set, the marketing team then reviews which ads performed the best. Some would even invest more money in improving these top-performing ads or creating new ads similar to them.

C. Once every quarter is complete, the marketing team then reviews data drawn from the entire marketing campaign. Things to look for are expenses, returns of investment, returns on assets, and other important metrics.

The key to success with paid marketing is to be specific with your goals in order to produce specific actions. For instance, each paid ad might be linked to a very specific page of your website such as the landing page, the sales page, or the products page.

Other specific actions you could drive with paid advertising includes:

- Improving returns on investment and assets.

- Making a specific impression on the various platforms you operate in.

- Hitting specific sales goals or, better yet, going beyond them.

- Optimizing ads in real-time.

- Testing marketing campaigns before full implementation to identify what parts make them effective (and where they might fail).

*However, the most **important** metrics you have to look out for in paid advertising will include:*

A. **Conversion Rates** - The traffic coming from your social media pages that not only engage with your web pages but would actually complete the sales conversion process (more on this later).

B. **Engagement** - The amount of likes, shares, views, and comments that each ad generates in a period of time after being published.

C. **Advertisement Type** - The types of advertisements that had the highest rates in conversion and engagement.

Where do These Advertising Types Fit in Your Marketing Campaign?

The one thing that you have to understand is that both paid and organic marketing actually complement each other well. There are even certain aspects where both advertisement types overlap into each other which can optimize conversion rates and incoming traffic in your main web pages.

However, the truth is that both advertisement forms are rarely used in tandem due to budget concerns. Paid advertising, as the name implies, requires you to invest more in order to generate tangible results.

On the other hand, even if you have a large advertising budget, you are not going to improve on your business's sales conversion if your content does not naturally engage with your target audience.

As such, it is important that you identify where you must use paid and organic marketing either in tandem or exclusively. Some of your marketing goals will rely on one form while others can be achieved if you used either type.

Once you have found a balance between paid and organic marketing, what you must do then is to constantly test and improve on your strategies throughout the entire campaign.

Some (Harsh) Social Media Realities That You Must Face

What you have to understand is that changes in consumer behavior has not only affected traditional marketing, but even online marketing. What worked for social media sites a few years back no longer applies today.

As such, if you want to truly survive in the world of social media, you need to face some realities about the current state of affairs.

Reality #1: Brand Recognition No Longer Means as Much as It Did

Traditional marketing has always been the act of telling the rest of the world that your business is the best of whatever it is doing or, at the very least, a fairly trusted brand in the field. But how does the rest of the social media market treat that same line whenever a company says it today? Noise. Loud, unnecessary, irrelevant noise.

The harshest truth you might face with social media is that nobody on there really cares about your business. And those that swear that they support your business won't be there for long if you start making mistakes here and there.

So, if the image you create is no longer important, what then matters for social media people? The answer is one word: solutions.

Simply put, marketing today is no longer about how well-known or trusted your brand is, but how applicable your offerings are in solving actual problems. As such, those that offer the best possible solutions to a problem, and at reasonable prices, tend to be at the top.

Reality #2: It's a Free-For-All

A few years back, the only kind of competition you needed to worry about came from the companies that offered the same products/services as you, or those that targeted the same demographics. Today, competition can come in any form or size.

In most cases, the competition you should take seriously today will come from smaller companies or lesser-known people. The reason for this is that they are closer to their target markets and can keep them engaged through a mixture of organic and paid marketing schemes (more so in the former).

In fact, you will find that less popular brands and individuals can garner stronger followings while big companies like Gap, Pepsi, and Spirit Airlines have to deal with backlash after backlash from their tone deaf social media strategies.

Also, the increase of volume in competition today gives rise to the problem of information overload for target markets. The more manufactured noise that similar companies generate on social media, the more people tend to ignore what they are trying to say.

Reality #3: Philanthropy is the New Form of Marketing

In a rather odd turn of events, marketing today has taken a rather altruistic tone. And no, this does not mean that companies have forgotten that they are capitalists by heart, as they still aim to make a lot of money from the markets.

What the shift means is that more and more people respond to marketing strategies that make them feel good. And what makes people feel good right now is if companies "stand up" for the "little man."

As such, you might notice that some companies are beginning to take up a stance in social issues, political topics, and even environmental concerns. By showing that they care for the rest of the world, companies give potential customers some value of sorts.

However, there is the drawback of becoming too political or ideological with your marketing. What you have to remember is that people don't like being talked down to. Whether it is you telling them how to live or making them feel ashamed for not caring too much, you can expect a lot of blowback from the market if the message you think is noble is perceived to be pushy and abrasive.

And there are quite a lot of brands out there that overdo it with taking a stand on social issues. The key to success, then, is to temper a business's newfound altruistic side with the notion that one is in business to give people what they want.

Either way, the point is that your brand has to give something of value if you want potential customers to trust it. Otherwise, you are not going to be as relevant in the years to come which, in turn, affects your visibility in the social media arena.

What this all means is that your marketing strategies in social media are utterly dependent on how people behave on them, whether you like it or not. And understanding the behavior of the modern day potential customer is crucial for the sole reason that, in order for your strategies to be deemed successful in social media, they must complete a step-by-step process of becoming paying customers.

Chapter 2: The Sales Conversion Process

Although marketing might sound complicated, it actually follows a rather simple and straightforward sequence. Here's the catch, though: Any member of your audience could be in either of these stages currently.

The 4 Stages: How a Prospect Becomes a Paying Customer

You have to know in what stage of the conversion process your audience is in to craft a message that would resonate with them well. So, how does one person go from an absolute stranger to your business to a loyal customer?

They do so in 4 steps.

1. *Attraction*

Since this is the start of the process, you can expect it to be the more labor-intensive phase compared to subsequent ones. This is where any business would have to introduce people to their products/services and give them the assurance that whatever they are paying for is good.

Of course, since this is the start of the process, the target audience at this phase absolutely does not know anything about the business. As such, the goal here is to inform and educate them by answering their queries. Visibility is a major factor in this phase which is why it is recommended that you adopt a rather aggressive strategy, especially if your business is relatively new to the world of social media.

2. *Conversion*

Once your social media pages are funneling traffic to your web pages, the focus shifts from introducing them to the brand to turning them into potential leads. Here, you may have to rely on your web pages' design and even the presentation of your content to give the push that your leads need to complete the conversion process. You should also have set up systems in your pages where you can easily retarget these people at a later date.

However, your social media pages will still play a crucial role in this part. Through your channels, you can offer them something of value like discounts and promises of access to high-end content if they subscribe or register to your brand.

However, don't go straight for a "hard sell" by immediately offering them all of your available products or services, as you want them to get to know your business more first.

In other words, the goal here is to entice the leads so they would stay on your pages long enough, and make them trust you to the point that they will trade their basic information for something that they can find value with.

3. *Closing*

Once you have your leads, the goal then is to turn these people into paying customers. Since you already have their basic information, retargeting your leads should be fairly straightforward now. Once you have a pool of potential leads to your site via those subscriptions to your social media profiles, you can provide them with even better offers so they would initiate the sales process.

This can be the most demanding part of the sales conversion cycle as you are now aiming to convince people to part with their money to try out something that you are offering. The chances of people bailing on the process is quite high at this part but those that are sufficiently convinced with your marketing at this point will have increased chances of closing a deal with you.

At this point, you can only rely on the quality of your marketing strategies in the first two phases as well as the ones you are publishing at this phase. If they are quite good, people will not only initiate a transaction with the business but would actually go through the entire process, resulting in a sale.

4. *Delighting*

Most business are content with turning one visitor into a paying customer. After all, the sales conversion process is technically complete. However, it would be better if you maintain a relationship with satisfied customers.

Once the main sales process is complete, the next phase will involve enticing these customers with even more offers. The goal for your marketing at this point is to give people a reason to come back to your channels.

The reason for this is quite simple: There is no better endorser to your business than people who actually tried your offerings and found them to be good. If all of your subsequent offerings live up to the promises in your marketing, you can establish a loyal customer base which will promote your business for you in their own little ways.

Nurturing Your Leads

Let's assume that you mastered the art of converting strangers into loyal customers and you know of strategies that can quickly drum up interest for your brand. So now, you have quite a lot of traffic going from your social media pages to your main website.

However, there is still one problem that you would have to face: Not all of those visitors actually become customers. In fact, the people that actually convert into customers coming from your social media pages don't even comprise 20% of your site's day-to-day traffic.

So why aren't visitors actually making important purchasing decisions when on your social media pages? The answer is simple:

Not Everyone Who Clicks Through Your Content is Ready to Make a Purchase

You could focus on generating leads all you want. But if you want to see noticeable changes in your traffic and conversion rates, you'll have to nurture your potential leads.

One key aspect here is that you must understand that each potential lead has their own story to tell. As such, they should be handled in different ways to make them convert into customers and then free promoters.

To perform lead nurturing properly, there are a few things that you have to keep in mind:

1. *Know What They Need*

As was stated, not every lead is the same. Because of this, your business has to directly interact with them to understand in what phase of the conversion process they currently fall into. Have they just discovered your business? From what social media pages did they come from? Have they filled out one of your forms or subscribed to one of your channels?

Knowing where they currently are in the conversion process will give you an idea if they are ready to try out what you are offering or not. However, just remember that just because a lead is not yet ready to make that final step towards conversion now does not mean that they won't do so in the near future.

2. *Communicate*

Once you know what they need, you then need to build a relationship with them. And just like in the real world, you can build trust with complete strangers if you initiate a conversion with them. Don't worry, though. These people are already subscribed to you so you should have no problems contacting them later on.

Having a direct conversation with your audience will actually help you appear sincere and genuine. You have to keep in mind that people today know if the "person" they are talking to online is an actual human being or is a program using a generic comment to get them to talk.

As such, you should learn how to personalize the content your business publishes on social media to build trust with your audience. The more your humanity shines through your social media content, the more people will give attention to you.

3. *Mind the Frequency and the Approach*

One surefire way to scare off a lot of leads from your business is if you are perceived as pushy. Leads often tune out any kind of content that immediately sells them stuff and appears more than once in a day.

Remember that marketing that relies heavily on spamming your message is going to infuriate a lot of people these days in social media.

If possible, limit your engagements with your leads to once or twice every week. Also, you have to have your content marketing designed to follow the sales conversion process. Stage 1 of the process might require content with informative tones while stages 2, 3, and 4 can go for a more promotional tone.

The point is that you should never drive your leads crazy with too much promotions that they would be turned off if they encounter your brand later on.

4. *Mold Your Message to the Platform*

The notion that there is more than one way to say a message is still applicable in the world of social media. When nurturing your leads, you have to adapt to how they speak and interact with each other depending on which social media site they usually hang out on.

What you have to remember is that each social media site acts as its own community with its set of guidelines and culture. And within the larger community lies smaller communities from where you can find specific customer personalities.

For instance, people coming from Instagram need to be reached out to in a visually-focused way while those from Facebook and Twitter need you to constantly interact with them through comments and the sharing of content.

Again, this all boils down to helping people see that there is someone operating that social media profile. And if they know that they are dealing with an actual human being at the other end of the line, they are more than willing to start a conversation with the business.

Granted, understanding the conversion process does not ensure that more people are going to respond well to your marketing strategies. However, what it does do is that it helps you understand that every potential lead needs to be approached in a manner that is unique and, more importantly, personal.

Why is this so? It's because intimacy is actually quite important in the world of social media. Regardless of whether that person uses Facebook or Twitter or YouTube, they are looking for an anchor from which they can connect to brands online on a personal level. And if you can provide that, then you have established a relationship with that person that ensures profit on your side and value on the other.

And, with that done, it is time to venture into the weird, wild world of social media.

Chapter 3: Marketing on Facebook Part I: Benefits and Successful Strategies

Arguably the largest social media platform currently on the Internet, Facebook, is used by an estimated 19 billion users—with 2.38 billion from 2018 alone. This is approximately 8% more than what statistics showed the previous year.

A highly diverse social media site, Facebook, can be used for a number of applications and can cater to a vast range of people. Whether you are a highly political activist in Malaysia or a budding entrepreneur in Romania, there's always something for everyone when they log in to Facebook.

Given its strong staying power and wide reach, it's hard to comprehend that Facebook merely started as a small program between friends at Harvard. And perhaps due to its wide reach, one can see quite a lot of potential from marketing their business here.

But before we go about learning how to do marketing on Facebook effectively, we have to address one question first:

What's in It For Businesses If They Market on Facebook Primarily?

To answer that question, let us look at six key benefits that the site offers.

1. Massive Exposure

As was stated, there are more than a billion people actively using Facebook across the world on any given day. Sure, there are some countries where Facebook is not as popular due to local alternatives, but the reach of the platform remains on a global scale.

This means that exposure for your business is also on a global scale. If you post something, and your profile's setting has all posts set to "Public," absolutely everyone can see your post in their news feed.

Of course, there are settings placed by the site so that not every public post would appear in your news feed. This prevents users from having to scroll through tons of posts from total strangers just to see what their friends are posting. However, the potential for global scale exposure for your marketing is still there.

And to make sure that the reach of your marketing is wide, Facebook offers several marketing platforms for businesses. This comes in the form of pages, groups, and your conventional online advertising channels.

For instance, your business can create a group page where you can promote community activities. Other people can then join in on this group and post their thoughts and ideas. With just one page, you can promote and interact with your potential customers regardless of where they are located currently.

And aside from these channels, Facebook does allow businesses to target specific demographics within the platform. Since people enter in information when registering to the site, the website then groups these people according to what they like according to their profile info.

One neat example of this would be Dove's campaign in 2013 called "Real Beauty Sketches." Featuring people getting their faces drawn by professional sketch artists, this campaign showed that people were rather overly critical on how they described themselves versus how other people actually describe them.

Apparently, that hit a nerve in a lot of people coming from a number of demographics (some of which did not even belong to Dove's target segments). And, as a result, the video received more than 100,000 comments and 6.3 million shares within two weeks after it was published.

And the best part about this is that Facebook's current design allows for content to "go viral" quickly (more on this later on). Recently, Facebook's algorithms can even predict what a user likes and auto-recommend several brands for them.

All it takes is for businesses to publish something good and for it to reach the right amount of people within a short time.

2. *Targeting Accuracy*

Facebook's current layout allows for businesses to target very specific people based on their interests. How they manage to get ahold of this information from people is actually quite ingenious. When a person registers to the site, they are recommended to list down the things that they like and what they are interested in.

Also, people have a tendency to create patterns when they interact with other pages on the site. In essence, every content you share on Facebook, along with the pages that you like and followe, and even the type of pages that you comment in, create a "profile" which allows you to be categorized under several demographics.

This profile, in turn, will be used by business owners to target specific people on the platform. For example, if your brand caters to young adults with some form of financial independence, you could choose several demographic options within Facebook when posting content. This include options like ages below 35, residing in metropolitan cities, and sharing interest in subjects like marketing, business, and careers.

The number of demographic options available on Facebook allows businesses to mix and match customer profiles to target multiple segments at once.

For instance, Ben and Jerry's could target men and women under the age of 40 with an interest in desserts for their ads. Or Victoria's Secret could target women ages 30 to 50 with an interest in fashion. Either way, you can be certain that your content will reach the right kind of people after you publish it.

Aside from targeting, Facebook also allows businesses to accurately retarget past customers. This is because their algorithm also looks into the interaction that people make with your main page.

So, in practice, Facebook allows businesses to automatically update past customers with new offerings and content without having to tediously build something like an e-mail subscription list.

3. *Cost Effectiveness*

The beauty with Facebook is that it can serve as your main website and official marketing channel. In fact, many small businesses (since they don't have the budget to set up a website) make their Facebook profiles their official business page.

Of course, there are the ad options which allow you to target potential segments of the market using information that Facebook has already gathered for you. Posting a paid ad on Facebook is going to cost you but the prices remain budget-friendly regardless of the size and reach of your business.

How Facebook charges you per ad can be done in a number of ways. The most popular of these are the **Cost Per Million** and **Cost Per Click** systems. Basically, you will pay for your ads by the exposure they get and not from the ad space you are renting (unlike in TV and radio).

The more engagements your ads generate and the click-through rate is high without people abandoning the ad as it is being shown, the more you will have to pay for them.

However, there are even cheaper payment methods available for businesses. There is the **Optimized Cost Per Million** rate where the site charges you based on the number of people coming from only the target demographic you have set for the ad.

The next option is the **Cost Per Action** scheme where you are charged only if people perform the specific set of actions after encountering your ad on their news feed. This includes liking your page or sharing the content you have just posted.

And if that is not enough, Facebook allows users to set the daily limit for their ad expenses. Of course, you can adjust the settings if you feel that your campaigns are not reaching the expected amount of people you are expecting. This way, you won't overspend for your Facebook marketing campaigns.

4. *Organic Brand Awareness (and Loyalty)*

Facebook encourages profile holders to directly interact with one another, regardless if that user is a private individual or a company. This direct line of interaction means that you can provide fast customer support which, on paper, should help in increasing awareness and loyalty to your brand.

What you have to understand is that more and more people are relying on Facebook now when making purchasing decisions. For instance, one person might be looking for a set of clothes that your business can supply.

To decide whether or not to do business with you, they look at your profile to see how quickly you can respond to queries. They want to know if you have been directly interacting with your customers, as this is a telltale sign that you can provide what they are looking for in the fastest time possible.

Engagement in Facebook is done through comments, private messages, and the content being published and shared on your page. And this, in turn, can lead to stronger connections with your prospective leads. Of course, a stronger connection increases the chances of conversion.

One other thing to consider here is that Facebook customers can make or break your reputation there. Users can place reviews and ratings on business pages which tells prospective customers how good (or bad) that business is to deal with.

And, also, people can tag in their own statuses. Whether that status is disparaging or praising your business, the reach of word of mouth on Facebook is quite wide and that could affect your brand in more ways than one.

5. *Funneling Web Traffic*

Integrating Facebook to your main online marketing campaign is easy. If linked properly, the Facebook profile for your business can be linked to your main website. If you think that making people go to another site can turn off potential leads, the truth is it doesn't.

What you have to remember is that people who click on any link that you provide do so willingly for 90% of the time. As such, they are more receptive to what you have to offer if they came first from your Facebook profile.

Once they are on your landing page, you can immediately shift to the third phase of the conversion process: Enticing them with offers that would make them start a transaction with you. As such, you can expose them to more direct calls to action or recommend they take a look at your products or services page.

6. *Insights*

The best advantage that Facebook gives to businesses is the ability to gauge how their content is being received in real time. The page of a business profile usually gives its users important information such as the number of likes for the page, engagement for each particular content, and the people who engaged with posts. All of that information is readily available when you click on their respective tabs.

This is quite unlike traditional marketing where you have to pay someone to get the data you need to improve on your marketing. And by the time you have received that data, there is a chance that response to your marketing campaign has changed again, rendering the data irrelevant.

Aside from on-page metrics, Facebook also has the Adverts Manager feature which lets business track how their advertisements are performing in the platform. The Adverts Manager can provide a number of valuable data including:

- Impressions - The number of times a single ad was shown.

- Reach - The number of people who saw the ad.

- Frequency - The number of people who visited your business page through the ad.

- Engagement - The number of times specific actions were done on your page by visitors. This includes liking the page or its posts, commenting on posts, and sharing content.

Granted, the data being shown to you will require an appreciation on the technical aspects of marketing in order to be valuable to you. However, Facebook does present the information to business owners in a manner simple enough that even those with no understanding of analytics could get the gist behind the figures.

The best part about Facebook's Insights feature is that it is completely compatible with the language used by Google's Analytics system. Using both, you can get an idea as to how your Facebook customer base is performing in relation to the wider marketing campaign you have implemented for the rest of the Internet.

7. *Boosting SEO*

The Search Engine Optimization (SEO) serves as the core of many marketing campaigns used currently. After all, marketing is about improving on your visibility and this is often made certain if your pages appear on the topmost results in the Search Engine Results Pages (SERPs).

This can be done naturally by having a key understanding of how search engine bots come up with their rankings for results. Basically, a search engine scours the entire Internet for information that would answer a query made in the search box.

So, if somebody is looking for Japanese restaurants in Los Angeles, the search engine would immediately look for pages that showcase the best places in that city where you could find that kind of food.

Facebook, in recent years, has been optimizing their layout so that their links would show up on Page 1 of the SERPs. If you were to look for your business pages in Google, chances are that your Facebook profile would come out in the top ten results on the first page.

This is good if people already know about your business's name. But what if they don't? Provided that you are constantly publishing content that people engage with on Facebook, the search engine bots might start noticing your page more and will give it a better ranking in queries that may not contain your name but definitely contain questions that your business might answer.

8. *Becoming Mobile Ready*

As of now, 60% of users on Facebook access the platform via their mobile devices. And as this percentage continues to grow, it becomes more important for your business to become optimized for mobile devices.

Remember that the navigation style for either desktop and mobile platforms are substantially different. Some sites are optimized for desktop, which means they are great to go through on a PC but are absolutely frustrating to do so on a mobile. As such, a good business owners needs to have their websites optimized for all types of devices and navigation schemes.

A good thing about Facebook is that it has been optimized for mobile devices. Your business page on the site is easy to access for both PC and mobile users. In fact, the mobile version might be friendlier for users as the most important information on your website is all placed up front. This includes:

- The hours that you are open for business (according to your time zone, of course).

- Your address.

- The reviews your pages get, along with some ratings.

- Phone number and other contact details.

- Your most recent posts.

The only drawback with the mobile version is for your part as the owner. The Custom Apps tab does not appear on the mobile unless you have the proper apps, like ShortStack, or access the site via mobile browsers that have the settings that allow the sites to be viewed via their desktop layout.

This means that monitoring your advertisement's performance through a mobile device is not as effective compared to the desktop.

9. *Monitoring the Competition*

One of Facebook's newest features for businesses is the ability to identify competitors within a specific area. Just below a business's page lies a tab that says "Pages to Watch."

If you click on the "+Add 5 Pages" option, you will be taken to another box which lists other businesses similar to yours operating in the same area as you.

And aside from informing you of your competitors, this feature also displays how these businesses are faring as far as their advertising is concerned.

And if you are wondering why this is quite useful, think of it this way:

Every business in the past has always wondered how their competition is faring in real time. If one of their advertisements was well-liked, a competitor would definitely want to know the figures that would show how effective that piece of marketing was.

It's even been a practice in companies in the past few decades to send "agents" as employees in rival companies just so that they could get hold of that company's advertising and sales figures.

So, if a new business page just popped up, you would want to know if their marketing strategies are effective. Things such as Likes, Comments, and Shares can tell you if that business is resonating with the local market which, of course, gives you an idea as to how to improve on your own marketing campaigns.

It is a bit like corporate espionage but perfectly discreet and legit.

Effective Facebook Marketing Strategies

So far we've only covered why Facebook is a great place to do your marketing at. However, we have yet to fully discuss how to effectively market your business on the platform.

So how does one go about doing that? Remember that there is hard and fast rule on doing your marketing on Facebook. However, there have been trends and tricks used by businesses in the past that allowed for a growth in their presence on the platform. Here are some of them:

1. Review Sharing

One of the best ways to stand out from the crowd on Facebook is something called "social proof." Basically, if your business can prove that what you say is true, people will trust it more.

That kind of proof, however, is not something that you can produce on your own. It only comes from people who are at the receiving end of what you offer: your customers.

This is where *review sharing* comes into play and you can implement it in two steps. First, you request that all your customers leave a comment on your business page. You can even offer an incentive for those that do leave their reviews, such as codes for discounts at your main website or a freebie that comes in their next order.

Once you have enough positive reviews, you must then take a screenshot of a review and post it as an image in your next status update. Don't forget to tag that customer and give them a sincere *thank you* for the review.

You can also use reviews coming from others sites like Google+ and Yelp. E-mails coming from satisfied customers also work, although you might have to ask permission from them before you post them.

And if reviews come few and far between, you can always use a customer's post regarding their experience with you. That works as social proof as well.

2. *Groups*

There are a number of benefits to expect from creating a Facebook group. This includes:

- More direct line of customer service.
- Multiple networking opportunities.
- Putting all your customer base on a single, well-connected community.

- Creating a list of products that you have currently available.

The beauty with groups is that you can give your customers a community where they can share thoughts and ideas with you having full control over the conversations as the administrator.

And since groups are comprised of people with similar interests, you can have your group focus itself on any subject that you will dictate when creating it.

For instance, if you are the owner of a scale model shop, you can create a group on Facebook for people who are interested in scale modeling. To keep the group alive, you might post some content like tips on how to build scale models or on repairing damages while also allowing community members to share their ideas and builds.

Once the group has reached a level of activity, it becomes its own self-sustaining community. This will open your business to more opportunities to market like local events and group meets (more on these later on).

An administrator, of course, has the added responsibility of controlling the behavior of group members and the content being shared there. You can approve or reject posts, add, block or reject members, and direct the flow of communication in every thread that is started in the community.

Handling a Facebook group can get demanding at times but you can be certain that the community you build will have a strong connection with your business in the years to come. That is, of course, if you constantly interact with the rest of the community and maintain a favorable relationship with them.

3. *Events*

Supposed that your business has some major event on the weekend like, say, an anniversary or a famous person is going to visit it. You can use Facebook to notify the rest of the world of what is going to happen with your business through the Events feature.

Creating an event on Facebook is rather simple. You only need to go to the Events tab and select the Create Event option. You will then be transferred to a box where you will fill in details like:

- The date and time

- The category of the event

- Event keywords

- Link to important websites for tickets or for more information

You can also add in a photo for the event like an official banner or any promotion related to it.

Once you have created the event, Facebook will do the rest to inform other people within your target demographics and your customers about it. People can even choose to respond to the notification by declaring their intent to go there.

Aside from Facebook doing the heavy work of promoting your event, you can also do things that will make sure that everybody else will know about it.

A. Add Directions - You'd want those people who have shown interest for your event to get there on time. Giving directions to your place tends to do just that.

B. Invite - Use your friends list to promote the event. Facebook allows you to manually invite people you know to an event. Once invited, they will be given regular reminders of the event until the day arrives.

C. Promote - Dedicate a post on your page everyday about the upcoming event. This way, those that have yet to be made aware of your event will be informed. However, do this promotion no more than three times per day. After all, you don't want to spam your message, as too much of this can turn off would-be-goers.

4. Go Local

If there's one thing that has always been consistent with Facebook, it is that people there love to celebrate things that are part of their local identity. You can use this to your advantage by coming up with content that celebrates every local landmark or any other noteworthy object in your area.

To do this, plan to publish content on your Facebook page that tackles your local culture. For instance, if you live in Idaho, you may link an article there that talks about all the weird stories coming from this region.

If your business offers events management services, you might publish articles about the upcoming events in your area. Or, if you are a restaurant, you might want to publish an article that highlights your city's local delicacies.

Giving your content a strong connection to your local culture would make it unique when compared to your competitors. Plus, people on Facebook love to share articles, especially those that cover things that have a personal connection with them.

5. *Tag*

To quickly build traction on Facebook, you can tag popular people, businesses, and other pages that share your interest in each post. For instance, if your post is about an upcoming event in your local area, you can tag the people that are coming there in your posts or you can name-drop whoever is going to make an appearance there.

Tagging is one way of quickly inserting yourself in a larger, ongoing conversation in your local area's social media circle. And, in line with the *going local* strategy, tagging is one way of increasing hype for an upcoming event, which also increases your prospects of entering into collaborations with other businesses.

Puma, for instance, is quite known for their aggressive social media marketing strategies. If they are sponsored in an upcoming athletic event, you can be certain that their official Facebook page will churn out content that promotes the event to the local people on a daily basis.

Also, you can tag upcoming local events to your posts. If you are helping set up a concert, tag that event. If you are manning a booth at a local convention for gamers and nerds, tag that event. If your Facebook group met each other in the real world for a round of drinks or dinner, post that meetup on your page.

The goal here is to give an impression that your business is actively networking itself to the local community. Showing earnest effort in making your business visible and relevant in the local area tends to resonate with a lot of potential customers, especially those that live and work near your place of business.

Warning: Tagging might be an effective marketing tool but it is also one strategy that could be disastrous for you if overdone. If you start tagging pages and other businesses in your post even if they have nothing to do with whatever your status update contains, chances are you are going to out yourself as a spam page. And if people see you as a spammer, they will immediately turn off your ads whenever they see it in their feeds.

As such, pick and choose whoever you are going to tag in your posts carefully. Pick the ones who are quite relevant to your status update and would provide the most impact with your audience.

6. *Scheduling Your Posts*

This might sound elementary, but you should be consistent with your posts. Constant activity does increase your visibility which brings attention to your page. And with attention comes engagements, and Facebook's algorithms do pick up on pages where people go to frequently.

Your posts should target a specific demographic by focusing on a central subject. Also, it should have the aim to either inform, entertain, or empower your audience.

So what are the best days to post something on your page? If you want to know that, head to your Insights page and go to the Posts tab.

There, you will be given the option to schedule your posts. If you hover over the day portion, you will be able to see the hours where people visit your site the most.

Aside from this, you can also use apps like HootSuite and Sprout Special to understand what type of content resonates with your audience the most. These apps can provide you with metrics and other information on which types of content have been liked and shared the most on your Facebook page.

On your part, you can also find ways to improve the presentation of your posts. As such, here are a few things to consider before you post a status update.

- **Use Emoticons Smartly** - For some reason, posts that use emoticons get commented at 33% and get shared 57% more times than posts that use bare text. However, you should find a balance between emoticons and text, as a focus on the former makes your status a bit hard to read through.

If possible, always put more focus on your text with the emoticons used only to enhance any point you want to get across.

- **Be Inquisitive** - Any post that takes the form of a question gets better engagement through comments. The reason is simple, a question is actionable by nature. It subtly encourages people to do something by satisfying the query it presents.

You can also use polls as an alternative to basic questions. The point is that any post that demands an answer tends to start a conversation, and conversations are one strong form of engagement on Facebook.

7. *Create a Contest*

Studies have shown that Facebook users love two things the most: participation and free stuff. This is where a contest comes into play, as it gives people the chance to enjoy both.

Setting up a contest on Facebook is not as hard as you think. For instance, your page might have this cool or weird picture and you want its engagement to increase. What you can do with that picture is share it with a "Caption This" status update.

Soon enough, your post should get more than a handful of comments if your audience base is quite large. Of course, you should offer something in return for all those people that commented something.

If your business is selling some products, you might offer one item for free. If you are running a service-based business, perhaps a discount on your service fees or a free consultation period could serve as a prize.

Then, you can promote this contest also through the Events tab or through your group. This way, your content gets shown frequently in the news feed of other users which should drive traffic to your page.

However, Facebook does have rules for anyone who wishes to hold a contest there. Before you set up one, you must know what you can't do. They include:

- Requiring contestants share your page or post or write something on your timeline.

- Requiring contestants to like YOUR page to enter.

- Requiring contestants to tag themselves in your post or image to enter.

There are several more things that you can't do for contests as listed out in Facebook's Community Guidelines page. Just make sure that you are quite aware of what Facebook deems acceptable for events so they won't shut your contest down.

8. *Improving "Foot Traffic"*

After all is said and done, you would want your Facebook followers to actually convert into paying customers. Sadly, this is where a lot of businesses are experiencing difficulties with.

You have to think of your Facebook profile as like a marketing email and your physical store as your website's sales page. In order to increase foot traffic, the path that turns digital engagements into real-world sales, you have to have a message that is compelling enough to make readers perform a specific action. This should be then partnered with, and to quote Don Vito Corleone of the *Godfather* saga, "An offer that they can't refuse."

There are ways that can encourage people to come into your store if they encountered your Facebook page. This includes, but is not limited to, the following:

- Creating a poll centered on your products and their uses.

- Run in-store events regularly and promote them on Facebook.

- Promote coupons that people can use in your store.

- Turning your Facebook page into an online shop or have it directly linked to your main website's sales page.

- Align your businesses with causes and charities that people care about in recent times.

In Summary:

Executing marketing tactics on Facebook will require constant experimentation. You have to always remember that even the best designed message might not be received by the public in a manner that you have expected.

Also, what works (and doesn't) for other businesses might not apply to yours. Take the time to understand how your audience behaves and what

Facebook deems to be acceptable. This is because Facebook, like any other social media platform, tends to change the rules from time to time.

Chapter 4: Marketing on Facebook Part II: Creating Your Own Marketing Campaign and Success Stories

Facebook, like any other website out there, wants to remain competitive. And to remain competitive, they must constantly reinvent themselves, which includes changing the rules for users.

In the early 2000s, the team at Facebook found out that a major percentage of their user base included business entities that wanted to reach out to a wider market. From small businesses to large corporate behemoths, every business out there wants a place on Facebook where they can discover a new community to turn into customers.

This has led to Facebook introducing some changes that were specifically meant for marketing a business. And whether these changes hurt or help your wider online marketing campaign is something that you must decide for yourself.

Crucial Components

So, this does give rise to the question: What has changed with Facebook? Here are some that you should pay attention to, as they involve the marketing aspects of your Facebook page.

1. *Customizable Audience Requirements*

Since July of 2018, Facebook has introduced new requirements when targeting custom audiences that were organized through customer files. In essence, when you collect information from Facebook for your marketing campaign, there are three new options made available for you. These include:

- Directly from Customers

- Directly from Partners

- Customers and Partners

How this change affects advertising is quite considerable. Whenever a user clicks on the "Why Am I Seeing This?" button on an ad, they would see how that business got ahold of their information. This would give power to the user to tune out any advertising that they don't like especially if they feel that that business got ahold of their information without their consent.

For businesses, however, this means that they must rely on the Business Manager feature to an even greater degree and must agree to newer terms in the Custom Audience tab if they want to get ahold of valuable user information.

2. *Power to the Audience*

Aside from flagging down business pages that got ahold of their information without their consent, customers are now given more options by Facebook to directly dictate the effectiveness of their advertising on the site. This can be done through the eCommerce Review tool which allows users to leave a rating on the business page after every transaction.

Although the Review feature is not something that is not exactly new to Facebook, the changes in it will help or hurt your advertising depending on the rating. If the ratings on the page are generally good, Facebook's algorithm will allow for your ads to show more in the news feeds of users.

If you start getting a few negative comments, Facebook will give you a notification informing you of such. Of course, as any smart business owner, you should take the notification as a reminder to improve on your services.

If, however, the negative reviews outweigh your positive ones to a considerable degree, you will find that the reach of your ads will be severely limited and the type of content you can publish will be restricted. Worse, Facebook might outright ban you if your page gets more than a handful of community strikes.

Just keep in mind that not every customer experience is going to be great. Some will give you glowing reviews and some will leave poor ones. This means that Facebook won't penalize you for one bad review over a hundred good ones. The restrictions only apply if Facebook notices a recurring pattern in the overall experience you give to your users.

3. *Other Algorithm Changes*

As of now, Facebook is still using the 5 Star scheme for their reviews. It's a fairly dependable system but it is quite notorious for resulting in massive shifts in the overall rating. For instance, if you get 2 to 3 star reviews, the overall rating for your business could change by several points and decimals even if you have 100 4 to 5 star reviews.

Facebook understands this and has been finding ways to make reviews even more reliable than what the number rating would imply. The review algorithm would now detect key phrases and words being left in your reviews as well as the testimonials and recommendations made by your customers.

As a matter of fact, scores right now would say something like "Based on the opinion of XXX people" or "Recommended by XXX people."

The implication for this is that Facebook will make sure that businesses that constantly provide good customer experiences will have better ratings even with the presence of a few poor scores. And if your business has been rating poorly in the past years, this gives you the chance to improve on your strategies on the platform.

Creating an Effective Facebook Marketing Campaign

Facebook's new rules can be daunting, especially if you haven't been using the platform as part of your wider online market strategy. The truth is that Facebook does not exactly demand that you follow a specific form of advertising to increase your brand's awareness there.

All it asks is that your campaign follows what it deems to be reflective on the needs and behavior of Facebook users. As such, when planning your marketing campaign on Facebook, there are several things that you have to keep in mind:

1. *Data is Important*

Any experienced advertiser knows that it is risky to venture into a new platform if you don't know the inner workings of that site. It is advisable, then, that you do your research first in identifying which markets have the highest possible chances in responding to any marketing you make, as this will save you a lot of time and money later on.

On Facebook, you have to always rely on the Insights tool, as it gives you a lot of data that will paint a picture as to how your target markets behave on the site. From when people engage with your content the most and the different demographic qualities that they share, the Insights tool can help you identify who you should target on the site and how to craft your message for them.

And the best part of the Insights tool is that it is free so you can do a lot of research without spending a single penny.

2. *Niche Down*

Generally speaking, mass appeal marketing has fallen out of favor in recent years as more laser-focused marketing styles are the norm. Fortunately for you, Facebook does offer some tools that allow you to improve on your ad's messaging so much so that a single ad can target different people differently despite carrying the same message.

For example, an owner of a Michelin-starred restaurant near a popular tourist spot in London might create two versions of the same advertisement. One might cater to people looking for a fine dining experience while another could cater to tourists and average food lovers.

In essence, the ad might say the same thing but it has been crafted in a way that it caters to three different mindsets. By identifying your niches and then molding your message according to those niches, you can ensure maximum engagement from your campaign without alienating one sector of your customer base.

3. *Stand Out Images*

In these times, a well-crafted message is no longer enough. That message has to be accompanied by something that can quickly catch the attention of your target audience.

This is where imagery comes into play, as a single image can be more compelling than one sprawling wall of text. That is regardless of how good a message that wall of text contains.

The good thing about imagery is that you are not exactly required to produce your own. All that is necessary is for the image to be relevant to the message that you are trying to convey. It also helps, however, if that image was legally acquired.

There are a number of sites out there that offer free stock photos for advertisers to use. You can also head to sites like Fiverr which helps you get in contact with image makers and photographers that can produce an image for your ad; for a reasonable price, of course.

And, with meme culture being quite thriving today (more on this later on), it is best that you take advantage of the fad and make your image meme-able. The more memorable it is, the more likely your advertisements will go viral on Facebook.

And we are all aware that going viral is synonymous with becoming famous on the Internet right now.

4. *Get Your Landing Page Right*

Always remember that any call to action you give in your message is only effective if you give your audience somewhere to follow through with their actions. A landing page allows your audience to learn more about your business while, at the same time, being exposed to more compelling offers.

Your landing page must be as well-designed as Facebook's current layout. This way, the experience that users have with your Facebook page remains the same when they click through your site. Also, it is at your site where most of your deals will be closed so make sure that navigating it is far from a frustrating experience.

5. *Focus on Sales, Not Clicks*

Engagement might be a strong signifier of an effective marketing campaign. However, it does not really assure your marketing campaign is helping people convert from audience members to paying customers.

There have been far too many instances when Facebook posts receive more than 100,000 comments, likes, and shares, but never translates to any action beneficial for you and your audience members. What good engagement is implying is that your ads are performing well. The question is if people are doing their part to enjoy the benefits you are claiming that your business offers on that ad.

What this only means is that you should never underestimate a good Call to Action. Create your CTAs so that they would actually prompt people to do something IMMEDIATELY after being exposed to your advertisements. On your part, you should also be diligent enough to track the sales of your business as soon as you publish your ads on Facebook.

Sales, after all, is the penultimate signifier that your marketing campaign on Facebook is truly effective.

You can craft all the compelling messages that you can think of. You can come up with the flashiest, meme-worthy ads on that platform.

But if none of those ads would result in people actually parting with their money to try out something that you have to offer, then you are wasting your time.

Facebook Live and How to Use It Effectively

The Live option on Facebook can make for a rather effective marketing tool if you know how to use it properly. It is one of way of keeping your content evergreen while also giving you the opportunity to interact with your target audience in real time while your live content is being aired.

So, is there a formula of success in using Facebook Live? Not really. How Live is used depends greatly on the message that you want to convey as well as the audience that you want to reach out to. However, there are a few things that you have to keep in mind to make the most out of this tool.

1. *The Introduction*

As odd as this might sound, you might want to greet your *replay* viewers first or, in some cases, only them. The reason for this is quite simple: Most live viewers don't exactly join you in the first few seconds after going live.

This also means that you should plan your script in as much as you would consider those who would re-watch your live feed in the future.

For your live viewers, you can easily greet them as they drop in. Facebook Live does offer you a tool where you can view the names of those that have just come into your feed. Keep your greetings short and mention your viewers by name (if you can, of course). Facebook users tend to connect with Live creators when they greet them by name in the middle of the broadcast.

2. *The Message*

This serves as the very core of your broadcast and should contain all bits of information that you want to talk about regarding a certain topic. First, you have to offer a brief description of what you are going to talk about. A few sentences should suffice in informing your audience about the nature of the discussion that is to follow.

For the sake of simplicity, divide your message into three or four main points. These sections allow your viewers to go through any sub-theme that they want on replay without having to go through the entire feed again.

Of course, this will help you once you are transcribing your live feed for use in other content that you will publish. By giving sub-topics to your discussion, you give your content creation team more topics to expound later on.

As for replying to comments, it is recommended that you get through your script first before you start engaging with your audience. Replying to comments can take up a lot of time and you run the risk of losing track of the topic you were trying to tackle.

3. *The End*

As you are about to end your live feed, try to wrap things up as neatly as possible. Give a summary of every topic that you have discussed, as this helps those who came in late to keep up with the rest of the group.

This is also where you can include your Call to Action. Suggest some actions that your viewers can do in response to the discussion that they have just taken part in. This might include subscribing to your page, buying your products/services, or heading to any other video or ad that you have on your page for more information.

If you are that particular with being consistent, you can also use this as an opportunity to announce when the next broadcast is going to air and encourage them to visit you on that date. With this, you give all your live feeds some form of coherence with one another, which keeps engagement high for all of your videos.

Preparing for a Live Broadcast

Facebook Live is a great tool for anyone who is used to being the center of attention. What happens, then, if you are not?

Being shy in your first ever Live feed is understandable. After all, you are entirely new to the experience and you might feel awkward with talking in front of a camera. Of course, there is still the need to keep the feed lively so your target audience does not disengage with you.

So, how can someone work through their stage fright and come out of a Live feed with their dignity intact? Here are a few tips to keep in mind.

1. ***Identify The Apprehension*** - What exactly is the reason why you are nervous in front of a camera? Is it because you are conscious with how you look, talk, and act? Are you afraid of the potential backlash you will suffer online?

The things that you are conscious about on a social level tends to answer why you are nervous with doing your Live feeds. Identify your fears first and your preparations would go smoothly from thereon.

2. ***Practice*** - This might sound cliché but practice does make perfect. Before hitting that Live button, make sure that you have gone through your script at least five times before. If you know what to say next, and are confident enough in saying it, you will fumble less once the feed starts.

Also, it would help if you can mentally condition yourself to the broadcast. Practicing gives you the chance to iron out any quirk you might have in delivering your lines as well as the expressions you subconsciously make when saying them.

3. *Improvise* - The one thing that you have to understand with live broadcasts is that even the best scripts can be ruined by unexpected happenings once the broadcast starts. Something might pop up in the middle of the broadcast, like your pet cat jumping onto your lap or you blurting out something stupid in the middle of your monologue.

This is where an ability to quickly recover from your mistakes would come in handy. You can actually learn a lot from actors and broadcasters who can take things in stride even if they are drifting off the script. As such, it is best that you watch online videos about news fails or improv comedy skits.

The point here is to reduce "dead space" in your broadcast while maintaining composure at all times. And speaking of dead space...

4. *Invest in a Teleprompter* - The one thing that can make any broadcast unnecessarily long is if you make constant pauses mid-sentence and use filler words like "um," "sort of," and "like." These fillers are usually uttered since your brain is trying to remember what to say next.

Practicing can remove a lot of these pauses and fillers but it would be better if you can invest in a teleprompter. This device can flash your script behind the camera to help you remember what to say next. And if a teleprompter is beyond your budget, you can always use the time-tested practice of having people flash "idiot boards" behind the camera during your broadcast.

Just remember that these tips will not ensure that your broadcast will go off without any problems. However, using these will help you deal with your own nervousness, which should make your broadcasts even more dynamic and lively.

Chapter 5: How to Market Your Business on Twitter

Twitter is home to 313 million active users every month, many of which belong to younger demographics. As such, generating enough of a following on this site depends greatly on how any business can adapt to the language and culture of the people using this platform.

Fortunately, starting a page on Twitter is a fairly straightforward affair. Once you fill out your bio, upload a picture, and come up with your Twitter handle, you can immediately start tweeting. However, what is not so simple is making your Twitter profile a potent marketing tool that generates leads and increases awareness of your brand.

So, how does one go about marketing their business on Twitter? There are many ways to do just that. But, before anything else, it's best to address a few issues first.

What Makes Twitter, well, Twitter?

Every social media platform out there requires a different approach and Twitter is no different. Basically, Twitter is a place where you are encouraged to share your thoughts within 140 characters or fewer.

As such, the platform focuses more on letting people engage with each other through active communication, not just publishing content for the consumption of the public. On sites like Facebook and YouTube, you are already good if you can constantly publish content at those sites through videos and status updates.

On Twitter, however, constantly tweeting is not enough. Your profile is expected to join in on conversations as they happen. It does this by replying to other tweets and sharing them. And you can expect for your own tweets to get commented and shared on, starting an entire conversation in itself.

Due to this, the primary name of the game on Twitter is *constant activity*. If you want to make your Twitter profile an effective marketing tool, you better have enough time in a day to make a status update on it.

And then there's the target markets you will find on the platform. And, like always, what you will be looking for here is constant activity.

So, in essence, you will not be looking for mere Twitter followers, but active ones as well. Where do you get these kinds of people? The answer is through Twitter Chats. These are moderated public discussions about a certain topic.

The Twitter Chats are filled with people who are constantly using their profiles to communicate with others in a certain sector of the platform. They are not just there to consume content but to do the one thing that Twitter wants its users to perform: Interact with other people.

As such, these are the kinds of people that you want to be exposed to your content as they are the ones that are going to reply, retweet, and share your content to their own circles.

There are Twitter chats for almost every topic and industry out there right now. If your business revolves around food service, you will definitely find more than a hundred Twitter chats dedicated to food. If your business sells toys and comic books, there are Twitter chats dedicated to all things found in Nerdom. And so on and so forth.

And what if you can't find a Twitter chat that fits your business? You start your own. This way, you carve out your own niche in Twitter's market which allows you to dictate the conversations that would occur there.

Marketing on Twitter the Right Way

So, you have a basic understanding of how Twitter is considerably different from other social media sites. So how do you go about marketing your business there? Keep in mind that what works for one business might not be so for another. Trial and error are to be expected in dealing with Twitter's ever-dynamic (and fickle) community.

But despite that, it's best that you learn what strategies other businesses have used to create awareness for their brand on the platform. Here are some of them:

1. Planning Your Tweets Ahead

Twitter's conversations are focused on the ***Now*** which is why it is recommended that you take a more active approach to your content planning for this platform. For example, if the Christmas season comes within a few weeks, you should already have planned the kind of content and tweets you are going to publish for that time of the year.

Planning ahead gives you the advantage of having enough time to craft your message while also coming up with hashtags that will most definitely trend for that season. For Christmas, we know that tags like #Christmas, #HappyHolidays, and #Mostwonderfultimeoftheyear will be definitely trending once December comes.

At best, you should have your campaigns ironed out three weeks ahead of the planned dates of their release. And once the big day comes, you can also follow up on other trending hashtags to go along with your more traditional marketing strategies.

The beauty with Twitter is that you can create content for events as they are happening instead of having to wait until they are over. This should keep hype and momentum for your campaigns at a high.

2. *Make It a Conversation*

A major gripe about business Twitter profiles is that their content is rather one-dimensional. What that means is that their tweets are simply broadcasts of whatever they want to send out to the community, not giving the community itself an opening where they can make that message into an active conversation.

This is not what Twitter is all about. Don't make your tweets just mere headlines with a link, a quote, or any brain fart that you can think of that day. Instead, give them a conversational tone.

There are several ways that you can do this which include the following:

A. **Make It a Question** - The reason for this is quite simple. Questions require answers which makes them perfect conversations starters.

B. **Reply** - If possible, allot 40% or 30% of your daily tweet responses to tweets made by other people. This helps you insert your business profile into ongoing conversations while also contributing to them. And speaking of contributing to a conversation...

C. **Add Your Own Insight** - If applicable, do not merely retweet somebody's content. Add your own insight into the statement regardless if you agree to it or not. Giving your own insight to tweets gives the impression that you have your own ideas and thoughts to share, like an actual human being that other people can interact with.

D. Talk TO Your Audience - Instead of the usual "Title of the Content-Link" format, try to make your links more of a conversation. You may start with a caption like "What do you think of this article?" before giving a link to that content.

The reason why you need to adopt a more conversational tone is that constant interaction increases your Twitter profile's activity. And the more active it is, the more visible it will be for Twitter's algorithms, which should increase your reach on the platform.

3. *Personalize*

Twitter folks love it when a business or a celebrity acknowledges their existence by responding to their tweets. As such, you should make the effort to respond to any tweet that tags you.

Granted, not a lot of these tweets require a response. Some are just looking for attention or finding an excuse to get refunded. Either way, people on Twitter need the assurance that you are listening to their complaints and opinions and are working on such issues to better improve your products/services.

Fortunately, Twitter gives you the option to craft a personalized response to customer queries and complaints. With this you can resolve any issue at a faster rate. This is also why Twitter is considered the best channel to air your customer complaints.

Granted, this does leave your business open to people who want to take advantage of your generosity. Look at the story of when a Twitter user tweets at Morton's steakhouse that he wants a porterhouse steak when he lands at the Newark Airport.

Sure enough, the user was greeted by a Morton's staff member with a plate of the porterhouse ready for consumption. This gave rise to a lot of copycats wanting their own personal slice of meat delivered to them at inopportune times. And so far, Morton's has yet to respond to succeeding requests, although the entire incident did generate enough good press for the business.

The lesson here is that you have to be careful with the tweets you are responding to and how you respond to them. The last thing that people expect is to have someone take their "joke" seriously, after all.

4. *Improving on Your Hashtag Game*

Hashtags are a core concept in Twitter's content sharing system as it can highlight certain hot topics and ongoing events, making your tweets relevant to the times.

And if somebody clicks on that hashtag, they will be linked to other tweets that talk about the same topic or subject. It's an easy way to embed yourself in an ongoing conversation while keeping your marketing up to date with the goings-on in your area.

However, it is also a fairly abused form of content and many business owners fail to use their hashtags effectively.

If you are planning to use hashtags in your Twitter marketing strategy, take the time to do it right. Keep the tags short and sweet, using only one or two words or short phrases.

For instance, if you are about to release some tweets that talk about preparing for winter, you can use words like #Winterready or, if you love pop culture references, a phrase like #Winteriscoming.

The point is to be creative and smart when using hashtags. The less boring your tags are, the more they will trend across the Twitter-verse.

5. *Use Visuals*

Twitter might be pushing for text-based content but that does not mean that images don't have a place on the site anymore. In fact, visuals are one way that you can spice up your tweets and keep their engagement at a high.

When making a tweet, find an image that would be relevant to the topic or is quirky enough to get everybody's attention. It doesn't even have to be an image that you produce on your own.

There are plenty of stock images on the Internet right now that you could get for free. Also, sites like Fiverr do feature professionals that can create an image for you for a fairly low price.

However, it is not necessary that every tweet comes with an image. A few image-centric tweets every five or ten texts, and link-based tweets, should be enough to break the monotony of your feed.

If done right, you should get thrice the engagement at most for your images compared to your other tweets.

6. *Use Humor*

Everybody loves a bit of levity here and there. As such, businesses that often inject humor in their tweets are most likely to get more retweets and comments than serious ones.

The reason for this is that humor is a language that almost everybody understands. Regardless of where a person comes from or what they believe in, they most definitely know what it takes to be funny.

There are a lot of Twitter profiles from businesses that use comedy to their favor. A chief example of this is the official Wendy's profile that started out tweeting mundane stuff but quickly adopted this personality of a sarcastic heckler when replying to tweets.

Another great example is Netflix, whose tweets contain a lot of inside jokes and references of their popular shows. And who could forget about Spirit airlines poking fun at themselves for any mishap that their flights encounter?

Warning: In as much as effective comedy is in improving engagement for your tweets, you must know the right kind of humor to use. There are certain jokes or phrases that could be misconstrued as offensive to a lot of people.

If possible, don't make light of subjects like race, religion, mental illness, gender identities, and physical disabilities. The best kind of clean humor today are cultural references and snarky comebacks, so use those if you have to be funny.

Also, it is best that you do not make light of a recent tragedy. Dark humor is not for everyone and those that do get offended by your quips will respond negatively. And there are no shortages of examples for people and businesses that got their Twitters shut down due to a tone-deaf tweet.

7. *Peak Hour Tweeting*

Depending on the time zone, there are hours in a day when users are the most active. This is where people are going to be the most likely to interact with your content.

As such, you have to know when your audience is going to be at their most active on Twitter. This way, you can time your tweets with their peak activity which boosts engagement and click-through rates for your content.

Research has shown that Friday going into the weekend is where people are at their most active compared with Monday to Thursday. Also, the times where people are at their most active span from 12PM to 6PM during the weekends and then 12PM to 3PM during the work days.

However, your peak posting time will also be dependent on the behavior of your target audience. If you are targeting teenagers, you can expect for their tweet hours to be more sporadic. Normally, teenagers are the most active before school starts, during lunch, and then after the final period of that day.

For adults, however, the 12PM-6PM range is more consistent due to work.

You can automate the scheduling of your posts through apps like Hootsuite and Buffer. These programs allow you to input a certain time and date where a tweet will automatically go live. This way, you can go about marketing your business without having to remember when and where you are going to publish a tweet.

8. *Use Twitter Video*

If images get a lot of attention, then videos get even more than what images could generate. Twitter right now has a function where profiles can upload an existing video footage or capture one live for the rest of the world to follow.

Studies have shown that videos are most likely to be retweeted six to ten times more than images and text. The reason for this is that videos have a multimedia appeal to them and have generally longer lifespans compared to other content as far as relevance is concerned.

Also, you could get to show more to your audience through a video than you would through text and images. With videos, you may give your audience a behind the scenes look at your business or allow them to know the people running your business more intimately.

If you are seriously considering producing video content, you might want to invest on proper recording equipment. A good camera and a microphone is a must if you want people to interact with your videos more. However, a decent camera phone would do the trick especially if you find yourself in the middle of an event that needs to be shared to Twitter.

9. *Optimizing Your Bio*

Although your Bio can only contain 160 characters, it can say much about your business's personality as well as its goals. As such, you need to create a bio that will catch anyone's attention, and this is a rather straightforward process.

When creating your bio, always think of that 160-character box as an opportunity to say to the world why this business exists and the goals you want to accomplish through it.

When creating your Twitter bio, there are a few tips that you need to keep in mind.

A. **Be Accurate** - Tell the people what your brand is about and what your business offers.

B. **Use Creativity -** Always inject a bit of creativity and humanity in your bio. Crack a joke, say something profound, or tell people what you love the most. The more relatable your bio is, the more engagement your page is going to experience.

C. **Brag** - It doesn't hurt to tell people what you have accomplished so as long as they are real. If you've been in the industry for quite a while, let the people know. If you've won some awards, let the people know.

D. **Target -** Write your bio so that it fits the language and the needs of your target audience. If your business targets teens, you can use an informal tone. And if you are targeting an older audience, a bit of formality wouldn't hurt either.

E. **Hashtag It -** This will link your bio to topics and events that your business usually covers.

10. *Do an Advanced Search*

Have you always wondered what people feel about your business or the kind of products/services that it offers? You can do this through Twitter's Advanced Search feature.

If you are not in the middle of tweeting or replying to somebody's tweet, take the time to feel how your industry is faring through Twitter's search engine.

For instance, if you run a clothing store, you can type terms like "clothes" or "fashion" or even "apparel" into the search bar. You will most likely find a person looking for someone that can provide them with those or what people in general think about businesses like yours.

This is a good way of determining whether or not your business has a sizeable audience on Twitter. And the tweet you discovered can be an opportunity for you to convert that user into a paying customer. As such, take the time to reply and answer their query.

11. *Start a Poll*

Polls are one of the most actionable forms of content in any social media platform right now. Fortunately, creating a poll is not hard as you only need to click on the Poll option when creating your tweet, and then add the options and the question.

Twitter polls have a double function if it is not apparent to you. First, they can boost engagement to your page, as the poll requires people to perform specific actions. This way, you can initiate a multi-layered conversation with your audience with just one tweet.

However, polls can also act as market research where you can get an idea as to which products people or service people consume the most as well as their purchasing decisions. With this, you can mold your future marketing campaigns to better resonate with your audience and even improve on your actual business offerings.

12. *End with a Compelling Call to Action*

Always remember that the point of your Twitter marketing campaign is to help generate leads and improve on your click-through rates. As such, if your marketing does not prompt people to do any action that would benefit them and you, your effort is pointless no matter how well-done it was.

Your Call to Action must contain a clear and concise statement as to what you want your audience to do after hearing the message. Whether it is subscribing to you or heading to your main website, the CTA must contain a request that people can perform easily.

When crafting your CTA, you might want to look into a few action phrases such as:

- Please follow us

- Visit our site

- Click here

- Download this file

- Go to our sales page

- Visit us at (insert your business address or website here)

- Learn more

- Don't forget to click like/retweet/share

An effective CTA is bound to drive engagement to your page which should funnel traffic to your main website. And if that CTA is then validated by equally good products and services, those coming from your Twitter page might just convert into paying customers.

What Does it Mean to Get Verified?

The process of receiving that blue badge at the end of your profile can be convoluted and demanding. And there are successful Twitter handles that have millions of followers and can funnel a large volume of traffic to their website without being verified by Twitter itself.

So, this does beg the question: should you want to be verified by Twitter? That is up to you.

But if you do want to become verified on the platform, you must know what you are getting yourself into.

A. <u>Advantages</u>

A key advantage in becoming verified is the assurance of an increase in followers. That blue badge/check mark on your profile does count as social proof as it implies that Twitter itself has checked your profile and found it to be legit and meeting their community standards.

And that social proof does make things easier on your part as a marketer. Since Twitter trusts your profile, people are going to become more responsive to your content. Also, content coming from verified users do experience a spike in engagement as their tweets get responded to, shared, and retweeted the most.

Also, verification does substantially change the layout of your profile. You might notice that there is now a separate column for mentions and follower notifications as well as a column for follows coming from other verified profile.

This way, you can easily identify the kind of engagement your pages are getting which should help you in improving your marketing campaign.

B. Disadvantages

As Uncle Ben would say: "With great power comes great responsibility." Becoming verified on Twitter, as such, comes with a number of responsibilities that you are expected to uphold.

One of these responsibilities is in making sure that your bio contains factual information. There have been far too many instances of verified

Twitter handles losing their status, as their bios are not accurately reflecting what that person is doing. You could not even change it frequently or you would risk losing your verified status.

Also, Twitter now is going to closely monitor your profile. Any infraction that would have otherwise been looked over in the past would now heavily affect your profile. As such, becoming familiar with Twitter's ever-expanding Community Guidelines is something that all verified handles are expected to do.

Another major drawback with the verified status is the sense of dilution it currently experiences. There are too many verified handles right now so the value of becoming verified is not as highly regarded as it was in the past.

Lastly, the increase of visibility comes with an increase to one's exposure to negative elements. Attacks on verified handles are far too frequent in recent years. In fact, Twitter recommends that you use a two-step verification process to protect your profile from the Internet's more insidious elements.

The Verification Process

Twitter has never exactly laid out how they verify profiles on their platform. They do not even give a specific timetable as to when accounts might get verified.

However, what is known is that the process of becoming verified involves several steps. This includes:

- Scanning and e-mailing a copy of documents that would confirm your identity and that of your business.

- Listing out a set of reasons why you are worthy of attaining a verified status.

- Links of outside sources that mention or confirm the existence of your person and that of your business.

Depending on how strong a case you present, becoming verified can take between two weeks to several years. This is because Twitter also has to double-check your background while also looking for duplicate accounts on their site.

So, in essence, becoming verified can really help in your marketing efforts. However, reaching that status also implies that you have to do more to appease Twitter's community standards while shielding yourself from negative online entities.

If you are willing to shoulder the risks it entails, then following the verification process might be a worthwhile effort.

Chapter 6: Dominating in YouTube

Being the second largest social media site in the world, you could definitely see how potent of a marketing platform YouTube can be. And if you are one that would like to get famous, let us just say that YouTube is the Internet's counterpart to Hollywood.

If set up right, your YouTube page can drive a lot of traffic to your websites which should improve your rankings on Google's SERPs.

Here's the thing, though. YouTube, in recent years, is not exactly known for being consistent or lenient. If you want to really make full use of the platform, you will have to play by YouTube's rules—whatever form those rules take.

So What Works in YouTube Now?

YouTube is quite malleable as a platform since it is always changing the rules of what is acceptable there. Since you are going to be improving on your presence there NOW, it is best that you know what would work on YouTube in the current year. This includes:

1. *Focus on Watch Time*

YouTube's algorithm used to rank videos by the number of click-throughs they received. The more clicks a video gets, the better its rank will be.

This, of course, led to an abuse of the system when users started posting clickbait to lure viewers in. This was quite the rage in 2014 when videos were titled with something ridiculous like "OMG! You Won't Believe What

Happens Next!" only for the content to show nothing that is unbelievable or out of the ordinary.

As a countermeasure, YouTube changed the algorithm by making it focus more on how long people stay in the video as opposed to how many times that video got clicked through.

For example, a 20-minute video would not rank well if people drop out of the page by the 5 or 10 minute mark. But a 5-minute video where people actually managed to reach the end of would receive better rankings on the search page.

For this reason, it can be seen why YouTube's recommended page is filled with movie trailers, music videos, talk show segments, and other shorter content that is easier to digest.

2. *Production Value is Rarely Important*

Don't get the wrong idea. It is still necessary that your video should be easy to go through. The video quality must be good and the audio loud enough to be picked up on any device.

It is just that interaction and consumption matter more these days than good production values. One big proof of this is the surge of podcasts and commentary channels on the page where every video is comprised of nothing more than one or a handful of people talking in front of a camera.

And then there are channels like the now-defunct FilthyFrankTV. Despite featuring videos shot in a dorm room and featuring people wearing cheap spandex onesies, Filthy Frank's videos get quite a lot of engagement even as of 2019.

The point is that people now don't care how much you spend in creating your videos. If the message you are trying to convey resonates with them a lot, your rankings should be decent in the search page.

3. *More Subscriptions*

As of now, visibility can also be affected by a channel's subscription count. How this works is actually quite simple: When a person subscribes to a channel, all of the videos that that channel has published will sporadically show up on their feed. And if that channel produces new content, its subscribers will get a notification of such.

In essence, YouTube is personalizing each user's feed by subtly feeding that user content that they think that person would like. If you, for example, would subscribe to a review channel like the Nostalgia Critic, you will also get recommendations for other similar channels like Red Letter Media, Jeremy Jahns, and Chris Stuckmann.

On your part, this means that you should really consider improving the content of your Call to Action. Reminding viewers to like, subscribe, and turn the notification button on is one way of making sure that the reach of your channel is optimized.

How to Get Better Rankings in YouTube

This might come as a surprise to you but the rules that apply in the Search Engine Optimization process also apply in YouTube's rankings. In essence, the ranking you will get there is going to be dependent on your content's presentation, relevance, and, to some extent, quality. To boost your content's rankings, there are a few tips that you have to keep in mind.

1. *The Title*

The first thing that a search engine bot in YouTube goes through when looking for content that answers a query is the title. As a rule of thumb, you have to make your title attractive enough but would reflect the content of the video. If, for example, you are about to publish a video about the top ten street foods in your local area, then the title should contain the words "street foods," "top 10," and whatever the name of your local area is.

Also, only be clever with your titling if it is really necessary. Save the sarcasm for the actual video because search engine bots are artificial intelligence and artificial intelligence still can't understand humor. Or nuance. Their purpose is to check if your title has the right keywords that would match the query being asked.

2. *Add Closed Captions*

People absorb information in different ways. Some are content with just video or audio but a lot of people cannot get a full experience of your content unless they also have something to read. Of course, there is the fact that some people are just hard of hearing or have bad sound systems.

This is where closed captioning comes into play, and it is best that you add them on the video itself or through YouTube's closed captioning feature at the options once the video is published.

With YouTube's closed captioning feature, you can add subtitles yourself or allow strangers to do it for you.

YouTube also has auto-generated subtitles, but they are a work in progress. They can't properly translate what you are saying, especially if you have an accent or speak too fast.

If possible, let another human being write your video's transcript so the message does not get lost in translation.

3. *Descriptions Matter*

The descriptions section in your video can help a person get the gist of the message without actually watching the video. This way, they can decide whether or not to continue watching your content.

When adding the descriptions of your video, always follow the rule of KISS: Keep it Short and Simple.

The reason for this is that YouTube tends to cut descriptions that are longer than 150 characters and hide the rest through the "Show More" option. This gives viewers another option whether to read the description or not. Most of them would choose the latter.

Also, it is at your discretion where you can direct your audience to your other web pages through a CTA. As such, make sure to link all the relevant pages of your site for your video there.

4. *Thumbnails Matter*

In 2018, YouTube ran an experiment where an automated program would decide on the thumbnail for a video using stills of the footage. Let us just say that it was not warmly received.

If possible, always create the thumbnail yourself. You can choose a certain section of the video, edit it, add enhancements, and then add your title. You can also use a separate image provided that you paid for it or ask permission from the image's owner.

Whatever the case, make sure that the image is of good quality and would also reflect the content of the video

.

5. *Every Minute Counts*

Many people think that YouTube is biased towards longer videos. The truth is that the algorithm now values videos that offer a lot of content per minute.

For example, if your video only has five minutes of actual content, then the footage you upload should have the same length. With this, viewers can find your content to be valuable, encouraging them to finish it. And if the stay time for your videos is high, they will rank better at YouTube's search page.

One thing you should never do is to add "blank space" in between or at the end of your videos to pad your content. Prior to the algorithm change, a channel by the name of LeafyisHere was notorious for adding minute-long blank spaces in their video to make it look like they have 10 minutes of content. Needless to say, engagement for the channel dropped severely when the new algorithm was put in place.

The Adpocalypse: How to Survive It

Aside from being a marketing tool, your YouTube channel can help you earn a bit of money through every advertisement being shown in the middle of your videos. However, YouTube insists that your content must be "ad friendly" if you want to monetize on it.

As of 2019, YouTube has experienced three Adpocalypses, events wherein all channels suffered from severe loss of monetization when their videos did not meet YouTube's current standards. Since an Adpocalypse acts like

YouTube's very own state of calamity, you need to survive these events. Here's how:

1. *Always Check on the Community Guidelines*

More often than not, an Adpocalypse is triggered whenever YouTube makes a change in their algorithm following changes in their community guidelines. The actual guideline is quite extensive but the point is that your video should be seen as friendly for advertisers in order to be monetized.

And what is ad friendly in YouTube now? This could mean a lot of things including not showing explicit content, not promoting violence, and is respective of current sensitive social issues. Also, keeping the language clean can help keep your videos monetized.

In early 2018, YouTube star Logan Paul was hit hard by one Adpocalypse after a series of videos involving playing with dead animals and showing a victim in Japan's infamous suicide forest. Other smaller channels were also hit the hardest for a single curse word, showing inappropriate items, and other things that YouTube finds offensive.

2. *Beware of Fair Use*

Using somebody's content without permission is another way of getting demonetized. When you use even a piece of footage or music owned by another channel/company, you will be hit with a copyright strike. If your channel gets struck out, you will find that you can't monetize on your video until the dispute is resolved. Worse, you may not even be able to upload content for weeks on end.

If possible, credit the people that own the music or footage that you are going to use for your videos, especially if such content lasts longer than five seconds. Another option is to use Royalty-free music such as the ones created by Internet artist Kevin Macleod. This should prevent your channel from getting a copyright strike or, at the very least, a legit one.

3. *Find Other Ways of Monetization*

Instead of relying on YouTube's ad revenue, some creators on the site have turned to places like Patreon for earnings. This way, they can directly interact with their audience and ensure that they have enough to stay afloat for the next few months.

Of course, since you already have a business, you can always use your videos to market your products and services. You can even use your offerings as the core subject for your videos. You may even teach people tricks on how to deal with certain problems, giving central focus to what your business offers.

If done right, the content you post on YouTube should help funnel traffic to your main web pages which should keep revenues coming from your online front at a high. And if your content matches what YouTube deems acceptable, you can even earn a bit of money on the side from advertisements.

What Content Should You Produce?

Of course, you are expected to publish videos on YouTube. The question is what kind of videos should you create for the site?

There is exactly no straightforward answer to this, as anything technically goes on YouTube. However, for marketing campaigns, your videos should find a balance between two different needs: the audience and your brand.

The Brand

What makes your brand stand out from the rest of the competition? What does it stand for? How do you make it competitive?

You could answer this by going to your business's vision and mission statement, which should also tell you of your brand's identity. What you should come up with, then, is a list of qualities that can give your content marketing plan a direction of sorts to follow.

Aside from your business's inner qualities, you should also find out what makes your brand ownable. What makes it resonate with the target market? What makes it appealing to people?

The Audience

Obviously, this is your target audience and finding them on YouTube is easy. Basically, they are more or less the same kinds of people that will form your primary target market. For example, if your brand is catered towards young adults, then your YouTube audience will be comprised of young adults.

By finding out who your audience is, you have an idea as to why they would visit your YouTube channel in the first place. And for this, you need to establish their intent.

For instance, if your business delves into carpentry and DIY home remodeling projects, your YouTube audience will come to your videos with the intent to learn new carpentry skills or how to complete certain DIY projects.

But intent is not always measured by tangible products and services. More often than not, your YouTube audience is there to feel good about themselves. Self-gratification is a major reason why people subscribe to channels. In fact, channels like Pewdiepie, h3h3, and Markiplier gain success by making people laugh and feel good about themselves.

The point is if you know what makes your audience tick, you should have no problems in determining what kind of content you should produce on your channel. Once this is done, all that is left to do is to plan on how you go about creating content for the channel.

Feeding the Demand

There is actually no way that you can satisfy the demand from your market with just one video. The trick with YouTube is to gradually build engagement with your brand through a growing library of content with different themes, messages, and even formats.

This may be a daunting task to look at but it is actually easy to pull off and manage. All you have to remember is three **C's: Create, Collaborate, and Curate.**

1. *Create*

This covers the content that you create for your channel. Your content should give the impression that it was made by people who understood the brand and would represent the brand.

Content can be made to perform various roles. It can invoke emotions, it can inform and educate, it can teach new skills, and it can entertain.

At this point, the goal is to be consistent with your goals for your YouTube channel and with your overall marketing campaign.

Large companies often use this scheme with their YouTube marketing campaigns by making their videos share the same message despite having different themes and formats.

Also, movie studios do this in promoting their big budget films. When a movie nears its release date, you might find that your feed will be bombarded with trailers, teasers, and clips promoting the same film.

2. *Collaborate*

If you have the resources and the clout, you can start doing collaborations with other content creators and promote both brands in tandem. The goal at this phase is to extend the reach and influence of your channel in YouTube's community of content creators.

One fine example of this is the Fine Brothers, who constantly invite celebrities to react to recent trends and memes. Even companies like Pepsi team up with smaller channels to create videos that entertain people while pushing up certain products.

3. *Curate*

Once you have built a library of videos on your channel, what are you going to do with them all? In most cases, small channels would have these videos removed but you can always use your audience to help you curate your videos.

For example, you publish a video that contains updates on a developing story. You can say in your CTA to head on to other videos where you covered the previous parts of the story (with links, of course). This is what is called curating and it is a good way to funnel traffic through each of your videos, which boosts the visibility of your channel.

Another thing that you can do is to give your viewers a chance to dictate what happens next in an ongoing story. For example, if a video gets X amount of comments, you might release another video following one story path but if it reaches X amount of likes, you follow a second story path.

Curation is a good way to keep your audiences engaged, especially if they know that they have a say in how your content flows. It's also one way to keep your old content evergreen while producing new ones constantly.

Clickbait and How to Avoid It

Clickbait is any form of content that does not reflect the one promised in the title. As far as YouTube is concerned, clickbaiting your audience is one underhanded way of increasing engagement for your channel and they don't tolerate it.

Why YouTube hates clickbait is quite obvious. YouTube has always been pushing to regulate the revenue streams on its platform and would encourage creators to grow their viewer base in the most natural way possible.

Basically, every click on that video is a potential source of revenue. Understanding this, a lot of content creators abused the system by creating undeserved interest for their videos.

Since YouTube is insistent that you grow your channel naturally, you must follow their community guidelines in titling and describing your videos. And to do that, there are a few tips that you have to keep in mind.

1. <u>*Honesty Is Always the Best Policy*</u>

Clickbait, by design, aims to mislead viewers. The problem became so prevalent in the mid-2010s that YouTube started a crackdown on clickbait, causing a lot of channels to drop in their rankings.

When creating your title, always follow the age-old policy in journalism: Keep things neutral and informative. If your video is about the seven ways that you can use floor polish, then the title should reflect that. If it is about the reasons why you should visit the Eiffel Tower, then the title should say so.

Nothing added, nothing taken.

2. <u>*Ease Up on the Hyperbole*</u>

Hyperbole and advertising used to go hand in hand but the overuse of exaggeration has hurt more brands in recent years. Words like "The Best" or "Greatest" are okay since they are still open to interpretation.

What is not okay, however, is if you start getting ridiculous with your title's wording. Phrases like "OMG!" or "Your Jaw Will Drop with…" or even "Number 10 Will Cause You to Faint" just reek of desperation on your part. It is as if you don't have enough faith in your viewers to find your content valuable as is.

The solution? Let your video do the talking. Make the title in such a way that it merely gives viewers an impression of what to expect if they click through the video's link.

3. *Drop the Exclamation Points*

Bangorreah is an annoying trend in storytelling where the creator relies too much on exclamation points just to get their point across or make things more dramatic than they really are.

Several years ago, you might have noticed videos with annoying titles like "Don't Try This at Home!!!!!!" or "What was He Thinking? Lolololol!!!!!" It's an eyesore at best and is a telltale sign of amateurish writing on the creator's part.

If possible, limit your punctuation to commas and semicolons. They can give viewers hints as to what to expect from the video without making the title needlessly long or dramatic.

And, as for the question mark, use this only if your content does encourage people to engage in a conversation. Also, Google loves question-type content recently as it matches the usual queries made in the search engine now.

To summarize, make sure that your videos are titled to encourage people to click through. But never, in any case, dupe your viewers into thinking that they will receive something when you have clearly another thing prepared for them.

In Summary

Out of all the social media sites out there, YouTube can look like the most unpredictable. What worked just barely a year ago would no longer apply with the platform's penchant for constant algorithm updates.

What you have to understand is that YouTube has its own interests to protect. With advertisers using the platform for their marketing, they would want to make sure that the content that they produce reflects things that the general public would find to be marketable and inoffensive.

What this means for you is to constantly toe the line if you want your channel to become an effective marketing tool for your business. Keep your content clean and ad friendly and you should not receive any serious strike. And, fortunately for you, you can make your channel visible on YouTube without having to betray the qualities that make your brand unique.

Chapter 7: Instagram and the Age of the Influencer

Out of all the social media sites out there, it seems that Instagram is the one that is the oddest. There is nothing about it that screams "great for marketing businesses" at first glance.

However, Instagram can make for a rather effective marketing tool if you know how to use it properly. But, before anything else, you have to understand why Instagram can make for a valid platform to market your business on. Here are a few facts:

1. It is the third largest social media platform with over 800 million active users every day. 80% of the population is made up of private individuals while the rest are taken up by businesses, large corporations, and other legal entities.

2. The biggest market segment here comes from people ages 18 to 30. this means that Instagram is frequented by teenagers and adults who are quite known for their active spending habits.

3. Approximately 51% of all known active users log in to their accounts on Instagram at least once every day.

4. Instagram stories have been used by nearly 37.5% of the user base and a third of these stories are generated by business profiles.

5. A highly visual platform, 58% of all recorded engagements on Instagram come from photos.

6. The most used hashtags on the platform are #fashion, #Instagood, and #love.

7. Engagement peaks at the platform during 4pm to 5am, regardless of the time zone.

8. There is no popular filter used in the platform, as the best engaged photos do not have one.

9. On a monthly basis, Instagram is visited by two million active users. As such, the potential for advertising is particularly strong on the platform.

10. A typical Instagram profile can net as much as 600 followers and can follow approximately 350 accounts. And this is even if the account is rarely visited on a daily basis.

So What Makes Instagram a Valid Marketing Tool?

On a more technical standpoint, what does make Instagram great for marketing? The answer will be different from one business owner to another. But, on general terms, there are three features that make the platform stand out from other social media sites.

1. It's Mobile-Friendly by Default

Since mobile users already take up a third of the population of Internet users today, it goes without saying that a website that is optimized for navigation through mobile devices is going to thrive. Instagram is not optimized for mobile devices per se. It was designed from the ground up to accommodate mobile users.

In essence, Instagram allows you to create your profile and start sharing content using only a few tools and, better yet, requires you to rely on only two fingers. If you set up your profile right, you can expose yourself to a near-infinite scroll of new content every time you are logged in to the platform.

2. *A Visual Medium*

It is kind of a standard now in marketing to use visuals due to their potential to generate a lot of engagements. Fortunately, Instagram's design encourages you to use visual content for your marketing. In fact, the best engaged content on the platform can be comprised of mostly images and with minimal alterations at that.

As for image sizing, Instagram automatically converts all images to the same size. This way, your images are not disproportionately too large or too small, giving your Instagram campaigns a sense of uniformity.

3. *Strong Staying Power*

What makes Instagram instantly distinct from other platforms is the sheer simplicity of using it. It has an interface that is easy to understand and most of its features are available with just a few clicks on different pages.

This makes the platform easy for younger demographics to express themselves and for businesses to do their marketing without having to master its technical aspects. It also helps that Instagram's online community has a vibe and a sense of togetherness that no other social media platform has managed to replicate...yet.

But not everything is well and good with Instagram. As with other social media platforms, Instagram has some quirks that users have to contend with. Here are a few of them:

1. *No Links*

You can't just include links in your posts at Instagram unless you find a way to embed them into your images. Alternatively, you can have your links placed on your profile but this means that you have to regularly change them if you want your audience to be directed to a specific page relevant to the campaign you are implementing.

The reason why Instagram does this is to prevent users from spamming links on their posts. If you want your campaigns to funnel traffic to your site from this platform, you will have to get creative.

2. *Text is Almost Worthless*

As a highly visual medium, any campaign that relies a lot on text will not be effective here. You have to understand that people come to Instagram for images that they can share to other people which means that you have to master how to deliver your message here using only a few words.

At best, incorporate your text as part of your images and keep them short. To say it differently, let your images do the marketing for you.

3. *No Dialogue*

Unlike other social media platforms, Instagram does not exactly encourage people to engage with each other in a conversation. The platform just wasn't designed for it.

If conversations lie at the heart of your marketing campaign, it is best that you find a way to change how your messages are being conveyed if you want to succeed on the platform.

How to do Marketing on Instagram

Despite its disadvantages, making your handle on Instagram stand out from the competition is not exactly complicated. Regardless of the marketing campaign you will come up with, there are some tips that you could follow to increase the reach of your profile and better engage with your target audience. Here are some of them:

1. *Get a Business Profile*

When setting up your Instagram handle, make sure that it is set up for businesses. Aside from helping people identify that your handle is for a legitimate commercial entity, a business profile has a few added benefits that are exclusive to this profile type.

- **The Contact Button -** This allows your followers to quickly contact you through the platform.

- **Insights -** Instagram gives business profile handlers the ability to gauge the engagement of their content as soon as it is published.

- **Advertising Tools -** Instagram gives businesses some tools to create advertisements and monitor them throughout the entire campaign. And the best part with these tools is that they are not as difficult to master as the ones currently found on Facebook.

- **Instant Exposure -** As a business profile, your handle has better chances of having its content seen in the feeds of your target audience.

2. *Collaborate with an Influencer*

An influencer can act as middleman between you and younger demographics and there are quite a lot of them on Instagram. So, the question: Which influencer is the right kind for your business?

To answer that question, you will first have to determine if both you and the influencer share the same target markets. It does not have to be a 100% match, mind you. You only have to make sure that you and that person have been reaching out to roughly the same kinds of people in your advertising campaigns.

Then, you will have to check if their overall style of communicating with people matches yours. You can see this from the way they express themselves and generate attention based on the topics that they usually handle.

Lastly, you have to make sure that their overall demeanor and language matches your image. If, for example, you have fashioned an image for your business as a professional establishment, you don't hire an influencer that goes out of their way to stir controversy. Of course, such styles would work for certain businesses but not for all.

3. *Cross Promote*

One way to easily increase traffic from your Instagram to your other web pages is to promote the fact that you can also be found elsewhere. Think of it this way: Most of your Instagram followers also have profiles on Facebook and Twitter and tend to frequent YouTube for videos. Also, they are quite active in surfing through the Internet.

So why not encourage them to look for you in other markets that you happen to be operating in too?

With cross promotions, you can increase the exposure for each of the content you publish on Instagram while also consolidating the traffic for all of your advertising channels and main web pages. If done right, you can even cut down on costs for creating new content, as you don't have to create content specifically for one site only.

Why Consider Using Influencers in Your Campaign?

The word "influencer" is casually thrown around these days but that does not mean that their overall impact on your marketing campaigns has diminished. In fact, your marketing campaign on Instagram (or in social media in general) can even be more successful if you are backed by a few influencers here and there.

So, this does give rise to the question: Why should you even consider letting these people into your marketing? Here are a few reasons.

1. Millennials Don't Trust Big Business

It might be because they were born at the dawn of the Internet Age that millennials are a rather cynical bunch. Millennials tend to look at advertising with a certain sense of disdain and are not too keen when businesses invade the social media sites that they frequent.

This means that you and other businesses will have to face the challenge of connecting with these people in a way that is not forced. And not only do you have to establish a connection with them, you will also have to find a way to make them convert into paying customers.

So, if advertisers and businesses are not as trusted as they were in the past, who do millennials trust? To put it simply, they tend to trust the people that they see the most online and can interact with their audience in a personal and direct manner. And that is where influencers have the advantage over you.

2. *Traditional Advertising is No Longer Effective*

If millennials are typically wary of businesses and advertising these days, it also means that the conventional ways of advertising products and services to them are not going to work. One good example of this is the fact that younger people don't watch as much TV today compared to older generations.

It's not that they can't access cable TV as older folks do. It is just that they tend to find the information that they need through the Internet.

And even conventional online marketing strategies have failed to generate considerable engagement from this demographic. Most people at the age of 18 and 30 now know what AdBlock is and have activated it for their browsers. This means that the chances that paid marketing content is going to show up whenever they browse through the Internet or watch a YouTube video is drastically lowered.

On the other hand, influencers can get younger people to listen to them. Whether it is because these influencers are millennials themselves or just know how to connect with younger people, there is the fact that younger demographics are more receptive to them today than your trusted advertising strategies.

3. *Clout*

When you collaborate with an influencer, you will notice that they can easily convince younger people to do what they want. The reason for this is simple: Influencers tend to bring a sense of humanity in social media which traditional advertisers lack. Of course, people tend to trust humans more than they do brands.

So, if an influencer can convince their audience to trust your brand, then younger folks will have no qualms about establishing a relationship with your business.

Of course, how strong that relationship is will be dependent on the influencer. But it cannot be denied that they enjoy a unique kind of trust that is placed on them by their very own audience.

Of course, even with all these reasons, there are some instances when an influencer is not necessary. There are even talks about the trend dropping recently due to some influencers abusing the trust that people have placed on them.

Despite that, it would be best that you give your brand a human connection. And in a platform that is dependent on visuals, having that human connection is vital to the survival of your brand there.

To Conclude

There is no denying that Instagram has its own set of quirks that you have to deal with. However, that does not mean that its viability as a serious marketing platform is diminished.

What is required from you is to understand the basic design of the website while also adapting to the unique culture its community has established for the platform. And if you do provide the kind of content that Instagram people consume the most, the rest, as they say and with no pun intended, will follow.

Chapter 8: PR in the World of Social Media

Believe it or not, a good public relations strategy goes hand in hand with any marketing push. However, not a lot of businesses can get it right.

It is either that they don't generate enough interest for their stories or have not properly established the channels necessary to get their PR across.

On the other hand, good PR can enhance any marketing campaign for even a fraction of the budget. This is made possible, of course, if you know the basis of it.

What Makes PR So Effective?

The first thing that you would wonder is why bother with PR in the first place? After all, it is not the only tool out there that you can use to generate enough of a buzz around your social media channels.

If there is one thing that PR brings that could be summed up in on word, it would be *credibility*.

How this works is actually quite clever. Any marketing campaign that you create is simply just that, an advertisement. This means that people can still tune you out, especially if the image you are projecting in your campaigns does not reflect your brand in real life.

However, if you put that same message in the context of something uplifting like, say, a news report, people will tend to be more receptive

The reason for this is that the mere mention of a product or service in a passive tone in a narrative tends to act as a subtle form of endorsement.

In fact, CTAs are more effective when done with PR as opposed to pure marketing content.

Public Relations and the Search Engine Optimization Process

The thing about PR and the SEO process is that you can synergize your efforts in both fields to come up with quite interesting results. A good PR-SEO strategy could yield you a number of benefits which include the following.

1. *Linking*

Linking remains a particularly important factor in search engine algorithms. The problem, however, is that getting good links is becoming difficult in recent years.

With PR, you can have your content linked to some influential websites, which can funnel quite a lot of traffic to your social media channels and web pages. For instance, a mere mention of your content at sites like Huffington Post can get your brand exposed to even more people, resulting in a significant boost in your web traffic.

2. *Better Brand Recognition*

The search engine bots scour information in a way that is seemingly similar to how we humans do it. Basically, they will look for any mention of your brand name through either your primary channels or through third-party sources. The more your brand gets mentioned, the more visible it will be in the SERPs.

It won't even matter if your business is small compared to larger, well-established companies. If your business gets mentioned in the same breath as the industry's most influential people, your pages should at least rank decently in the results pages.

3. *Improving on Your Reputation*

How do people typically encounter a new business or brand? If you answer "reviews," then you are correct. For instance, the reputation of restaurants and their ability to get more people in is utterly dependent nowadays on what people say about them on websites like Yelp.

Chances are that people would even trust whatever those reviews say more than what you say about yourself in your marketing campaigns.

The obvious problem here, of course, is that people can be notoriously fickle. There have been far too many instances in the past where businesses have been "review bombed" on third-party websites just because the owner said something that they didn't like.

This would naturally lead to rankings for that business dropping in the SERPs.

However, this is where a PR strategy would come into play, as it can alleviate most of that negative impact brought about by poor reviews. With enough mentions of your web pages, your ranking should remain at the first SERP.

In essence, good PR helps you gain a bit of control over your reputation in the online community, even if a lot of people still don't like you.

4. *Social Proof*

So what is your normal reaction if some big business or third-party website mentions your brand? Of course, you are going to brag about that.

What you have to remember is that big sites like Huffington Post, New York Times, or other publications with handles on social media are considered reliable sources of information. As such, a mention of your business makes your business even more trustworthy.

In other words, people will hesitate less in engaging with your business if it has appeared in stories published in major publications.

Of course, that story has to show you in a positive light. When Amy's Baking Company appeared on Kitchen Nightmares in 2013, they received a lot of negative press over the way they interacted with customers and Gordon Ramsay.

Due to their antics, they became the first and only restaurant in the series where Ramsay walked away from. Naturally this opened to a lot more bashing from people online and more news articles regarding the restaurant.

Unfortunately, the couple that owned that restaurant decided to double down on the negativity by harshly responding to critics on their Facebook page and behaving erratically on TV.

This started a downward spiral where negative press resulted in more bizarre antics which further generated negative press. Ultimately, the couple's reputation were in tatters and the restaurant had to be closed.

5. *Establishing Authority*

Even if a journalist has done all their research with regards to a certain topic, they still would welcome the input of an expert in that field. This is why they often ask local businesses for opinions on certain matters.

For instance, if a reporter comes to you for your opinion on the local economy and you give an impression that you know how things work, you help the journalist finish their article while also establishing yourself as an authority on the matter.

However, what you must remember is that the information you are going to provide is only going to help you if it can capture the attention of the audience. For instance, backing your opinions with hard data and making sure that your information is correct will make you sound even more credible.

If done properly, your opinion as shown on that article will increase your brand's visibility on social media and funnel enough traffic to your web pages.

The Art of Using Press Releases

The Press Release might look like this remnant of a bygone era in PR. In actuality, it is a rather effective tool for marketing, especially through social media.

However, in order to really make full use of press releases in the Internet Age, you have to understand that there have been considerable changes in the concept. Here are some of them:

1. Search Engine Visibility

To start things off, you have to understand that search engine bots now can differentiate between promotional, educational, and news-related content. This can mean two things. For audiences, they can discern whether or not that content was published to either provide information or promote a certain brand.

For marketers, this allows you to monitor what type of content your target audiences will resonate with the most.

One telltale sign that your PR in social media is effective is if the search engines feature your press releases first, followed by your social media content, and then your main web pages. Not only does this mean that your presence in the search engines is quite strong, this allows your audiences to quickly go through whatever content you put out there.

2. *The Narrative*

Of course, press releases should tell a story. However, they also need to provide continuity and this is where a lot of brands fail when making press releases on social media.

Think of it this way: If the movie that Disney released after *Black Panther* is *Avengers: Endgame* instead of *Infinity War*, and you are wondering why they are leapfrogging through time to save their dead friends, the first question you'd be asking is "What happened in between?!"

This is the same for press releases. In essence, a press release should be an opportunity for you to showcase to your audience how your company has grown through the years.

For example, if one press release talks about you breaking into the market, then the next press release should cover what you have achieved since then. And the press release after that would be your company appearing in big trade shows, collaborating with other businesses, and showing off new products.

By making your stories follow a coherent narrative, you give the impression to potential customers (and investors) that you have something potentially groundbreaking in your business and it would be wise for them to start dealing with you now. Without that narrative, all your press releases would sound like boring updates to your company.

3. *Frequency*

One question often asked is "How often should one publish a press release?" There is actually no formula for press release frequency but it is recommended that the gap between your press releases span only months, not years.

If you are going to publish a press release in August of 2019, then maybe the next one would be in November of the same year, or January 2020.

On the other hand, it is not recommended that you put out press releases every week. Social media algorithms often regard that as spam, as not a lot of companies have newsworthy content to share on a weekly basis.

As such, a good pace for your press releases would either be once a month or once every quarter.

4. *Finding Leverage*

Timing is also crucial for your press releases. If possible, make one before you take part in a major event. And, if you are the first brand to talk about that upcoming event, you can funnel a lot of traffic to your web pages as people follow you for blow-by-blow coverage.

Also, being one of the first businesses to be quoted by a third-party article gives the impression to audiences that your brand has some clout. This could increase interest for your brand which naturally leads to an increase in site traffic.

5. *Content Marketing*

Your press releases should be incorporated into your content marketing strategies for all your social media profiles. You can do this by actually dedicating a slot for them in your content creation schedule and assigning writers who are proficient with journalistic-style writing.

With this, your staff can devote a portion of their time creating your press releases as opposed to it being an afterthought. And the less forced your press release sounds like, the more effective it is in creating a narrative that your audience can follow.

Lastly, this gives your staff an opportunity to master the art of creating a press release. Not every press release you put out has to only tell your readers that your company has grown considerably in the past few months.

More often than not, it gives your staff an opportunity to look back and take note of how the content they are producing has changed in quality over time. Your staff might be surprised as to how their content has changed in tone and style through the years.

Dealing with Online Backlash

Although you can do your best to remain on everybody's good side, there is still the chance that you will find yourself in a rather tricky situation with social media. It's expected that you will make mistakes on your social media campaigns along the way, but the bigger problem is if that mistake generates a lot of negative publicity.

Fortunately, there is a way for you to weather through the negative press and come out with your dignity intact. And to do that, there are a few tips to remember.

A. *Be The First to Know*

Set up alerts and notifications on your social media pages to know if negative press is building up on you. Your social media team should make it a habit to periodically scan your channels to see if a person has any issue with your business. Legitimate or otherwise.

You can also use Google alerts and other similar apps to notify your team in case any mention of you is made is made by a third-party entity.

B. *React Quickly*

Customers use social media to complain, as this is the fastest way they can get attention to their grievances. If you know something is raised up against you, be the first to respond and find a way to address that situation with the person to the best of your ability.

If a lot of people have already seen that negative comment, the best that you can do is to address the situation publicly by issuing a statement.

The worst that you can do is to delete those comments as people can track if any omission has been made on your part. Treat a complaint as an opportunity to do the right thing and solve the problem effectively.

C. *Make Yourself Accountable*

In a case when you did make an honest mistake, the best thing that you can do is to own up to it. A humble response to a criticism gives the impression that you value the opinion of those that have been loyally consuming your products and services.

One good example of this is YouTube celebrity Jojo Siwa. When her products were discovered to have harmful substances in them, she was the first to apologize and promised to revamp the standards in her products. She even promised refunds for anyone who has already purchased her product.

D. *Actually Fix the Problem*

The most important thing that you can do when dealing with online backlash is to actually address the situation presented. This is the most labor-intensive part of the process, as you will have to look up where you made the mistake and how you can avoid similar instances from occurring in the future.

If the problem stems from issues in your product, the most obvious solution is to recall your products and investigate where things went wrong in production. If the problem is a tweet or status update you made, the best that you can do is to order a redaction or issue a formal apology.

Whatever the problem, the responsibility of fixing always lies with your business.

To Conclude

Without a doubt, handling the PR for your brand in the age of social media can be demanding. Do it wrong and you open your brand up to a lot of negative backlash.

However, that is not to say that public relations will remain a difficult aspect to handle in your business. All that is required of you is to keep track of what has changed and to always find a way to keep your audience interested in the story behind your business.

Chapter 9: Social Media Success Stories: Organic and Paid Marketing Strategies that Work

After all is said and done, the one thing that you would want to ask would most likely be this:

Will all of these strategies work for me?

There is no definitive answer to that, as only you can determine what strategies will work the best for your business. However, that is not to say that some companies have not managed to use marketing strategies to gain a foothold in the social media arena.

In fact, there are quite a lot of brands and people out there that managed to make their marketing strategies work for them. And to give you just a bit of inspiration for your upcoming campaigns, here are their stories.

I. *Facebook Promo*

This paid marketing campaign follows the typical conversion goals, specifically encouraging their audiences to sign up for a trial for a series of Internet marketing lessons.

But, instead of merely settling for the usual text ad with a CTA, Promo decided to produce a ten-second video with a baby dancing on an open track next to a boom box.

As of 2019, Promo's campaign has reached 2.2 million views, 4.2 thousand reactions, more than 590 comments, and 500 shares. And aside from an increase in engagement on their Facebook profile, Promo also saw an increase in their click-through rates by 42% and a decrease in their cost per action by 28%.

Why Promo's ad worked is quite simple. First, it targeted a very specific demographic: people running small businesses. Second, it laid out the problem and the solution in one paragraph so people don't have to overthink and overanalyze.

And lastly, it used an eye-catching video to get people to click through.

MobileMonkey

Facebook's Messenger feature has become a semi-platform for marketing in 2018 and this campaign proves just that. MobileMonkey's campaign in 2018 was optimized for the Messenger app in the sense that clicking it would direct you to a chatbot.

But marketing a chatbot conventionally is not exactly appealing so MobileMonkey had to find a way to get everybody's attention first. How they did that was through a shockingly unusual image of a multicolored mechanical unicorn. It's enough to make everyone do a double take on their news feed just to process the imagery.

But MobileMonkey's cleverness did not stop there. Their CTA just says "Type: Send Me the Secrets." It's direct enough to tell people what to do but is vague enough to not spoil whatever offer MobileMonkey has in store for those that clicked through.

This is one great example of gamification where you make your content highly engaging by offering something tangible as an incentive for those that follow your commands.

And how did this campaign helped MobileMonkey? Its engagement was quite high that the company's cost per lead for this campaign was a measly $5.00. That's thirty times less than what they used to spend for their ads in the past.

Grammarly

One problem that has often plagued advertisers is getting their message across to their audience without becoming spam. Grammarly managed to do just that with their organic advertising campaign way back in 2018.

The goal of the campaign was very simple: to do branding. But Grammarly told a rather relatable story in a two-minute video that ended with a rather compelling message: Write the Future.

Storytelling works great in selling a product or service, especially if the thing that you are selling feels complementary to the story itself. In Grammarly's case, the ad did not shove their service right at the forefront but included it in the story in a manner that is natural and non-intrusive to the theme of the narrative.

And, aside from a compelling CTA, Grammarly also added an element of social proof as they linked a *Forbes* article mentioning them in the video's description.

Needless to say, the campaign reached more than 5 million people with their cost per click reduced to roughly $0.50 per complete views. It also is important to note that Grammarly's cost per million for this ad was 76% cheaper than their usual ads.

Airbnb

What is the best way to promote yourself while also building rapport with your customer base? Use their experiences as the core of your advertising, of course.

Airbnb's marketing on Facebook is reliant on the content generated by their satisfied customers. Simply put, the company uses photos of exotic locations that their customers have taken, which they would otherwise have not enjoyed were it not for Airbnb's services.

What you have to remember is that the algorithm used on Facebook actually favors visual content over hard linking. As such, any marketing campaign that takes advantage of visual media is expected to reach a lot of people organically there.

In 2018 alone, Airbnb managed to triple their return of investment while also lowering their ad's CPA rates by 47%.

Toyota

Being authentic and having a strong connection with your user base tends to make any ad campaign more effective and Toyota's "Feeling the Street" campaign is proof of that.

This ad is a cross-platform contest wherein Toyota would use images generated from street musicians in Instagram and Twitter for a series of visual ads on Facebook.

By showing the culture that their products can live in, Toyota managed to make the central focus of their ads more of the people that can use their product than their actual products.

As a result, Toyota's Feeling the Street campaign managed to generate 1.2 million engagements in 2018 alone. That is a 440% increase in engagements over their ad campaigns in the year before that.

II. *Twitter*

Netflix

Technically speaking, Netflix is not marketing their services or shows on Twitter. But that hasn't stopped their Twitter handle from being one of the most visited and engaged channels on the site today.

This is because Netflix does not market itself conventionally through Twitter. Instead, it uses its handle there to celebrate pop culture and the Internet community.

Aside from the usual updates and retweets, Netflix's Twitter profile is almost dedicated to sharing memes and pop culture references. And, if you are well versed in millennial humor, you would know that those two things resonate with younger folks a lot.

One lesson to be drawn here is to never underestimate entertainment values for your content. Any profile that can speak the language of Internet users and generate content that celebrates online culture is bound to make itself popular on any platform it markets on.

Oberlo

This B2B company caters to small businesses and rookie entrepreneurs. And, given that rather small reach, you'd expect for Oberlo's Twitter marketing to be rather generic and uninspired.

However, a look at Oberlo's Twitter handle would prove that it is anything but those two. Its content is filled with motivational quotes and soothing images that one tends to expect from a life improvement coach or philosopher.

The reason for Oberlo's Twitter campaign is to give its audience a healthy mix of motivation and information. And anyone who is still trying to break into the market knows how important those two things are.

So, by tapping into needs that their audiences can relate to, Oberlo managed to generate a strong following on Twitter. And most of these leads have actually converted into customers.

PlayStation UK

A reactive content strategy is where one adapts to the language and culture of the platform. And in Twitter, one can easily find themselves in the middle of a cultural shift.

PlayStation UK understands this and thus constantly provides content that reflects changes in Internet culture. For instance, if a new form of meme pops up, this handle would then mold their messaging to fit the format of that meme or, at the very least, give a nod to it.

And the best part about this is that PlayStation UK manages to constantly remold their advertising to adapt while still following Twitter's character limits.

Wendy's

When it comes to humor, no other Twitter handle could match the biting sarcasm of Wendy's. In fact, the content found on the profile is a mixture of the usual company update and the profile engaging in Twitter "beefs" with other people, or roasting other competitors like McDonald's.

As of now, the growth of Wendy's Twitter handle in terms of popularity is quite baffling. Perhaps it could be traced back to the fact that Internet humor is quite unpredictable. If you force yourself to be funny online, it wouldn't generate as much interest. But whoever is in charge of Wendy's profile knows when and how to drop a one-liner.

Or perhaps it could be traced back to the fact that the profile, though rather scathing with its remarks, tends to hold back on the more offensive stuff. This way, it keeps a certain level of goodwill with its target audience without becoming needlessly abrasive.

What could not be denied, however, is the fact that Wendy's Twitter profile has more than 970,000 new followers as of 2018, many of which are awaiting which hapless fast food chain Twitter profile it is going to start a tussle with next.

Casper

Cross-platform marketing is something that is highly recommended these days since it consolidates all the traffic coming through your different social media channels. Casper is one company that does this but takes things even further by linking their Twitter handle on popular platforms.

In a bid to help people sleep, Casper created the Casper Sleep Channel which can be found on YouTube, Spotify, and IGTV. They would then provide teasers and updates of whatever content they have produced on these channels on their Twitter along with their Facebook and Instagram handles.

The only draw here is that Casper is now spending more just to keep multiple social media fronts active. However, this does pay in dividends as the following for their brand has significantly increased across all platforms, which easily translates into increased profits.

Google Maps

Being a highly visual app, it is expected for Google Maps to use a highly visual approach for their marketing on Twitter. But how does Google Maps exactly make its handle there stand out from the competition?

First, there is consistency. When Maps would announce changes in the app, their next tweet would be designed in such a way that it looked like a smartphone app but with the changes in Google Maps highlighted there.

What makes this strategy effective is in its simplicity. Using the most basic of tools on Twitter, Google managed to convey their message across despite the platform's inherent limitations.

The other factor is their ability to provide additional content despite the word limit on Twitter. Whenever they provide an update, Google Maps will also include a link where their audience can find a better explanation of the changes. And if the link does not suffice, Google will always place a GIF or a video in their updates.

This way, Google Maps managed to catch the attention of people who are looking for an in-depth explanation of their changes or are content enough with the basic announcement.

Lastly, Google keeps things fun and exciting. For instance, if their announcement falls on a quirky holiday like, say, Spaghetti Day, Google will make a quick reference to the celebration in their tweet.

It's practically a situation where everybody wins. On one hand, Google manages to inform their audience about the changes in their Maps app to the best of their ability. On the other hand, they keep their audience engaged by presenting such important information in a way that is interesting and funny.

III. *YouTube*

Reebok

In conjunction with their #HonorYourDays campaign, Reebok released a video called 25,915 days. It featured the life of a woman in reverse as she ran a Spartan Race (with Reebok shoes, of course) to the day that she was born.

The message of the video was quite simple. The average human being lives for an average of 25,915 days and one must use those days to push their body to the limit.

And just like any good video campaign, the main product serves only to complement the story, not steal the spotlight from a rather moving narrative. And, to top it off, it ends with a strong CTA with the words "Calculate Your Days."

What makes Reebok's ad work is that it creates a sense of urgency without making things bleak. And urgency is a particularly strong motivator which makes any message you convey all the more actionable and compelling.

GoPro

Not every marketing campaign you create for YouTube has to directly relate to your brand or your products/services, and GoPro's "Fireman Saves a Kitty" video is proof of just that.

The premise of the video is quite simple. It just shows a random firefighter saving a kitten from a burning building. What makes it unique is that

GoPro is never one to show modern day heroism, as their brand is more about adventures and extreme sports.

However, it did prove to be one of the company's most successful and engaging YouTube videos to date. The only takeaway from this campaign is that one must never hesitate to explore the different facets of their brand's image.

By showcasing the work of a firefighter, GoPro is subtly implying that there are other thrills found out there and ones that can actually inspire and uplift.

Plus, it also helps that it showcases a cat and it's an open secret that almost everybody on the Internet loves cats.

Coachella

It's typical for big events to be advertised on YouTube. But what if that actual event would not only be advertised there but also broadcasted?

This is what the organizers of Coachella did when they decided to stream the entire event Live on YouTube. For several days straight, viewers could see the performances in the music festival at the comfort of their own homes, and practically for free.

The end result? Coachella's first ever livestream on YouTube garnered 4 million views and the numbers have only risen in the years that followed.

Old Spice

When targeting two different demographics for the same line of products, it would be best that you convey the same message differently.

Old Spice did this when they marketed their line of products to adult males with the "The Man Your Man Could Smell Like" campaign, featuring Isaiah Mustafa encouraging ladies to make the man in their life use the company's body wash.

Needless to say, the campaign became one of Old Spice's most successful commercials in the 2000s which gave rise to other campaigns featuring Mustafa and his sultry voice.

By the 2010s, however, Old Spice decided to target younger male demographics. And to do that, they came up with the "Smells Like Power" campaign featuring Terry Crews in a series of insane, reality-bending advertisements. It was bright, loud, and weird and each 30-second video would net in views by the millions after publishing.

In 2015, everything came to a head when Old Spice decided to feature both stars in a crossover campaign called "Make a Smellmitment" which advertised the Timber and Bear Glove scents.

Featuring a clash between the sophistication of the Mustafa campaign and insanity of the Crews campaign, the campaign also became Old Spice's most successful advertisement for the latter half of the decade.

Sephora

In these days, telling your audience why your brand is the best is no longer enough. You also have to show them how your products and offerings can be applied in real world situations.

In Sephora's case, their YouTube channel does not only feature the usual product promotions but also step-by-step tutorials on how to achieve certain makeup effects using their products.

Then, to generate traffic to their web page, which leads to sales, Sephora includes links to their website in the description for each video.

The main takeaway from Sephora's strategy is that if you insist on highlighting your products for your campaigns, you have to make sure that they are presented in a manner that makes them relevant to the message that you are trying to convey.

And, of course, never forget to make sure that the video actually generates enough traffic to your main pages. This can be done with the help of a strong CTA partnered with a working link to your sales page.

Adidas

One great way to market yourself in social media is if you allow your brand to become an opportunity for the public to directly interact with celebrities and influential people. In 2014, during the FIFA World Cup, Adidas published a series of videos called The Dugout which was a series of interviews with popular football players, managers, and other influential people in the industry.

Here, and for the first time in the history of the World Cup, people had the opportunity to have their questions answered by stars like Luca Moura and have them directly answered in a virtual press conference of sorts.

The Dugout became one of Adidas' most successful video campaigns to date, with more than 1.5 million views on the platform and with an increase in subscriptions to the channel by 300%.

IV. *Instagram*

ESPN

News programs often have it hard on Twitter. It is as if the constant stream of news is turning people off which leads to fewer engagements the more frequent a news handle posts there.

Back then, ESPN used to get in between 300 to 3,000 comments for their posts but this all changed when they started using polls for their Instagram posts.

The strategy is quite simple: ESPN asks a question with several different answers. Of course, sports fans would not only pick any of the questions but would defend their answer in the comments with their opinions.

No matter how polarizing an issue gets, the engagement ESPN receives from their online quizzes is quite considerable with comments going well beyond the 30,000 mark and more than 1,000 shares.

The lesson here is to find ways to make your audience interact with you. Polls and online questions can often do this because they require answers. And answers start a conversation, which increases engagement for your content.

Lego

What if your company is in the middle of a rather uneventful stretch? What if the industry you are part of has no major events or issues that need tackling? What if everybody's attention is on another event/issue happening in another part of the world?

Lego's answer to that on Instagram is quite simple: Jump on the bandwagon.

For instance, when everybody was focused on the Royal Wedding in May 2018, Lego published a picture depicting the couple made from Lego blocks and with the trending #RoyalWedding hashtag.

The end result is the picture garnering Lego more than 300 comments and well over 100,000 views.

Why this worked is quite simple. Events trend in the online world because people are interested in whatever has happened or is going to happen. You can take advantage of this brief shift of focus in the online community by showing the rest of the world that you know what's trending.

The thing with Lego is that it has a rather malleable image due to its products. Basically, since everyone can create anything with pieces of Lego, the company can also market itself in almost every known event happening across the world right now.

Casper

Pillows and contests sound like two things that don't go hand in hand but Casper managed to find a way to bring these two things together. Wanting to reach out to a lot of people, Casper launched an interactive campaign which is best described as an online pillow fight.

The premise is simple: On a website they set up, users can hit each other with an online pillow. They would then promote the pillow fight on Instagram using videos showing the online fight.

The result, obviously, was that people started tagging their friends to come to the website to have their pillow fight. The more long-term result was that Casper retargeted their old customers while bringing in droves of new ones who have become aware of their line of pillows and mattresses.

What lesson that could be drawn from here is that there is absolutely no limit as to how you can market your products in any platform that you operate on. In Casper's case, they turned a sleeping accessory into a tool where people can interact with each other through the Internet.

By keeping your campaigns interesting, you are bound to keep your brand relevant and more people will become aware of it. And with an increase in brand awareness comes multiple opportunities to convert your audience into loyal customers.

Rent The Runway

Picture this scenario: Your company is going to launch an update to your app. Naturally, app updates are boring content since they contain mostly technical stuff.

So, how are you going to market it? By making it look like the app was in response to customer comments.

Rent The Runway did this when they announced a new update for their app which allows people to see whether or not the clothes they are about to purchase has pockets.

Naturally, this announcement would not generate much buzz among fashionistas but, luckily enough, Rent the Runway has a picture of a comment from one of their customers asking if pockets can be one of the filters for their app.

And so Rent the Runway posted their announcement with a screenshot of the comment, explaining in the caption how they came to the decision to add that feature. And, soon enough, the announcement would manage to net 10,000 likes.

Using feedback generated by your customers is not only a creative way of selling your products or announcing changes in your services. It's one way of subtly saying that you do care for their needs. By giving the impression that you are interested in providing what the people need, you naturally endear yourself to the public.

Citrix

Marketing on a highly visual platform can be difficult if the product you are selling is highly technical. This is the problem faced by Citrix, a company that provides remote device access services to their customers.

Their product is targeted towards people who are interested in cloud-based storage and data protection, which is the demographic that is not as prominent in Instagram when compared to other platforms.

Their creative workaround to this problem? Wordplay. Simply put, Citrix's promoted their app by linking it to an issue that almost every adult can relate to: a cluttered physical workspace.

So, by making people understand that their app is to online databases what sorting and cleaning is to physical work spaces, Citrix bridged the gap between them and their customers, resulting in tons of engagement on their page.

When having to market a fairly complicated and technical product/service, it is necessary to keep things simple and relatable. Find a way to make the crux of the problem your marketing is trying to solve into something that people can instantly understand.

Whether it is a mundane walk to the business or having to file taxes, there are quite a lot of situations out there that can be analogous to the problems your products are trying to solve. Finding that link and marketing your brand in a highly visual platform should be easy.

Conclusion

After everything has been said and done, there is still one question that you need to answer:

What is the ultimate measure of success for your social media campaigns?

Some would say it is the increase in your brand's awareness. The instant that more people know about you compared to a few months ago, then your social media campaign is a success.

Others would say it is the increase in web traffic. Granted, all the strategies that you have read in this book have been designed to funnel and consolidate all traffic coming from your social media pages to your main web pages.

And then there are others who would claim that it is the increase in engagement in your content. This could hold some truth, as an increase in activity on your social media pages is a telltale sign that there is considerable interest in your brand. And where interest lies, profit will soon follow.

Then there are people who say that it is in the discovery of new segments in the market. This is a sign that your products and services can actually be made to fulfill needs that you haven't thought of before. And, of course, knowing that other demographics like your brand is a sign that your range of influence in the field of social media has expanded.

The truth, however, is that all of these metrics are all telling that your marketing campaigns are working. However, there is one other factor that trumps them all: conversion.

Conversion begins when a person becomes so interested that they visit your channels and are convinced by what you are offering. This interest is then followed by a willingness to visit your sales page or your physical business.

Once there, they will then be convinced enough to start a transaction with your business and part with their hard-earned money in return for what you are offering.

If they find value in what you are offering and would want to consume more of it, then and only then can you declare that all your marketing campaigns have been effective.

Sure, marketing in a field that is as dynamic and fickle as social media has its ups and downs. Even the best-laid plans that you have designed can be derailed by a single misfire.

However, the beauty with marketing is that there is always room for improvement. If you do fail, there is that chance to learn from where you messed up and start all over again.

The risk of stepping out of your comfort zone in the hopes of offering something that people will find value in does reap some rewards. And you will know that your efforts did pay off when your brand's name alone is enough to convince people to start doing business with you.

I would like to thank you and congratulate you for finishing this book!

I hope all that you learned here will help you in making your business stand out from your competition in the world of social media.

The next step here is to actually implement whatever strategies you have thought of and measure your success.

I wish you the best of luck!

Thank you

Before you go, I just wanted to say thank you for purchasing my book.

You could have picked from dozens of other books on the same topic but you took a chance and chose this one.

So, a HUGE thanks to you for getting this book and for reading all the way to the end.

Now I wanted to ask you for a small favor. **Could you please consider posting a review on the platform? Reviews are one of the easiest ways to support the work of independent authors.**

This feedback will help me continue to write the type of books that will help you get the results you want. So if you enjoyed it, please let me know!

Click here to leave a review!

https://www.amazon.com/review/create-review/

www.ingramcontent.com/pod-product-compliance
Lightning Source LLC
Chambersburg PA
CBHW081801200326
41597CB00023B/4109